READING SHAKESPEARE
HISTORICALLY

Lisa Jardine is one of the most renowned and popular Renaissance scholars writing today. This collection of her essays charts ten years of her thinking on the relationship between early modern history and the period's canonical texts. At the same time, the essays provide a fascinating account of the rise of feminist scholarship since the 1980s, and the diversifying of 'new historicist' approaches over the same period. Throughout, the book is written with a sharp sense of how present social and political concerns pose questions to the past while recognising that they must not write the answers for the past.

Each chapter makes a surprising discovery. The laws and practices of defamation help the reader to see something new about Desdemona and her failure to protect her sexual reputation against Othello. The laws of prohibited degrees in regard to marriage and the rules of succession help to show Hamlet's grievance in a new light. The rhetorical rules for letter writing help us to understand the breakdown or misuse of communication in *King Lear*. The sexual availability and the nature of male friendship and clientage help us to place the powers and vulnerabilities of male/female love in Shakespeare in a new perspective. Moving away from Shakespeare to contemporary dramatists, unease about the parallels between commerce in money and goods and commerce in knowledge and information adds to the intensity of events in Marlowe's *The Jew of Malta*, while the competing loyalties of companionate marriage and male friendship intensify the gender conflicts in Middleton's *The Changeling*.

Reading Shakespeare Historically will fascinate and provoke students of Shakespeare and his historical age, and general readers with an urge to understand how the culture and history of our past illuminates the key social and political issues of today.

Lisa Jardine is Dean of Arts and Professor of English at Queen Mary and Westfield College, University of London, and Honorary Fellow of King's College, Cambridge. Her many publications include *Still Harping on Daughters: Women and Drama in the Age of Shakespeare* and *Erasmus, Man of Letters*. She is a regular presenter for BBC Radio.

READING SHAKESPEARE HISTORICALLY

Lisa Jardine

London and New York

First published 1996
by Routledge
11 New Fetter Lane, London EC4P 4EE

Simultaneously published in the USA and Canada
by Routledge
29 West 35th Street, New York, NY 10001

Routledge is an International Thomson Publishing company

Typeset in Garamond by Datix International Limited, Bungay, Suffolk
Printed and bound in Great Britain by Clays Ltd, St Ives plc

British Library Cataloguing in Publication Data
A catalogue record for this book is available from the British Library

Library of Congress Cataloguing in Publication Data
Jardine, Lisa.
Reading Shakespeare Historically/Lisa Jardine.
Includes bibliographical references and index.
1. Shakespeare, William, 1564–1616 – Political and social views.
2. Shakespeare, William, 1564–1616 – Contemporary England.
3. Literature and history – England – History – 16th century.
4. Literature and society – England – History – 16th century.
5. Women and literature – England – History – 16th century.
6. Social problems in literature.
7. Historicism.
I. Title.
PR3024.J37 1996
822.3'3–dc20   95–35506

ISBN 0–415–13489–7 (hbk)
ISBN 0–415–13490–0 (pbk)

for Rachel

CONTENTS

ACKNOWLEDGEMENTS

A version of Chapter 1 appeared in Margaret Tudeau-Clayton and Martin Warner (eds), *Addressing Frank Kermode: Essays in Criticism and Interpretation*, London, Macmillan, 1991, pp. 124–53.

A version of Chapter 2 appeared in Francis Barker, Peter Hulme and Margaret Iversen (eds), *Uses of History: Marxism, Post-Modernism and the Renaissance*, Manchester, Manchester University Press, 1991, pp. 123–39.

A version of Chapter 3 appeared in *Shakespeare Quarterly*, 1987, vol. 38, pp. 1–18.

A version of Chapter 4 appeared in Susan Zimmerman (ed.), *Erotic Politics: Desire on the Renaissance Stage*, London, Routledge, 1992, pp. 27–38.

A version of Chapter 7 appeared in Susan D. Amussen and Mark A. Kishlansky (eds), *Political Culture and Cultural Politics in Early Modern Europe: Essays Presented to David Underdown*, Manchester, Manchester University Press, 1995, pp. 234–54.

A version of Chapter 8 appeared in Betty S. Travitsky and Adele F. Seeff (eds), *Attending to Women in Early Modern England*, Newark, University of Delaware Press, 1994, pp. 123–44.

A version of Chapter 9 appeared in Deborah E. Barker and Ivo Kamps (eds), *Shakespeare and Gender: A History*, London, Verso, 1995, pp. 316–26.

INTRODUCTION

It is more than ten years since I first grappled in print with the relationship between history and the plays of Shakespeare.[1] In that time I have been able to participate in an extraordinarily productive debate amongst scholars of the English renaissance on both sides of the Atlantic. This debate has been broadly concerned to develop our understanding of the ways in which a historically situated study of the works of Shakespeare plays a central part in studies of early modern text and culture. At the moment when western culture as a whole reconsiders the fragments of its heritage and searches its history for some point from which to see itself, once more, reassuringly whole, Shakespeare studies too are preoccupied with the relationship to the past. In both cases the task is not nostalgic reminiscence, but a fresh understanding of the rootedness of our present uncertainties, derived by some kind of engaging dialogue with the textual residue of history.

The process of development of my own thoughts on Shakespeare has been shaped by that vigorously developing debate, and coloured by its various and varied contexts and locations. It has also inevitably been marked by the strong way in which my personal intellectual history (within which literary studies form only a part of an academically diverse collection of interests and areas of expertise)[2] has intersected with those of others pursuing alternative lines of thought, sometimes in entirely different fields of inquiry.[3]

I have learnt more than I would ever have imagined possible from people with intellectual agendas entirely different from my own, and with interests derived from distinct cultural formations. What has characterised the debate as a whole has been a shared energy, and a passionate commitment to deepening our intellectual grasp of the present we inhabit, and of contemporary issues which challenge our understanding. The differences of opinion (occasionally the head-on confrontations on public platforms) have been as important and as formative as the agreements. The alliances formed have at times been unpredictable, the disagreements correspondingly unexpected: in discussions of gender and power, feminists have crossed swords with new historicists; on other occasions specialists in gender studies and those in history have found themselves together proposing alternatives to arguments expounded by deconstructionists and post-structuralists.[4] Over the same period, what used to be termed new historicists have clarified their intellectual practices and emerged as two distinctive schools of thought: one predominantly committed to a study of Shakespeare determined by text criticism and psychoanalysis, the other more inclined towards a study framed by recent work in anthropology and in economic and social history.[5] If pressed to identify my own practice and affiliations as a Shakespeare critic I would probably declare myself as inclining to the latter group of interests.

My own developing work on Shakespeare has been shaped by a number of preoccupations arising directly out of the context in which I live and work. The first has undoubtedly been the strong impression made upon me by dialogue about the theory and practice of Shakespeare studies with professional colleagues and with students on both sides of the Atlantic – in Britain and in the United States. It was North American Shakespeareans who responded immediately and enthusiastically to *Still Harping on Daughters* – North American feminist Shakespeareans, specifically, who generously included me in the vigorous discussions about gender and power which took place at the annual conferences of the Shakespeare Association of America in the mid-1980s.[6] These debates were a far cry from the dignified exchanges of views which took place annually under the auspices of the International Shakespeare Association, run by the Shakespeare Institute at Stratford-upon-Avon in England. The ISA's annual conference was an 'invitation only' affair, whose carefully circumscribed topics and interests were selected by a small group of distinguished, mostly European Shakespeareans. The delegates at the SAA's huge annual meeting, by contrast, came from schools of English in colleges and universities across the length and breadth of America (and beyond). For every one of these delegates Shakespeare was the lodestar figure on their intellectual map, and the purpose of the conference each year was apparently to decide, as a matter of urgency, where the vital centre of Shakespeare studies currently lay in relation to American literary and cultural studies as a whole. Practically any issue of the day was available to be thrashed out in a small crowded seminar room, or before a large, excitable audience on a plenary platform at the SAA, and thrashed out such issues were. It took very little time, then, for me to discover that Shakespeare studies stand in a very different relationship to the totality of cultural studies in the United States from the one we take for granted in Britain.[7]

The second shaping influence on my thinking about Shakespeare has been my academic move from Jesus College, Cambridge to Queen Mary and Westfield College (QMW), in the University of London. Teaching is the cornerstone of our intellectual formation as scholars and critics. If your students cannot follow your train of thought, then you probably haven't yet got it quite straight yourself. If your students will not accept your argument, then you need to ask yourself what you are overlooking which stands between them and agreement (since, on the whole, students are more generous and

2

more likely to give you the benefit of the doubt than academic colleagues). At Cambridge it was easy never to ask the question, 'Does Shakespeare matter?' Teaching there at the very heart of British high culture, one took entirely for granted in one's teaching the centrality of his plays to a literature course. I could assume that my students would claim familiarity with the entire corpus of works (including the poems).[8] Most of my students had already formed opinions on the worth of the major plays in the Shakespeare canon, and would confidently offer views as to the relative merit of specified passages of blank verse.[9] It was, in fact, extremely difficult to coax students into confessing ignorance on any point of textual detail in a play under consideration – such was their expectation that as élite students they ought to be able to master Shakespeare.

My London students, by contrast, are quite comfortable confessing ignorance of all but a small number of Shakespeare's plays (*Hamlet, Lear, Othello*, their set text for their A-level examination), and voluble in their willingness to admit that they have difficulty construing the lines on the page. Most important of all, they require persuading that the study of Shakespeare is as important as I persist in insisting it is. What is the study of Shakespeare for? Arguing the case for Shakespeare with my students at the University of London has forced me to scrutinise my own motives and assumptions. I have been obliged to make explicit the fact that I believe that the continuing presence within British culture of the texts of Shakespeare's plays – familiar, quotable – has laid down a kind of cultural sediment which marks our everyday communal life in telling ways. That is why an appeal to Shakespeare on the part of a British politician or public spokesperson continues to resonate.

I once set as an assignment for my class at QMW the instruction that they should listen to television or radio news bulletins – it was the season of political party conferences – and try to identify tags from Shakespeare used to give authority to a politician's pronouncements. As I left the college that day, I turned on my car radio to hear the then Chancellor of the Exchequer, Kenneth Baker, exhorting the party faithful of the Conservative Party not to lose confidence in Conservative economic policy, in spite of the fact that mortgage interest rates had just been raised for the third straight month in a row. What was needed, he insisted, was unflinching commitment to the Party, and courage in the face of adverse pressures affecting even their own pocketbooks. In conclusion he urged them not to lose heart, to stand their ground in the face of press criticism and public hostility:

> . . . he which hath no stomach to this fight,
> Let him depart.[10]

A direct, deliberate quotation from the St Crispin's Day speech in *Henry V*, in the full expectation that his audience would 'hear' a rhetorical call to arms in the face of impossible odds. Many of my students also tuned in to the speech (designed as a 'sound bite' by its author, and much repeated on bulletins throughout that day), and picked up the reference. When we assembled for the next class, all my students were prepared to admit that an author whose texts could still be used vividly and reliably to particular political effect could not be deemed a 'dead' author.

Which brings me back to the differing significance of Shakespeare as a curriculum author – a canonical author – in the United States and in Britain. Cultural appeal to Shakespeare in the United States is significantly different from that made in British public life. In an editorial on the deepening international crisis in Bosnia in the *International Herald Tribune*, which I happened to pick up in the summer of 1993, Shakespeare's *Henry V* was again invoked in a rallying cry. The editorial began:

> The West's worst moral and political disaster since the Nazis is coming to a climax. And just as many politicians and institutions paid for the failure to stop Hitler, so many of them will pay dearly for allowing the Serbian tyrant, Slobodan Milosevic, to destroy Bosnia.[11]

The piece accused Europe and the United States of a policy of appeasement in Bosnia worthy of Neville Chamberlain, and of standing by and watching crimes against humanity on a scale which, in 1945, the West had promised would never again be tolerated. It concluded:

> [Whatever happens now,] the inhumanity will remain unhealed. Looking at the scene in Bosnia, we should say what Shakespeare, in *Henry V*, had the French noble say as he looked down at the shattered field of Agincourt: 'Shame and eternal shame, nothing but shame!'

Here Shakespeare's *Henry V* is invoked as a moral touchstone: Shakespeare says, 'Shame and eternal shame, nothing but shame', and so ought we all to do, before the humiliating spectacle of the Bosnia débâcle. But a number of features distinguish this, North American, appeal to Shakespeare (I think, quite typically) from the kind of use made by the British Chancellor of the Exchequer. In the first place, the reader is not asked to take a tone drawn specifically from the play mentioned. *Henry V* is a triumphalist play (however Shakespeare tempers its message in his dramatisation). If you want to awaken in your readers a deep communal sense of the unacceptability of ethnic slaughter in petty partisan disputes, why choose to refer to a play about a nationalist victory on the grand scale? There is, in fact, something curious about quoting the French version of Agincourt in the play at all, since, in the interests of the structural coherence of the play, the dramatisation of French military action consists in fleeting moments of delay, indecision and poor judgement, punctuating a full and exhilarating depiction of the unexpected victory of a small, bedraggled band of plucky Britons over a highly organised, well-equipped French army. In the second place, the editorial writer's choice is not a 'memorable' quotation: it is not a familiar Shakespearean tag, nor even a passage from a much anthologised soliloquy. Until our attention was drawn to it, we might never have recalled this passage in Shakespeare at all (it is the leader writer who alerts us to its belonging to the canon, 'we should say what Shakespeare . . .').

And indeed, in a sense, I suspect, this phrase as used in the *International Herald Tribune* editorial is not a quotation from the play at all. It is a quotation from Kenneth Branagh's box-office-success film of the play.[12] It can be found significantly highlighted in Branagh's published screenplay, where a brief Shakespearean glimpse of the French commanders' dawning realisation that they have lost the day becomes a studied piece of moralising in the midst of the graphic carnage of the battlefield.[13] Branagh publicly said that his version of Shakespeare's *Henry V* was an anti-war film; here the quotation selected is part of the material deliberately highlighted cinematographically so as to focus that theme.[14]

It is worth staying with this example a little longer. Since the appearance of the Oxford Shakespeare edition of *Henry V*, edited by Gary Taylor, that edition has become, for many Shakespeare specialists, the standard reference edition. At the time that I read the *International Herald Tribune* editorial it was the edition I had to hand, the edition I turned to when I wanted to reflect upon the implications of the use of the quotation. It was interesting, therefore, to look up Taylor's text for further illumination on 'Shame and eternal shame, nothing but shame!' and to find that this line does not figure in the main body of Taylor's edited text at all.

All editions of *Henry V* are based on the 1623 first folio version of the play, as opposed to the 1600 quarto.[15] In his compelling introduction to the Oxford Shakespeare edition, Gary Taylor explains clearly why he has chosen to integrate the quarto version of the 'Shame and eternal shame' scene with the hitherto universally accepted folio version, to produce a hybrid from which the 'Shame and eternal shame' line is missing. The reasons he gives for doing so are given in his Appendix A. He argues that the Dauphin ought not to figure in this scene, on grounds of the structural coherence of the plot, and emends the text accordingly. Justification for drastic editorial revision here, in other words, boils down to the fact that (as Taylor sees it) this scene is inconsistent with the revised focus of the play. In other words, Taylor 'edits out' 'Shame and eternal shame' because, in his view, such sentiments no longer accord with the strongly British nationalistic focus of the folio play, and have survived only as a kind of shadow or echo of an earlier version. We may be shocked that an editorial decision should be taken on such overtly critical (and therefore by definition subjective) grounds, but that is material for a whole other discussion. What is relevant here is that for Taylor the scene and the sentiment are 'unShakespearean', in the sense that in some way (which Taylor is prepared to treat as critically definitive) they are at odds with the play as a whole. So what is happening when the *International Herald Tribune* invokes it as a canonical moral touchstone?

I did not choose this instance in order to disparage an American columnist for not knowing (or, in Taylor's terms, not being sufficiently critically sensitive in relation to) his *Henry V*. I actually think the use made of Shakespeare here is a valid one within the American cultural frame. The appeal is to a consensus view of civilised human behaviour, and Shakespeare stands for that shared recognition. The cultural advantage of using Shakespeare is, I think, that here is a cultural reference point older than the United States, which is not, however, parochially American, but in some unspecified sense 'universal'. In my British example, the purpose of the Shakespeare allusion was to trigger an immediate recognition, a sense of cultural belonging. According to Raymond Williams's view of culture and ideology, that sense of belonging does not require that you know the reference, but merely that you share with those around you the sense of its being a shaping part of your landscape of beliefs.[16] In the American case, the appeal is to an authority – to a named figure whose ethical insights, as expressed in his surviving texts, ought to be taken seriously by 'right-minded' people. And in the American case, since the persisting centrality of Shakespeare to the culture is neither agreed upon nor widely felt, the appeal to a particular passage from a particular play leans heavily on the expectation that many readers will have seen the film version starring Kenneth Branagh and Emma Thompson, in which that passage is memorably framed by the screen action (evocative in its graphic, mud-splattered misery of news footage from Sarajevo).[17]

To claim the continuing importance of Shakespeare in contemporary American culture is a more delicate affair than drawing attention to the ease with which he can continue to be conjured up as an emotional reference point. In particular, it can readily be argued that to claim Shakespeare as a cultural touchstone, a canonical text, in North America, is to affirm the priority of Western European culture at the expense of all the other cultures which have gone into the American 'melting pot'. Recent North American Shakespeare criticism has been typified by an interest in the many ways in which key contemporary issues (gender, power, race) can be made to reverberate by juxtaposing our twentieth-century version with Shakespeare's early modern treatment of the same themes. Not, of course, that Shakespeare ever catechises on gender, power or race, but new historicist criticism has brilliantly excavated the way in which a kind of issue-grounded *explication de texte* or close reading can elucidate our own cultural assumptions. The desire to 'speak with the dead', which Stephen Greenblatt so memorably made the starting point of his own Shakespearean negotiations is, surely, the desire to initiate a conversation about burning questions in the here-and-now with the thoughtful past, as it survives in the textual residue of a 'great author'.[18]

So much for anecdotal attention to responses to *Henry V* on either side of the Atlantic. What would constitute a more properly historicised response to this most paradigmatic of the English history plays? In a book with 'history' in its title there must surely be some treatment of a Shakespearean history play. And indeed I do consider it a crucial part of my critical argument for 'reading Shakespeare historically' that my approach will produce a distinctive version of *Henry V* – a play with a historical theme, received first in a period historically distinct from our own, and with its reception now coloured both by the Branagh film success and by the much publicised information that Branagh's stage performance in the role reduced to tears the heir to the British throne, Prince Charles.[19]

I have spoken about the strenuously 'British' (in fact, English) strain in *Henry V*, which has lent itself to propaganda use in contemporary Britain.[20] Yet when we look at the play today, what strikes us first is the counter-currents and fissures which cut across the ringing confidence of the Harfleur or St Crispin's day speeches. We may choose to pause with this notion of flawedness, faultlines and ideological counter-currents – and that, indeed, has been a tendency in a significant amount of recent criticism of quality.[21] But we may choose instead to register 'indeterminacy' (ideological or otherwise) as a sign that we should listen attentively to the multiple resonances of the text, for thematic points of contact between early modern culture and our own. 'Indeterminacy' alerts us to the fact that when we 'speak with the dead', our own historical moment presses us to choose as the subject of our conversation topics which have only now once again come into cultural view, after a period of occlusion. It is no accident, and may turn out to be the tragedy of our own time, that readings of *Henry V* at the present historical moment stumble repeatedly at the complexity of representation within the play of nationalism and ethnic identity.

If we had not watched with horrified fascination on the evening news bulletins as an integrated, multi-racial, multi-faithed community in Old Yugoslavia disintegrated into territorial fragments of so-called 'pure' ethnicity and separate religious beliefs, we would not, I contend, be able to recognise as sharply as we currently do the problems lurking within *Henry V*'s depiction of fervour for English nationalism. Now, however, it is the pathos of the contradiction between Henry's proud boasts of 'Englishmen' pure and true, and the fact that his own progeny will be hybrid Anglo-Gallic, which attracts our critical attention. And when we take up our conversation with the play text – interrogating the lapses into silence produced by the accidents of the historical process – the play itself responds with confirmation that this is indeed a vital theme, and one which we can use to animate the action, and to see more deeply into the plot's construction.

Like the opening scene of the play, the closing scenes of *Henry V* direct the dramatic spotlight onto the issue of royal lineage. Henry's elaborate naming of the French royal house as his close kin (brother, sister, cousin) contrasts starkly with the adversarial and oppositional language of the body of the play – a play centred on conflict and warfare. It ushers in the wooing scene, in which Henry contrives to gain the 'love' of his 'cousin' Catherine, a wooing which confirms a match which is a crucial part of Henry's demands in settlement of his triumph at Agincourt:

> *King Henry.* Yet leave our cousin Catherine here with us.
>   She is our capital demand, comprised
>   Within the fore-rank of our articles.[22]

England's seizure of the French crown by force is to be cemented and endorsed by a marital alliance, an alliance which Henry is anxious to represent as a consensual one.

At the moment of marital alliance with which *Henry V* draws to a close, women (the perpetual onlookers thus far in the action) are finally given a voice:

> *Queen Isabel.* So happy be the issue, brother England,
>   Of this good day and of this gracious meeting,
>   As we are now glad to behold your eyes –
>   Your eyes which hitherto have borne in them,
>   Against the French that met them in their bent,
>   The fatal balls of murdering basilisks.
>   The venom of such looks we fairly hope
>   Have lost their quality, and that this day
>   Shall change all griefs and quarrels into love.[23]

'Love' and 'happy issue' belong to the language of courtship, and thus reintroduce the matter of inherited claim to title so prominent in the play's opening scenes. Throughout this final scene such language is consistently juxtaposed with the terminology of peace treaty and contractual rights exacted under duress. His private wooing over, Henry negotiates his bride-to-be's acquisition with her father openly as part of a territorial transaction:

> *King Charles.* We have consented to all terms of reason.
> *King Henry.* Is't so, my lords of England?
> *Warwick.* The King hath granted every article:
>   His daughter first, and so in sequel all,
>   According to their firm proposèd natures.
> *Exeter.* Only he hath not yet subscribèd this:
>   where your majesty demands that the King of France, having any
>   occasion to write for matter of grant, shall name your highness in this
>   form and with this addition: (*reads*) in French. *Notre très cher fils Henri,
>   Roi d'Angleterre, Hériter de France*, and thus in Latin, *Praeclarissimus filius
>   noster Henricus, Rex Angliae et Haeres Franciae.*
> *King Charles.* Nor this I have not, brother, so denied,
>   But your request shall make me let it pass.
> *King Henry.* I pray you, then, in love and dear alliance,

> Let that one article rank with the rest,
> And thereupon give me your daughter.[24]

Consent has here acquired a curiously coercive tinge. The French King has 'consented' to all the terms of the treaty forced upon him by France's humiliating defeat at the hands of the English. Kate has become an 'article', the first in a sequence 'according to their firm proposèd natures'. She figures in an inventory of goods exchanged, which includes the designation of Henry, 'heir to France' – not *his* heirs, but he himself endowed with the legal right to the French crown.

The point here is not the by now commonplace one that, in spite of courtship rituals, early modern marriage is unproblematically regarded as a 'traffic in women'. Rather, I draw attention here to the sleight of the dramatist's hand. 'Consent' to the marriage alliance between France and England blurs the blatant aggression of the seizure of France in a war fought on tenuous legal grounds. The audience's assent to the proposition that England has 'won' France legitimately is effected dramatically by the scene in which Henry woos Kate. As part of the dramatist's strategic plan for shifting the audience's attention from warfare to wooing, Shakespeare alters both history and his source and tacitly erases the legitimate French heir. In Shakespeare's version of the historical narrative's final resolution the Dauphin – the first-born son of the King of France, legitimate natural heir to the throne of France – vanishes.[25] His disappearance makes the emergence of a new heir – Harry, King of England – apparently unproblematic. In the absence of a male heir the throne of France passes through the female line (the route of all the dubious lineal connections in the play). The new husband of France's only daughter claims the throne of France by way of a love-match marriage.

As a rule, the marriages which provide the final plot resolution in a Shakespearean play bind up the loose ends of the story, and resolve the difficulties for lineage which the passions of individuals have created.[26] On the face of it *Henry V*, too, draws to a close to a chorus of commitments to family, and to the alliances of major landholdings which marriages between great families confirm and consolidate:

> *King Henry.* Peace to this meeting, wherefor we are met.
>   Unto our brother France and to our sister,
>   Health and fair time of day. Joy and good wishes
>   To our most fair and princely cousin Catherine;
>   And as a branch and member of this royalty,
>   By whom this great assembly is contrived,
>   We do salute you, Duke of Burgundy.
>   And princes French, and peers, health to you all.
> *King Charles.* Right joyous are we to behold your face.
>   Most worthy brother England, fairly met.[27]

But the situation is by no means so clear in the case of kinship between royal families. In the formation of national identity there is an inevitable tension between royal marriage (in which the two partners come from different nations, and may effect a cross-national territorial merger) and the passing on of the crown by lineal descent; and there is a straight contradiction between lineage and conquest. If the monarch is a 'true born' son of the nation, what is the status of his heirs if he marries a foreign princess? What if the monarch is a true-born daughter, who legally becomes part of the line of her husband should she marry? None of these tensions would seem strange to a public whose cultural memory included the strain of the marriage of Mary Tudor to Philip of Spain, and anxiety over the (unsuccessful) courtship of Elizabeth by the French Duke d'Anjou.

As Shakespeare's *Henry V* draws to its dynastic conclusion, these tensions are articulated explictly by none other than Harry himself:

> *King Henry.* If ever thou be'st mine, Kate – as I have a saving faith within me tells me thou shalt – I get thee with scrambling, and thou must therefore needs prove a good soldier-breeder. Shall not thou and I, between Saint Denis and Saint George, compound a boy, half-French half-English, that shall go to Constantinople and take the Turk by the beard? Shall we not? What sayst thou, my fair flower-de-luce?
>
> *Catherine.* I do not know dat.
>
> *King Henry.* No, 'tis hereafter to know, but now to promise. Do but now promise, Kate, you will endeavour for your French part of such a boy, and for my English moiety take the word of a king and a bachelor.[28]

As Henry woos Kate to declare herself his wife of her own volition (attempting to extract a private promise of commitment from her),[29] he articulates the obvious fact that their offspring will be of mixed nationality – 'half-French half-English' as he puts it.[30] Here woman is that site where the male fiction of the pure and proper blood-line is both founded *and* undermined. Her fecundity guarantees the posterity of the family, but her alienness threatens to taint its ethnic purity.[31]

In *Henry V* Shakespeare fudges the issue of pure lineal entitlement to the crown, and the taint of foreign blood.[32] To tease out the ingenious slippages in the plot a little further, let us return to the wooing scene. Why is this scene so fraught with sexual anxiety – specifically an anxiety about masculinity?[33] My short answer is, because the stage representation of Catherine as a sexual subject problematises the crucial plot fiction of the smooth transition from nationalist conquest to the triumph of pure lineage. By interrupting the smooth transition from military victory to seizure of the throne with a courtship, Shakespeare introduces a *doubt* about the general possibility of effecting such lineal transactions without the weakening intercession of women (inevitably necessary to continue and consolidate the line).

Long before it is certain that Henry will be victorious, Catherine has apparently transferred her allegiance to the English cause. What else is her enthusiastic attempt to learn the rudiments of English but a capitulation in advance of the fact?[34] The sexual innuendo of the 'English lesson' transposes the impending 'conquest' of France into a 'conquest' of France's women – into the familiar proposition that women are 'won' in battle (as Tamburlaine wins Zenocrate's affections as well as her body in Marlowe's *Tamburlaine*).

The editors find the English lesson at 3.4 charming, but we might want to consider its timing, and, in particular, the tone of the scene which immediately follows it. Realising the gravity of the military situation, the French Dauphin rails against the loose women of France, whose sexual exploits with Englishmen have produced the doughty descendants of the Normans who now threaten the French with defeat:

> *Dauphin.* By faith and honour,
>   Our madams mock at us and plainly say
>   Our mettle is bred out, and they will give
>   Their bodies to the lust of English youth,
>   To new-store France with bastard warriors.[35]

There is a heavy genealogical irony in his outburst, which is given added emphasis by the confusion of the syntax. The Dauphin maintains that it is the fault of French women that the English troops are cross-bred to combine the dour tenacity of the English with the 'quick blood' of the French. The true-blooded Frenchmen are fit only for 'the English dancing-schools' – their purity of line is also their weakness. But are the 'bastard warriors' already fighting on the English side, or are they future products of the 'rape' which will be France's imminent defeat?

The Dauphin's outburst picks up all too clearly from the bawdy language which Alice and Catherine inadvertently introduce into their language lesson:

> *Catherine.* Comment appelez-vous les pieds et la robe?
> *Alice. De foot*, madame, et *de cown*.
> *Catherine. De foot* et *de cown*? O Seigneur Dieu! Ils sont les mots de son mauvais, corruptible, gros, et impudique, et non pour les dames d'honneur d'user. Je ne voudrais prononcer ces mots devant les seigneurs de France pour tout le monde. Foh! *De foot* et *de cown*! Néanmoins, je réciterai une autre fois ma leçon ensemble. *D'hand, de fingre, de nails, d'arma, d'elbow, de nick, de sin, de foot, de cown.*[36]

> [*Catherine.* How do you say 'the feet' and 'the gown'?
> *Alice.* 'foutre' (fuck) and 'con' (cunt), madam.
> *Catherine.* 'foutre' and 'con'? Heavens! These are words which sound so bad, corrupt, gross and immodest that it is unseemly for a gentlewoman to use them. I would not dare speak such words before the

nobles of France for the whole world. Phew! 'Foutre' and 'con'! Still, I'll recite my whole lesson one more time . . .]

Is Catherine one of the 'madams who mock us' here?[37] Already punning on sexual intercourse with the English aggressor, she seems too readily to invite the accusation, made immediately afterwards by the Dauphin, that all inter-national royal intercourse is shameful lust, the products of such sexual activity bound to undermine the integrity of the nation state. It is as a result of cross-breeding between Norman women and English men that an English stock has been produced which is currently trouncing the French on the battlefield:[38]

> *Dauphin. O Dieu vivant!* Shall a few sprays of us,
>   The emptying of our fathers' luxury [lust],
>   Our scions, put in wild and savage stock,
>   Spirt up so suddenly into the clouds
>   And over-look their grafters?[39]

Weakening of national stock is regularly laid at the door of women as the prospect of a seepage, a loss of integrity of blood through their lineal involvement. In 4.5, Bourbon's outburst at the prospect of military humiliation at the hands of the English (whether or not it includes explicit expressions of national shame)[40] diverts attention deftly on to French women. The stain of defeat to masculine honour is vividly captured by the prospect of carnal intercourse between the two nationalities – an intercourse in which women carry the shame (and blame) as bearers of cross-bred bastards:

> *Bourbon.*   Once more back again!
>   And he that will not follow Bourbon now,
>   Let him go home, and with his cap in hand
>   Like the base leno [pimp] hold the chamber door
>   Whilst by a slave no gentler than my dog
>   His fairest daughter is contaminated.[41]

By contrast, integrity of nation amongst men alone is consistently represented as a struggle in which national differences are clearcut (no blurrings or leakages), and unions considered and intentional. Catherine's English lesson is immediately preceded by a scene in which the united 'English' troops deconstruct themselves into an Englishman, an Irishman, a Welshman and a Scot, distinct in their speech, attitudes and interests, and at loggerheads, uncovering the fiction of a 'pure' English nation, and provoking the passionate cry from the Irish MacMorris: 'What ish [is] my nation?'[42] Under conditions of shared interest – here a shared benefit to be gained by acquiring France as adjunct to the British Isles – alliances may be forged between the separate nations, but these supposedly stop a long way short of assimilation into one nation state with intermingled ethnicities and shared social practices.

This fictional distinction between the inevitable outward flow of blood through marriage and the inward, non-mingling integrity of race can be clearly seen in *1 Henry IV* – a play in which the conflicts and pragmatic alliances between the separate territories of Ireland, Wales, Scotland and England are dramatically central.[43] Douglas of Scotland, Glendower of Wales, Hotspur for the northern territories of England and Mortimer for the south form an abortive alliance against Henry IV, an alliance which is always doomed through mistrust and lack of commitment on the part of its participants. Because of its inherent weakness (deliberately emphasised to offset the 'true' alliance of interests which supports the king), there is a clear tension between Henry IV's rhetoric of single (English) nationhood and unique national identity, and the actuality: Wales claimed by the Tudors (Henry V is Prince of Wales)[44] but contested by Owen Glendower; armed conflict with Scotland in which Henry Percy on behalf of the crown has temporarily subdued the Scots, and continued resistance to English settlement in Ireland (where an earlier attempt at subduing the Irish, we are reminded, led to Richard II's downfall).

In this play, the language difficulties which complicate Henry's courtship of Catherine in *Henry V*, and which critics sentimentalise, are used to make it clear that the union of interests which Mortimer, Glendower and Hotspur claim to have made is a shallow strategic convenience. While holding Mortimer to ransom after he has failed to put down his Welsh rebellion, Glendower has married him to his daughter. In the very scene in which Glendower, Mortimer and Hotspur carve up the map of mainland Britain between them,[45] the fiction of their integrity is sharply underlined by the entry of 'the ladies', their wives: Mortimer cannot understand a word his Welsh wife says, unless his father-in-law acts as interpreter.[46]

In *Henry V* the tension between the pure race and the aspiration to territorial expansion is a constant source of rhetorical anxiety, from the Archbishop of Canterbury's fudged endorsement of Henry's claim to France onwards. Henry's claim rests precisely on the *impurity* of his blood – his French ancestry. Nor is this thematic resonance an accident of the play: its contradictions are fundamental to all expansionist nationalism.

The fundamental contradiction at the heart of expansionist nationalism is dissolved in *Henry V* by appealing to the inevitability of female fallibility. Were women pure, the suggestion seems to be that that would guarantee the continuing purity of the nation; because women are inevitably 'impudent', the sullying of national stock is also inevitable. From the very start of the play the fissure which opens up in nationhood and its territorial rights stems from claims through the female line. However complex and deliberately confusing the Archbishop of Canterbury's account of Henry's claims to the throne of France under Salic law, what comes clearly through is the litany of women's names enabling the supposed transfer of rights from one line of male heirs to another.[47] And it is Catherine's susceptibility to being 'won' – willingly

13

joining her French stock to Henry's English – which covers for the possible illegality of Henry's seizure by force of the French crown at the end of the play. In spite of Kate's protesting that alliance with Henry betrays the French cause, verbal sleight of hand allows Henry to shift to her the responsibility for capitulating to England, and surrendering France's territory:

> *Catherine.* Is it possible dat I sould love de *ennemi* of France?
> *King Henry.* No, it is not possible you should love the enemy of France, Kate. But in loving me, you should love the friend of France, for I love France so well that I would not part with a village of it, I will have it all mine; and Kate, when France is mine, and I am yours, then yours is France, and you are mine.[48]

In 1600 no unified Britain existed. England, Wales, Scotland and parts of Ireland were not incorporated into an economic and political unit, with perceived common European objectives and a shared desire to preserve their insular integrity against threats of annexation by external forces. The differences amongst the people of the nations manoeuvering for advantageous alliances which would ultimately produce the 'United Kingdom' were as fully in play and as visible as the likenesses. As we now know, the cohesiveness of such a union is underpinned by a carefully fostered fiction of 'sameness' (of cultural practices and religious belief) – my jewishness, your scottishness are not at issue as long as the Britain we inhabit remains intact.

The Shakespeare criticism which emerged during the Second World War as part of the British 'war effort' attended vigorously to the parts of the history plays which prefigured union, and resolutely ignored those which mirrored the antagonisms amongst the constituent peoples.[49] The nationalistic Shakespeare 'industry' – the commercial exploitation of the image of Shakespeare, and his history plays in particular as quintessentially British, now a main plank in the 'propaganda' version of Shakespeare's cultural centrality – is in the direct line of descent from this war era Shakespeare/Harry.[50]

The first critics explicitly to recognise this were, I think, the British critics Graham Holderness and Terence Hawkes, who reinserted key secondary works and interpretations of Shakespeare into the social and political context from which we have traditionally separated our own critical activities.[51] Their work prepared us for the (for me) startling shift of attention which we critics have made in recent years in our work on Shakespeare's history plays. I find it hard to believe, personally, that I failed for so long to see the fractures in the plays' nationalistic rhetoric. As the Eastern bloc has collapsed, as the Soviet Union has been dismantled into its constituent faiths and ethnicities, and as the knock-on effect has led yet again to the disintegration of the Balkan States, the precariousness of the nation state has re-emerged as an issue in those very plays which had supposedly stood for the permanence of union. We are beginning to interrogate Shakespeare's texts for clues to our understanding of ethnic conflict in an unstable political world. In just such critical shifts in our dialoguing with the texts of the past lies the historicity of the reading of Shakespeare.

The essays in this collection chart both my own shifting relationship with a historicised Shakespeare, and a series of precise moments of engagement with issues thrown up by the historical process itself.

The intellectual place of women in history was a topic which absorbed much attention on the part of feminist academics in the early 1980s. The earliest essay here, 'Cultural confusion and Shakespeare's learned heroines: "These are old paradoxes"', arose from my interest in the significant role allowed to intellectual women in the fifteenth century, but intriguingly denied them (and denied in the historical account) in the twentieth century.[52]

By the mid-1980s, text critics were becoming intrigued by the fruitful collaboration of social historians and social anthropologists, which was yielding an entirely unexpected, vivid version of everyday life in the early modern period. The 'making strange' of our own past, on the model of Clifford Geertz's engagement with other cultures, opened up the possibility of dialogue between ourselves and our own cultural precursors. Out of that historical moment came 'new historicism' – much misunderstood by literary critics, but, with hindsight, a recognisable response to the invitation to treat our forebears as 'other'. The two pieces of work with which this collection of essays opens belong to that exciting moment in Shakespeare studies: '"Why should he call her whore?": Defamation and Desdemona's case', and '"No offence i' th' world": Unlawful marriage in *Hamlet*'. In both I draw on archival material uncovered by social historians, of a culturally unfamiliar kind, but which turns out to set up reverberations with key textual moments in the plays under consideration. It was 'new historicist' work of this kind which opened up the possibility of constructive exchange between historians and text critics, an exchange which will undoubtedly continue to deepen our understanding both of history and of texts.

Both these pieces, it should be said, caused a good deal more of a disturbance in the text critical community than I had expected (or than readers may consider credible, since they now seem to me quite 'tame'). There was something fragile about the alliances that were formed at that time under the general rubric of 'new historicism' – alliances between men on the left of criticism, and feminists; alliances between deconstructionists with historical leanings, and cultural materialists with a healthy suspicion of purely textual abstractions. The first version of '"Why should he call her whore?"' was delivered on a panel with the title 'Gender and Power', at a meeting of the World Shakespeare Association held in Berlin in 1986. It deeply offended some of the 'power' participants, because I took issue directly with 'new historicist' critics who had, I alleged, overlooked problems of gender in their treatment of power and authority in the Elizabethan and Jacobean drama. The first version of '"No offence i' th' world"' was written for a conference of historically-minded text critics held at the University of Essex. Once again, unexpected differences arose between those whose historical approaches were fundamentally textual and theoretical (for whom 'history' tends to mean the distinctive mentalities manifested in texts of different periods), and those for whom the historicity of texts resides more in those features which share the strangeness of that textual residue of any period accidentally preserved in archives and record offices.

The first version of 'Twins and travesties: Gender, dependency and sexual availability in *Twelfth Night*' was written for a plenary session of the Shakespeare Association of America meeting in 1989, and subsequently included in a volume edited by the convener of that plenary, Susan Zimmerman, entitled *Erotic Politics*.[53] The occasion is probably remembered by participants in the session more by the fact that Peter Stallybrass and I enacted stage cross-dressing there and then by exchanging jackets before delivering our papers, than for what we either of us had to say. In my own work, however, I think this was the point at which I acknowledged that historicist text studies and psychoanalytical text studies did have things to say to one another (a recognition which has, I hope, borne fruit in my more recent work, particularly since I have had the benefit of Professor Jacqueline Rose as colleague and friend at Queen Mary and Westfield College).

The stage cross-dressing which we had been told in the 1970s that we should ignore as a historically specific stage convention, in the 1980s that we could detect as generating a current of sexual innuendo circulating in the texts of the comedies, was suddenly foregrounded as a crux for our understanding of renaissance identity-formation. As was usual (for critics of my generation), the first step towards such an understanding was taken by Stephen Greenblatt in his article 'Fiction and friction', which drew psychoanalytical criticism more straitly into conjunction with social history and anthropology.[54] For myself, a shift in the centre of critical focus led helpfully to my being able to reassess and revise my own position on what is to be learned from the treatment of cross-dressing in a play like *Twelfth Night*. Anyone who recalls my discussion of travesty in *Still Harping on Daughters* will recognise that 'Twins and travesties' represents a change of heart on my part – one informed by the changing relationship between my reading and our history.

Between 1988 and 1993 most of my scholarly energies were taken up with an intellectual historical study of the Netherlandish humanist Desiderius Erasmus. This work culminated in a book entitled *Erasmus, Man of Letters: The Construction of Charisma in Print* (Princeton University Press, Princeton, NJ, 1993). 'Reading and the technology of textual affect: Erasmus's familiar letters and Shakespeare's *King Lear*' is a spin-off from that work, and owes its inception to my colleague at Queen Mary and Westfield College, Dr Lorna Hutson, who read my Erasmus book in manuscript form while the two of us were co-teaching the first-year course on Shakespeare. She

16

pointed out to me the way in which my enriched understanding of letter-writing as a Renaissance cultural practice had direct implications for our understanding of the plot of a play thick with exchanges of letters, like *King Lear*, and provided me with a wealth of detailed suggestions which I was able fruitfully to pursue.

The closing pieces in this collection of 'essays' – attempts at historicising my reading of Shakespeare – drift away from the plays of Shakespeare to those of near-contemporary playwrights, and to broader issues concerning the attempt to merge historical and text critical practices. All that we have learned from our engagement with the quintessentially canonical dramatist of the early modern period in Britain turns out to revivify and intensify our historicised sense of Shakespeare's distinctiveness, which in turn proves fundamentally illuminating for the period as a whole. I use Christopher Marlowe's *The Jew of Malta* and Thomas Middleton's *The Changeling* to enlarge and thicken the strangeness which I discovered in the Shakespeare plays, restoring them to meaningfulness for us. The resulting essays – 'Alien intelligence: Mercantile exchange and knowledge transactions in Marlowe's *The Jew of Malta*' and 'Companionate marriage versus male friendship: Anxiety for the lineal family in Jacobean drama' – confirm for me the impossibility of any longer isolating a re-historicised Shakespeare from the richly suggestive culture and history of the period in which his plays were produced.

Throughout this book the disciplines of history and of literary studies are interwoven to produce a single narrative which historicises the renaissance text. The most recent and groundbreaking work in history confronts the most recent critical pronouncements on canonical literature. As I have gone on, however, I have found there to be an asymmetry in this conjunction. Because I write here primarily as a specialist in Shakespeare, I am bound to use 'history' as if that discipline were less available for scrutiny and critique than literary studies. 'History' here tends to validate and confirm textual insights, pinning them to the 'solid ground' of a revered pursuit less 'subjective' than criticism.

As a historian myself at other times and in other places, I have felt the need to register here the fact that historical studies themselves are currently poised ready to respond as text studies already have done to the diversifying of western thought, the burgeoning discovery outside the traditionally dominant discourse of other worlds and other voices.[55] My penultimate chapter addresses that diversity with a piece I delivered as the plenary lecture at the groundbreaking 1991 Conference 'Attending to Women in the Early Modern Period' at the University of Maryland – a piece entitled 'Unpicking the tapestry: The scholar of women's history as Penelope among her suitors'. In this way I can at least gesture towards the fact that as I write, whole new fields are opening up in historical research which will change the shape of early modern historical studies as radically as text studies. Here is yet another reason why the engagement with the canonical text becomes ever more demanding and complex – acknowledging the positioning of the historian as participant in the historical process rather than detached observer of the passing of time adds a further dimension to the proliferating preoccupations with which the critic is asked to deal.

London, June 1995

'WHY SHOULD HE CALL HER WHORE?'

Defamation and Desdemona's case

Emilia. Why should he call her whore? who keeps her company?
What place, what time, what form, what likelihood?[1]

My concern in this work is to use the textual traces of early modern social relations as the point of encounter with early modern agency – specifically the agency of those whose point of view has tended to be excluded from dominant cultural production (non-élite men and all women). My proposal is that the social relations in the community, as conveyed to us in the 'shaped' accounts which come down to us, position the self (the subject) at the intersection of overlaid maps of acknowledged interpersonal connections. This in turn can helpfully sharpen our response to the dramatisation of interpersonal relations on the Elizabethan and Jacobean stage, if we regard stage dramatisation as the focusing of otherwise inchoate 'experience' into socially constructed units of meaning, for the purpose of clear and distinct transmission of plot to audience. So the present piece of work is not just offered as one more novel way of enhancing our reading of Shakespeare's texts; it is proposed as a very particular way of recovering some sense of connection between the textual and the social – recovering, perhaps, a distinctively *cultural* dimension in early modern textual production.[2]

The shift towards such a cultural dimension has come, in my own case, from a sense of limitation within textual studies. Specifically, in some recent 'historical' work on *Othello*, a commitment to textuality has seemed to carry the consequence that the critic is no longer to be held responsible for distinguishing verbal suggestions of Desdemona's guilt which enter the play as interpretations or anticipations of her actions, from the 'tale' (the construction as plot, in the text) of those actions themselves. The result has been that Desdemona has come increasingly regularly to be 'read' as guilty by association (with what had been said of her), and her death has been presented as punishment (ideologically and individually), instead of tragic injustice.[3] In my view, methodologies which erase the agency of any main protagonist so effectively from the interpretation are fundamentally flawed.[4] It is one thing to suggest that, textually, female figures are deprived of the power and

19

authority to control the interpretation and evaluation of their actions (that texts place them permanently in the object position in the narrative); it is quite another to continue to sustain the traditional historical view that the lived experience of women down through history has been as objects.

In seeking to develop a methodology which would restore subject status (subjectivity, even) to the female figure in history, one significant objective seemed to be to find some means of distinguishing in a text between casual verbal formulations involving women, and what I shall specify as *events* in which women participate. Here I take *event* to be a configuration of circum-stances and persons which was perceived as having a shape, so that it carried a shared meaning for the early modern community: although our access to such a configuration is necessarily via surviving textual remains which give it shape, we are able (I shall argue) to distinguish such an event as socially and culturally meaningful in the flow of incidents and social interactions.[5] Take, as an extreme case of the former, the following piece of scurrility on Iago's part, in the opening scene of Act 2 of *Othello*:

> *Iago.* [*Aside.*] He takes her by the palm; ay, well said, whisper: as little a
> web as this will ensnare as great a fly as Cassio. Ay, smile upon her,
> do: I will catch you in your own courtesies: you say true, 'tis so
> indeed. If such tricks as these strip you out of your lieutenantry, it
> had been better you had not kiss'd your three fingers so oft, which
> now again you are most apt to play the sir in: good, well kiss'd, an
> excellent courtesy; 'tis so indeed: yet again, your fingers at your lips?
> would they were clyster-pipes for your sake.... [*Trumpets within.*] The
> Moor, I know his trumpet.
> *Cassio.* 'Tis truly so.[6]

Lewd innuendo at Desdemona's expense enters the text without on-stage acknowledgement; and the overly-courteous Florentine Cassio's reply adds to the joke, as he apparently assents to the implied unchastity of her behaviour (*Iago.* 'The Moor, I know his trumpet'/*Cassio.* ' 'Tis truly so'). None of us, I think, imagines that this piece of wordplay weighs very heavily in the balance of the play's developing value-system; indeed, we do not imagine that the figure Cassio, on the stage, has heard the pun. Yet the play on words is there (as it is also, at equivalent moments, in *Troilus and Cressida* and in *The Merchant of Venice*) and, in the increasingly intricate games that Shakespearean critics play with the text, it is made increasingly to count as part of a case against Desdemona – a case for making Desdemona take the critical blame.[7]

Play on words in itself does not damage a reputation; innuendo alone does not shift the emphasis from potentiality for blame (an incautious marriage, provocative behaviour) to blameworthiness. Reputations are damaged by harm-ful accusations made under socially significant circumstances. At the other pole of the scale of cultural meaningfulness for which I am concerned to construct a methodology stands substantial *defamation* – an offence against an individual which had consequences, historically, in the community, which was an *event* with a kind of concreteness and stability to which we are able to give our critical attention, in a specifically historical sense (and making such a distinction is, for me, crucially what it means to read Shakespeare historically).

If we treat Desdemona simply textually – as a 'representation', in a uniformly illuminated discourse (without the light and shade of historical context) – then the vectors of agency (who acts, and upon whom) will necessarily end with her as object to some male subject.[8] Yet, in history, agency is a dynamic in relation to women and to men (both women and men have acted, have been acted upon). It is this historical *agency* which I am concerned to retrieve, in theory as well as in practice. The distinction between scurrility and an accusation which requires a formal hearing (offensiveness and substantial offence) is designed to retrieve the category of agent, as the intersection of a set of social relationships and cultural expectations.[9] To understand what happens in *Othello*, I shall argue, it is important to distinguish an offensive remark or gesture (of the kind which remains all too accessible and current) from what was once an indictable offence (but one which, as an integral part of the system of social relations of the early modern period, we no longer recognise).[10] It does not just matter *that* a woman is called 'whore', it matters *when* and *where* she is.[11]

If we fail to sustain that dynamic relationship between history and text, we may mistake the shared textual conventions of a period for an authentic Renaissance subjectivity (because separate subjects share access to matching cultural conventions). That in turn may be taken as evidence as to the intrinsic nature of the event these conventions represent (the closest to the 'real' to which the textual can give us access).

The lure of such a textual 'authenticity' can be illustrated with an example which turns out to be particularly relevant to Desdemona's case in *Othello*. A recent article on *A Midsummer Night's Dream* juxtaposes a passage from the private diary of Simon Forman, which draws attention to the biological femaleness of the ageing Queen (dated 1597, when Elizabeth I was in her sixties) with two passages of description of the Queen from the journal of Hurault de Maisse, ambassador extraordinary of King Henri IV of France (also dated 1597):

> I dreamt that I was with the Queen, and that she was a little elderly woman in a coarse white petticoat all unready; and she and I walked up and down through lanes and closes, talking and reasoning of many matters. At last we came over a great close where there were many people, and there were two men at hard words. One of them was a weaver, a tall man with a reddish beard, distract of his wits. She talked to him and he spoke very merrily unto her, and at last did take her and kiss her. So I took her by the arm and put her away; and told her the fellow was frantic. And so we went from him and I led her by the arm still, and then we went though a dirty lane. She had a long, white smock,

very clean and fair, and it trailed in the dirt and her coat behind. I took her coat and did carry it up a good way, and then it hung too low before. I told her she should do me a favour to let me wait on her, and she said I should. Then said I, 'I mean to wait *upon you* and not under you, that I might make this belly a little bigger to carry up this smock and coats out of the dirt.' And so we talked merrily and then she began to lean upon me, when we were past the dirt and to be very familiar with me, and methought she began to love me. And when we were alone, out of sight, methought she would have kissed me.[12]

The descriptions of the Queen's appearance by de Maisse are also from a private journal:

She was strangely attired in a dress of silver cloth, white and crimson, or silver 'gauze', as they call it. This dress had slashed sleeves lined with red taffeta, and was girt about with other little sleeves that hung down to the ground, which she was for ever twisting and untwisting. She kept the front of her dress open, and one could see the whole of her bosom [*gorge*], and passing low, and often she would open the front of this robe with her hands as if she was too hot. The collar of the robe was very high, and the lining of the inner part all adorned with little pendants of rubies and pearls, very many, but quite small. She had also a chain of rubies and pearls about her neck. On her head she wore a garland of the same material and beneath it a great reddish-coloured wig, with a great number of spangles of gold and silver, and hanging down over her forehead some pearls, but of no great worth. On either side of her ears hung two great curls of hair, almost down to her shoulders and within the collar of her robe, spangled as the top of her head. Her bosom [*gorge*] is somewhat wrinkled as well as [one can see for] [*sic* in text] the collar that she wears round her neck, but lower down her flesh is exceeding white and delicate, so far as one could see.

As for her face, it is and appears to be very aged. It is long and thin, and her teeth are very yellow and unequal, compared with what they were formerly, so they say, and on the left side less than on the right. Many of them are missing so that one cannot understand her easily when she speaks quickly. Her figure is fair and tall and graceful in whatever she does; so far as may be she keeps her dignity, yet humbly and graciously withal.[13]

[In a second audience, the Queen appeared] clad in a dress of black taffeta, bound with gold lace, and like a robe in the Italian fashion with open sleeves and lined with crimson taffeta. She had a petticoat of white damask, girdled, and open in front, as was also her chemise, in such a manner that she often opened this dress and one could see all her belly, and even to her navel [mistranslation of: *luy voyait-on tout l'estomac jusques au nombril*]. Her head tire was the same as before. She

22

had bracelets of pearl on her hands, six or seven rows of them. On her head tire she wore a coronet of pearls, of which five or six were marvellously fair. When she raises her head she has a trick of putting both hands on her gown and opening it insomuch that all her belly [*estomac*] can be seen.[14]

The critic maintains that juxtaposition of these passages shows how 'the virginal sex-object' of Forman's dream 'corresponds with startling accuracy to descriptions of Elizabeth's *actual* appearance in 1597' (my emphasis). And in a revealing comment on what is meant by 'actual' in relation to the Queen's appearance as described here, he observes:

Elizabeth's display of her bosom signified her status as a maiden. . . . Like her bosom, Elizabeth's belly must have figured her political motherhood. But, as the French ambassador insinuates, these conspicuous self-displays were also a kind of *erotic provocation* [my emphasis]. The official portraits and courtly blazons that represent the splendor of the Queen's immutable body politic are nicely complemented by the ambassador's sketches of the Queen's sixty-five year old body natural. His perceptions of the vanity and melancholy of this personage in no way negate his numerous observations of her grace, vitality, and political cunning. Indeed, in the very process of describing the Queen's preoccupation with the impact of her appearance upon her beholders, the ambassador demonstrates its impact upon *himself* [author's emphasis].[15]

The 'erotic provocation' belongs, I am suggesting, to the text, and its cultural conventions – the shaping in the telling which refracts and intensifies 'experience' into expression – not to the event (that is, to any of the Queen's many public appearances).[16] What the two 1597 accounts of the physically female Elizabeth share is a common set of motifs denoting sexual availability. Both texts dwell on a prominence of breast and stomach (ambiguously prominent, though not necessarily naked), which takes the eye of the observer, and troubles decorum in its possibilities for suggestiveness (most clearly to be seen in the obscene fecundity of woodcut 'whores' of the period).[17] In the case of the Catholic Hurault de Maisse's two descriptions, glimpses of female flesh – neck, throat, and (in veiled *décolleté*) suggestions beyond – cannot be accommodated to his version of female decorum. The detailed richness of the dress, furthermore, in conjunction with the suggestions of indecency, reinforces the anxiety about 'whoredom' (since finery and extravagant dress was customarily associated with prostitution).[18] In the case of the Forman passage the whore/harlot connotations are readily mobilised when 'Queen' is heard (in the familiarity of tone of the account) as 'quean' (prostitute).[19] Forman's dream fantasy of female 'power' overwhelmed inverts the culturally dominant iconic versions of Elizabeth as Diana (chaste goddess), as Penthesilea (virgin amazon warrior), as phoenix (reproducing without a mate), all of which iconographically stress chastity as her *virtù*, and occlude as far as possible her 'actual' sex.

What is interesting about this example (from an article by a critic for whom I have a great deal of respect) is that while it invokes history, it slips, at the point of comparison between the two accounts, into an exercise in intertextuality, and the critical mistake (equating 'actual' with 'textual' versions of Elizabeth) is a direct consequence. Textual 'equivalence' (the words weighing equally),[20] I suggest, does not automatically confirm that there is a common historical 'actual', in which both texts are grounded. In this case the discourses are undoubtedly shared: both texts make use of contemporary cultural versions of 'woman spoken badly of' (specifically, spoken of as *fallen* woman – harlot, whore).[21] But then, the *occasion* for both accounts is the same: the appearance in public, in a position of authority rather than of deference, in her own right, of an unmarried woman – in early modern terms an intrinsically indecorous event, and one to which the two early modern authors respond in the kind of unseemly terms which they consider are licensed by her (the Queen's) breach of acceptable female behaviour.

Forman's erotic dream encounter with the Queen seems to tell us more about Forman's own preoccupations than about Elizabeth;[22] the Sieur de Maisse's recorded observations are more complicated in their relation to the occasion to which they give expression – the preoccupation with visible flesh which shapes his description of the Queen's appearance is structured by conventions of decorum which are, perhaps, the ambassador's response to the fundamental lack of *respectability* involved in a woman's occupying the throne of England (unthinkable under French Salic law), and suggestions of her as 'harlot/whore of Babylon' in reaction to her further public prominence as head of the English church.[23] Neither text gives us (the twentieth-century reader) access to Queen Elizabeth as historical subject and agent.

There are two reasons why I have considered this example to be important enough to treat it at some length. One is that the culturally constructed figure of the whore or harlot, as a response to a 'forward' woman which stands behind this example is particularly appropriate (in its yet more culturally specific form of 'whore of Venice') when we come to look at *Othello*. The other is that what surfaces very clearly in this example is a tendency in textual criticism to privilege for analysis texts which are concerned with desire and sexuality. And the very plausibility of the critical case made suggests that the temptation to claim two culturally homologous textual versions of 'woman spoken badly of' as 'actual' is then particularly strong. Here, I think, the 'historical' becomes troublingly entangled with the theoretical version of subjectivity in which subjectivity is the unconscious, and which takes the self to be constructed in discourse – a discourse in which unconscious desire is uttered in an endless process of aspiring towards a fulfilment that is permanently deferred. This version of subjectivity allows the 'shaping fantasy' of the Forman and Sieur de Maisse texts to be 'actual', not in the sense that that

was how Elizabeth 'really' was, but in the sense that Elizabethan male subjects expressed (and therefore consciously experienced) their selfhood in
those (explicitly sexual and desirous) terms.

But, strikingly, distinctions in female agency in history seem to have a
strong tendency to collapse into a transhistorical textual identity when we
concern ourselves as critics with utterances which centre on woman's sexuality. Or, to put it another way, if we require discoursing subjects to produce
themselves in terms of desire, in order to recognise those subjects as persons
in our modern sense, then we seem already to have disadvantaged early
modern women.[24] This is a marked tendency in *Othello*, a play in which
sexually charged utterances concerning women play a remarkably prominent
part in the action.

In *Othello* three women, of three distinct social ranks, figure prominently in
the plot. Desdemona is the daughter of one of Venice's most senior and
influential citizens. Bianca is a Venetian courtesan – a woman of substance
who supports herself and her household by her liaisons with men of rank
(notably Cassio, Othello's second-in-command).[25] Emilia is the wife of
Othello's third-in-command, Iago, and personal maid to Desdemona.[26] As
women playing active roles within the community the three are occupationally
distinct. All three are wrongfully accused of sexual misdemeanour in the
course of the play; all three, though unequal in their rank-power, are equally
vulnerable to a *sexual* charge brought against them: although the incidents
which provoke the slander may be presumed to be of separate and distinct
types (as befits the differing social situations in which the three women find
themselves), they yield the identical slur, the identical charge of sexual promis-
cuity – the most readily available form of assault on a woman's reputation.[27]
Each takes the accusation (once made) extremely seriously; but the ways these
accusations are dealt with by the women themselves have very different consequences, and this is crucial, I shall argue, for a 'historical' understanding of
the outcome of the plot. In the substantial part of this chapter I shall propose an alternative approach to the 'defamatory' in *Othello* as part of a general
argument for the need to consider the relationship between text and cultural
context in 'historicist' approaches to Shakespeare.

The Ecclesiastical Court records which survive for England in the early
modern period contain a profusion of examples of cases in which individual
women believed their reputations had been harmed by imputations of unchastity, and what they felt it necessary to do about them. To be more precise: the
depositions laid in defamation cases in the Ecclesiastical Courts (throughout
England, though I shall use the Durham records because of their comparative accessibility) show us how it was expected that a story would be shaped
in relation to public accusations of unchastity – the sort of occasion, the
nature of the accusation, the circumstances of the incident, and above all
how these were put together as a 'convincing' tale for the presiding clerical
official. Throughout the period, ordinary people who had been publicly

accused of social misdemeanour sought restitution in the Ecclesiastical Courts (the courts which had jurisdiction over violations of acceptable practice in domestic, marital and sexual matters).[28] The offended party made depositions (sworn statements) which if substantiated in court led to the offender's doing public penance, paying a fine, or (in extreme cases) being excommunicated. The charges of adultery, whoring, bastard-bearing, scolding, petty theft, etc. were such, however, that if the defamation were allowed to stand the person defamed (the offended party of the records) stood in danger of being charged in their turn in the courts. In other words, the defamation, if it went unchallenged, could become an 'actuality'. I shall argue that we can use the evidence of the Ecclesiastical Court records to make good sense of what does and does not happen with regard to such accusations in *Othello*.[29]

One of the conclusions to emerge from these records is that 'when women defended their reputations through defamation suits in the ecclesiastical courts, they were more concerned with their reputation for chastity, not for submissiveness, obedience or being a good housewife. . . . [By contrast] [m]en worried about insults to their social position, their honesty or sobriety as well as about their sexual behaviour.'[30] In a sample survey of the York records, for example, 90 per cent of cases concerning a female plaintiff involved her sexual reputation.[31] Ritual sexual banter, including lewd mocking rhymes and fairly explicit romping at weddings, was an acceptable part of social practice.[32] But there was a point at which it was understood that lewd talk became defamation – when the accusation, circulating publicly, endangered the individual's reputation. The impact of defamation is most graphically illustrated by citing some cases (here taken from the Durham records).

On 26 October 1568, Margaret Nicolson ('singlewoman') made a deposition against Agnes, wife of Robert Blenkinsop, claiming that she, Margaret, had been defamed as follows:

> Hyte hoore, a whipe and a cart and a franc hoode, waies [woe is] me for the, my lasse, wenst [wilst thou] have a halpeny halter for the to goo up Gallygait and be hanged?[33]

On 7 December 1568, Ann Foster made a deposition against Elizabeth Elder:

> That the wyfes of the Close wold say that she was a spanyell hoore.[34]

Here the *circulation* of the defamatory accusation is the substance of the accusation, but (by implication) it emanates from Elizabeth Elder. Janet Steilling lodged a complaint against Margaret Bullman for defamation which shows how the charge of 'whore' is apparently substantial, where other charges of dishonesty are not. In this case Agnes Wheitley (wife of Robert Wheitley, of Segefield, aged 33 years) made deposition on Steilling's behalf as follows:

> As this examinate was commyng forth with her skeill she hard Bull-

man's wyffe caul Styllynge 'noughtie pak' [baggage, worthless person (according to the *OED*), but often 'whore']; who answered, 'What nowtynes know you by me? I am neyther goossteler nor steg [gander] steiler, I would you knew ytt.' And then Bullman's wyff said 'What, noughty hoore, caull thou me goose steiler?' 'Nay, mayry, I know thee for no such' saith Stillinge wyffe, 'but I thank you for your good reporte, whills you and I talk further.'[35]

In this deposition it appears that mutual accusations of thieving take second place to the central slandering 'noughty hoore' by Bullman against Steilling.[36]

A case in which the shaping of the tale is more obviously a crucial element is the one brought by Katherine Reid against Isabell Hynde, in 1569. Two depositions were made in this case, both on behalf of Katherine Reid, the woman against whom the defamation has been uttered. It will be clear that the accused woman, Isabell Hynde, is the more vulnerable of the two, and has no one (perhaps) to speak on her behalf. The first deposition is made by Agnes Dods ('late wife of Edward Dods of Newcastle, shipwright, aged 23 years' [a widow?]):

> She saith that, the weik byfore Easter last past, one George Dawson and the said Isabell was in this examinate's house, what other certain day this deponent cannott depose, at what time the said Isabell spoke to a baster [bastard] litle boy of the said Isabell, which the said Georg bygatt of hir and put to this examinat to boor [board], thes words, 'Thow shall not caule Katherine Reid mother, for she caul me hoor, and I never maid fault but for this christen soull, and they wyll nott dytt [stop] ther mowethes with a bowell of wheit that wold say she had bore a barne in Chirton.' – She said the said Dawson, that shulde mary the said Katherin, was present.

Here the scenario is explicitly socially fraught: the slander is perpetrated by the unwed mother about her ex-lover's wife-to-be (in the presence of the woman with whom her child boards, while she herself works to support him). The second deposition shows how by repetition it is reinforced and becomes more serious. This deposition is made by Helinor Reid ('wife of John Reid of Newcastle, merchant, aged 26 years' [sister-in-law of Katherine Reid]):

> She saith that the said Katherine haith been sick thes 2 last yeres, and for the most part this twelmonth haith bein in house with this examinat, hir brother's wyf. And that the said Kathren toke on very hevylye for that she had gotton knowled that the said Isabell had slandered hir, and that she had bome a barne in Chirton. Whereupon this deponent said 'Suster Kathren, be of good cheir, and cast not your self downe again for any such talk; And, for ease of your myend, I wyll myself goo and question hir of hir words.' And therupon this examinat went to Mr

Th. Clibborn house, and the wench Isabell was out a doores. And to [until] she came yn this deponent was opening the matter to hir dame. And at last the said Isabell came in, to whome hir dame Clibborn's wyfe said, 'Thou hast brought thyself in troble with this good wife's suster,' pointing to this examinat then present, and said, 'Thy Mr will not be in troble therwith.' And the said Isabell maid answer, 'What, Katherine Reid?' 'Yea,' saith this examinat, 'she will have you to answer the sklander that ye have maid upon hir, which was that she had borne a barne in Chirton.' And the said Isabell annswered, after many folish words, that that which she had sayd she wold say ytt again, for that she had one wytnes for hir.[37]

The point in invoking these depositions is not that they are 'documentary', but that as texts they are explicitly *purposive* – they shape the story told to a desired outcome. As this last example shows particularly clearly, they are told to the clerk so as to 'make a case': someone's good name has to be shown to have been damaged, by an accusation which must be shown to be false (what would happen to Katherine Reid's engagement, if Isabell Hynde's defamation were allowed to stand?). The apportioning of blame is constructed into the telling: the deponent for the person slandered acts as character witness for them, and endeavours to show that the slanderer is unreliable.[38] What helps our understanding of the case against Desdemona in *Othello*, is that the depositions show how some ostensibly verbal incidents between individuals, as they spill over into the community space (the village green, the pump, outside the house)[39] become recognised as events, which generate particular expectations on the part of the audience (for the local community is surely both onlookers and audience): whatever the audience thought heretofore, the event in question introduces competing versions of fault and blame, which must now be resolved in order that the individuals concerned may be reintegrated into the community.

In *Othello* the crisis point in the play's presentation of Desdemona comes in Act 4, scene 2, when Othello publicly defames Desdemona, and Emilia repeats and circulates the defamation (thus reinforcing and confirming it). The seriousness of the incident is explicit, in strong contrast to the earlier easy, casual impugning of Desdemona's honesty amongst male figures in the play, in private, and in her absence:

> *Othello.* Impudent strumpet!
> *Desdemona.*   By heaven, you do me wrong.
> *Othello.* Are not you a strumpet?
> *Desdemona.*   No, as I am a Christian:
>   If to preserve this vessel for my lord
>   From any hated foul unlawful touch,
>   Be not to be a strumpet, I am none.
> *Othello.* What, not a whore?

Desdemona. No, as I shall be sav'd.
Enter EMILIA

Othello. Is't possible?
Desdemona. O heaven, forgiveness.
Othello.   I cry you mercy,
   I took you for that cunning whore of Venice,
   That married with Othello: you, mistress,
   That have the office opposite to Saint Peter,
   And keeps the gates in hell, ay, you, you, you!
   We ha' done our course; there's money for your pains,
   I pray you turn the key, and keep our counsel.[40]

When Othello accuses Desdemona of unchastity he sends Emilia away, giving her expressly to understand that the conversation between himself and his wife is to be private and intimate: 'Leave procreants[41] alone, and shut the door, / Cough, or cry hem, if anybody come' (4.2.28–9). It is her premature return which results in her overhearing Othello call Desdemona whore. But once the defamation has been accidentally uttered Emilia's outrage on her mistress's behalf consolidates it:

Emilia. Alas, Iago, my lord hath so bewhor'd her,
   Thrown such despite, and heavy terms upon her,
   As true hearts cannot bear.
Desdemona. Am I that name, Iago?
Iago.   What name, fair lady?
Desdemona. Such as she says my lord did say I was?
Emilia. He call'd her whore: a beggar in his drink
   Could not have laid such terms upon his callat.[42]

'Speak within doors', cautions Iago – 'speak lower; "you don't want the whole street to hear"', reads Ridley's note – underlining the fact that the charge has moved from the intimacy of the bedroom to the public space (4.2.146). And the very forms of Emilia's repetition of this 'slander' (4.2.135) indicate first, the seriousness of the accusation, and second, the necessity for formally rebutting it:

Emilia. Why should he call her whore? who keeps her company?
   What place, what time, what form, what likelihood?[43]

This is technical defamation, which invites direct comparison with the cases in the Durham records. In historical and cultural terms this is the point in the play at which Desdemona's culpability becomes an 'actual' issue, in the sense that the depositions in the Ecclesiastical Court records suggest: the verbal has been constituted as event in the community by virtue of the circumstances of utterance, its location in public space, the inclusion in its performance of persons not entitled to hear what is uttered in privacy or intimacy. Just as the tale is told so as to enhance these features of the alleged *causa diffamationis* in the records, so Act 4, scene 2 of *Othello* is shaped, I am suggesting, so that the audience at this point is party to a slander, 'audiently' uttered, and hears it repeated and circulated.[44]

The point is reinforced in the play by what immediately follows: Emilia reminds Iago that (as the audience already knows) Othello was once suspected of sexual misdemeanour with Emilia ('it is thought abroad, that 'twixt my sheets / He's done my office' (1.3.385–6; also 2.1.290–4)). But now she specifies that in that case she too was a victim of a defamation:

> *Emilia.* Why should he call her whore? who keeps her company?
>   What place, what time, what form, what likelihood?
>   The Moor's abus'd by some outrageous knave.
>   Some base notorious knave, some scurvy fellow; . . .
>   Oh, fie upon him! Some such squire he was,
>   That turn'd your wit, the seamy side without,
>   And made you to suspect me with the Moor.[45]

Unlike the noblewoman Desdemona, Bianca and Emilia understand the need actively to counter defamatory utterance against their reputation. In Act 5, scene 1 (and surely in deliberate juxtaposition with Desdemona's defamation?) Iago accuses the courtesan Bianca of keeping a bawdy house, and Emilia publicly calls her strumpet; Bianca's retaliation is immediate:

> *Iago.* This is the fruit of whoring; pray, Emilia,
>   Go know of Cassio where he supp'd to-night:
>   What, do you [Bianca] shake at that?
> *Bianca.* He supp'd at my house, but I therefore shake not.
> *Iago.* O, did he so? I charge you go with me.
> *Emilia.* Fie, fie upon thee, strumpet!
> *Bianca.* I am no strumpet, but of life as honest
>   As you, that thus abuse me.
> *Emilia.*   As I? faugh, fie upon thee!
> *Iago.* Kind gentlemen, let's go see poor Cassio dress'd;
>   Come, mistress, you must tell 's another tale.[46]

Bianca, in spite of her 'profession', retaliates against the slanderous 'strumpet'.[47] Bianca is uncomfortably 'like' Desdemona at this point in the play: both women of independent spirit (and means), both Venetian women of some rank and status, both accused of being 'whores of Venice', when Venetian whores were a recognisable *topos* of literature and art, both associated negatively with Cassio's Florentine manners and 'proper manhood'.[48] Textually a critic might note their 'equivalence'; but there are considerable consequences to their occupying entirely different rank positions in the community, with differing sets of social relations.

I am proposing that Desdemona's case is altered from this point forward in the play – in the telling of the tale of Desdemona's relations with a community which includes the play's audience – not because of any alteration in Desdemona's own conduct, but because she has been publicly designated 'whore' in terms damaging enough to constitute a substantial threat to her reputation. From this point on there is no casual innuendo, no lewd comment on Othello's wife's behaviour or supposed sexual appetite. Desdemona's two remaining scenes focus on her now supposedly culpable sexuality, culminating in her suffocation on her bed, in a state of undress – a whore's death for all her innocence.[49]

Desdemona's defamation has no substance at all; at the moment of her own death Emilia testifies to her mistress's chastity: 'Moor, she was chaste, she lov'd thee, cruel Moor, / So come my soul to bliss, as I speak true' (5.2.250–1).[50] Yet in spite of her private protestations of innocence, Desdemona does nothing formally to restore her now 'actually' impugned reputation. It might be said that she does nothing because she does not know of what she is accused (reminding us that calling your wife 'whore' is common abuse, whatever the offence):[51] 'If haply you my father do suspect / An instrument of this your calling back [to Venice], / Lay not your blame on me', she says, whilst begging Othello forgiveness on her knees (4.2.45–7). She cannot even bring herself to utter the word used against her ('Am I that name, Iago?' 'What name, fair lady?' 'Such as she says my lord did say I was?'; 'I cannot say "whore": / It does abhor me now I speak the word').[52] In striking contrast to the innocent Desdemona's inaction, the worldly Bianca recognises the affront, and its damaging consequences, and retaliates.

Many critics have observed that Othello treats Desdemona as a prostitute in 4.2. Indeed, the scene is often described as the 'brothel' scene. But that, I am arguing, is once again to miss the distinctions between shaped and meaningful events, and the persisting innuendo and suspicion which shrouds the action of the play from the moment Desdemona marries against her father's wishes, and for love of a man whose 'ugliness' (ethnicity) makes it clear she can be drawn to him by lust alone. 'Leave procreants alone' may be lewd talk, it may be unworthy of a man of Othello's standing in relation to his wife, but it does not have bulk and density as the uttering of the words 'I took thee for that cunning whore of Venice / That married with Othello' does, 'audiently'. Whether or not Emilia physically enters, or whether she simply and pedantically circulates the defamatory utterance (like the wives of the Close in one of the examples I gave from the Durham records), it is from that moment an accusation in public space.

To sharpen this last observation a little more: there is one further, curious deposition in a case of defamation in the Durham records which we may usefully set against this account of *Othello* 4.2. In the early 1570s John Hunter, 'of Medomsley, husbandman, aged 50 years' who 'partes bene novit a suis cunabulis' (knew the parties well as neighbours), made a deposition on behalf of the supposed utterer of a defamation, in the case of Helen Johnson, wife of Simon Johnson, against George Allenson, as follows:

> Upon his consciens he beliveth that the said Elinour is a veri honest woman, and so named and reportyd within the towne and parish of Medomsley of all the inhabitors there, saving hir owne husband, who, beinge a very suspecious man, haith some tyme audiently caulde the said Elinor 'Skott's hore'. He saith, upon his oothe, that he never harde the said Allenson say at any time any suche wordes as is articulate. Mary, he saith, that, about St. Elenmas last past, to this examinate's remembrance, the said Helen [alias Elinour] Johnson, by report, satt downe of hir knees in the church porche of Medomsley, upon a sonday or hallydaye, after service, when many people were assembled in the church yarde; at what tyme the said George Allenson came to this examinat, being then talking with one John Stevenson, of Bierssyde, and requierd this examinate and one Androo Hunter to here what he, the said Allenson, wold say, and examon the said Helen upon which had satt down in the kirke porch, and asked a vengeance of hym, the said George. At whose request this examinate and the said Androo went with the said George to the aforesaid Helyn Johnson, and in the presence of 30 persons moo, then, this examinate and Andro Hunter questioned and examoned the said Helene, what fault he had maid hir or hir husband to ax a vengeaunce upon hym, the said George Allenson? to whome the said Helyn answerd and said then, 'whye dids thowe caule me — hoore?' and then the said Georg aunswerd hir, the said Helyn, and said, 'Thou knowist best whither thou art a hore or noo: thou was never my hoore'. And she, the said Helyn, still said that the said George had cauld hir so. And then the said Allenson offerd to make amends yf she culd bring in aither honest man or woman that wolde prove thoise wordes. 'Yeis', quodth the said Symon, 'Thou caulde hir hoore to my face at the well grein'. And then aunswerd the said George and said, 'Loke, what I caulde hir afore, that will I caull hir againe'; and so the parties departyd. Examined whither he, this examinate, haith harde the said George caule the aforesaid Symon cookhold or noo, he aunswerethe negatively.
>
> Signum + JOHANNIS HUNTER[53]

The deponent testifies that 'the said Elinour is a veri honest woman', but suggests her reputation is damaged by the fact that 'hir owne husband, . . . beinge a very suspecious man, haith some tyme audiently caulde the same Elinor "Skott's hore"' (and perhaps the suggestion is that this leads to others repeating the slander). 'Audiently' (presumably the clerk's interpolation – it comes from an educated vocabulary) – captures perfectly the way in which words uttered in the privacy of the home are altered as they are 'heard' in public – whether deliberately, or overheard. It is the spilling-over of private exchange into a public space ('Thou caulde hir hoore to my face at the well grein [green]') which alters the nature of the incident, and turns it from verbal abuse into event in the communal sphere.

If we read *Othello* in this way, locating our analysis at the disciplinary interface between history, culture and text, we (the twentieth-century explorers of the past) begin to see a web of social relations, a mesh of interpersonal tensions, given meaning by the social events which rendered incipient feeling actual and acknowledgeable in the community. The shape of the tale becomes structurally significant, as it matches the shapes of other tales, told in the early modern community to other, more occasional, judgemental ends. We do not thereby access 'truth' or 'reality', but we do begin to recognise the shared cultural conventions where 'lived experience' was given expression and acknowledgement. So the process can (I maintain) yield a submerged intensity and explicitness in interpersonal feeling which can helpfully position our twentieth-century attention and perhaps give us back a point from which to respond to culturally significant incidents which no longer have meaning in this early modern sense. This, at least, is what I am arguing in the present case.[54]

In conclusion, I want to suggest that if we allow a historical reading to direct us towards substantial defamation as the crux of the plot in *Othello*, then we are also led towards a revised reading of the instrumentality of Othello's 'jealousy'.

I suggest that once the substantial defamation stands against Desdemona, Othello murders her for adultery, not out of jealousy.[55] If we retrace the play to Act 3, scene 3, we find jealousy contrasted both with ignorance of dishonour on the part of a husband, and with certainty. Jealousy is the humiliating condition of doubt in relation to your own honour and your wife's obedience. It is linked from the outset, by Iago, with 'good name':

> *Iago.* Good name in man and woman's dear, my lord;
>   Is the immediate jewel of our souls:
>   Who steals my purse, steals trash, 'tis something, nothing,
>   'Twas mine, 'tis his, and has been slave to thousands:
>   But he that filches from me my good name
>   Robs me of that which not enriches him,
>   And makes me poor indeed.
> *Othello.* By heaven I'll know thy thought.
> *Iago.* You cannot, if my heart were in your hand,
>   Nor shall not, whilst 'tis in my custody:
>   O, beware jealousy;
>   It is the green-ey'd monster, which doth mock
>   That meat it feeds on. That cuckold lives in bliss,
>   Who, certain of his fate, loves not his wronger:
>   But O, what damned minutes tells he o'er
>   Who dotes, yet doubts, suspects, yet strongly loves! . . .

Othello. Think'st thou I'ld make a life of jealousy?
  To follow still the changes of the moon
  With fresh suspicions? No, to be once in doubt,
  Is once to be resolv'd . . .
  I'll see before I doubt, when I doubt, prove,
  And on the proof, there is no more but this:
  Away at once with love or jealousy![56]

Later in the scene Othello reiterates the view that cuckoldry is not theft until it is public knowledge ('Let him not know't, and he's not robb'd at all' (3.3.349)). And what he demands of Iago is knowledge, to end his doubt (and his jealousy):

Othello. Villain, be sure thou prove my love a whore,
  Be sure of it, give me the ocular proof . . .
  Make me to see 't, or at the least so prove it,
  That the probation bear no hinge, nor loop,
  To hang a doubt on.[57]

In the crafted narrative of the play, Othello's doubt is ended, and with it his jealousy, when a case of defamation is perpetrated against Desdemona and the case is not answered – 'She turn'd to folly, and she was a whore' (5.2.133).[58] From that point he acts with complete certainty of her guilt.[59] 'It is the cause [the case, adultery]', he says, as he prepares to murder her (5.2.1–3), and as he murders her, his cross-examination is couched in the terms of the lawcourt: 'If you bethink yourself of any crime . . . solicit for it straight'; 'take heed of perjury'; 'confess'; 'O perjur'd woman'; 'He hath confess'd . . . That he hath . . . us'd thee . . . unlawfully'.[60] In other words, doubt has given way to certainty – a certainty built not on 'ocular proof', nor even on the misinterpretation of his eavesdropping on Cassio, far less on the persistence of Iago's lies. Certainty, for Othello, the certainty that entitles the cuckolded husband to seek retribution upon his wife,[61] hinges on that substantial defamation perpetrated by Othello himself – who 'beinge a very suspecious man, haith some tyme audiently caulde . . . [his wife] "hore"'.

Finally, let me return to that matter of agency, and its retrieval for those traditionally excluded from the historical account. The present case conveniently illustrates the fact that what I am concerned to do is to find a way of including the possibility of agency, a reciprocity of activity such as we experience ourselves. As I said earlier: 'In history, agency is a dynamic, in relation to women and to men (both women and men have acted, have been acted upon). It is this historical agency which I am concerned to retrieve, in theory as well as in practice.' In my exploration of *Othello* I have not been able to give back to Desdemona power to accompany her activity – but I have, I believe, repositioned our attention in relation to the events which take place on the stage so that representation no longer overwhelms the interpersonal dynamics of an early modern community to which the text gives expression.

2

'NO OFFENCE I' TH' WORLD'
Unlawful marriage in *Hamlet*

Hamlet. Madam, how like you this play?
Queen. The lady doth protest too much, methinks.
Hamlet. O, but she'll keep her word.
King. Have you heard the argument? Is there no offence in't?
Hamlet. No, no, they do but jest – poison in jest. No offence i' th' world.[1]

Each of the chapters in this book sets out to bring historical studies and text studies into constructive tension with one another, to encourage us to 'read historically' in something stronger than a ritual genuflection towards the past. One of my aims is to prompt a dialogue with others writing similarly reflectively in both fields. Since this is work intended for an audience of both text critics and historians, I pause here for a moment on the whole idea of 'historicism' in relation to text studies. In an article entitled 'Literary criticism and the return to "history"', David Simpson argues that the attention currently being given by text critics to 'history' is merely a convenient kind of academic valorising. In fact, he maintains,

> the status of historical inquiry has become so eroded that its reactive renaissance, in whatever form, threatens to remain merely gestural and generic. 'History' promises thus to function as legitimating any reference to a context beyond literature exclusively conceived, whether it be one of discourse, biography, political or material circumstance.[2]

In other words, he believes that many so-called historicist critics are using the catchword 'history' to mask a quite conventional (and conservative) commitment to a set of unscrutinised, idealised premises about a past already modelled on the ideological requirements of the present.[3] The implication of that idea of 'return', then, is that there is something retrograde, and above all something positivistic about the undertaking – that is, that in invoking history we are privileging something called 'facts' or 'real-life events', whereas in truth we are all now supposed to know that there are only texts, that our access to facts and to history is only and inevitably textual.[4]

I start my own argument by making it clear that I do not regard the present endeavour as either a turn or a return. I do not think that we should let the marketing tag, 'new' (targeted at eager academic consumers, after the latest product), suggest fashionable change, any more than we should allow 'historicist' to suggest retroactive, backward-looking positivism (once historicism always historicism). What we should be looking at, I suggest, is the converging practices of social historians, intellectual and cultural historians, text critics and social anthropologists, as they move together towards a more sensitive integration of past and present cultural products. It is to this generally progressive trend or development that I consider my own work belongs.[5]

Historians and text critics have absorbed some crucial methodological insights from recent text theory. We do, indeed, now begin from that position of understanding that our access to the past is through those 'textual remains' in which the traces of the past are to be found – traces which it will require our ingenuity to make sense of. Nevertheless, it is by no means the case that this inevitably leaves us in a position of radical indeterminacy. In fact, I begin to believe that it only appears to lead us in such a direction if we are committed (wittingly or unwittingly) to the view that what textual remains yield, in the way of an account of the past, is evidence of individual subjectivity. In this case, indeterminacy is apparently doubly inevitable. For what we recognise as individual subjectivity is the fragmented, partial, uncertain, vacillating trace of first-person self-expression. And if we take on board Stephen Greenblatt's suggestive idea of self-fashioning – an aspiration on the part of the individual, embedded in past time, towards a coherence of self, which is inevitably endlessly deferred and historically incomplete – it can be argued that what the cultural historian can retrieve and reconstruct of the past will of necessity be correspondingly incomplete and indeterminate. Here, Greenblatt's primary model is an anthropological one, his methodology that of the social anthropologist (and with it some of his assumptions about the strangeness of other selves).[6]

But those of us who are committed to social and political change may consider that we have another agenda altogether, the focus of which is group consciousness (and intersubjectivity).[7] In my recent work, I have emphasised that the specified grounds for my own textual and cultural interpretations is a strongly felt need to provide a historical account which restores agency/ participation to groups hitherto marginalised or left out of what counts as historical explanation – non-élite men and all women. That means the focus of my critical attention is interpersonal, social relations within a community (loosely defined). For it is in such 'events' – shaped and made to signify for the group – that those members of the community without authority nevertheless figure. So the shaping of events in telling the tale is part of the given of the kind of excavation of the past I am engaged in.[8]

In other words, I find that I am able to accommodate competing accounts of a set of textually transmitted events (competing versions of what makes collections of incidents in past time culturally meaningful), without discarding as illusory the lost incidents in past time which gave rise to them. That is a methodological matter to be negotiated, the very fabric out of which perceived social relations are constructed, not a breakdown or paradox within the community as such. Texts may be generated by individual, gendered selves, but we may nevertheless choose to give our attention to the way in which in any period, membership of a community is determined by a shared ability to give meaning to the shifting unpredictability of everyday life. This is the group consciousness on which social practice depends, and which provides the boundary conditions for individual self-affirmation and action.[9]

The counter-position to non-participation is active participation, but not (without falsifying the account) power. In my excavation of the defamation of Desdemona in *Othello* (which in Act 4, scene 2 shifts the focus of blame/guilt from Iago/Othello to Desdemona herself, and destroys her reputation), I was not able to give back to Desdemona power to accompany her participation – but I was able to reposition our attention in relation to the events which take place on the stage, so that representation no longer overwhelmed the interpersonal dynamics of an early modern community to which the text gives expression.[10] Insofar as I was successful, this retrieval of agency for Desdemona was achieved by my treating the individual subject in the drama as a 'cultural artifact':[11] the play gives us a tale of Desdemona's participation in what one might call 'artifacted incidents' (recognised, acknowledged, shared), whose 'shape' incorporates assumptions about *outcome* and *subsequent action*. We can retrieve that recognition, I argued, by juxtaposing the tales told in contemporary court depositions (where the recognition of the infringing of shared codes of behaviour is the essence of the story) with the dramatic text – both being 'performances' before 'audiences' in that same community/group.[12] Our access to something like 'who Desdemona is' is given by learning to 'read' in the social relations dramatised, those situations which were meaningful – which established or expressed Desdemona's relationship to her community in ways acknowledged as socially significant. Those 'events' (as I choose to call such socially meaningful sets of relationships) are the expressed form of Desdemona's 'lived experience', and I mean that, since in my view it will not make a significant difference whether the 'person' who is presented via this shaped version of experience is real or fictional.[13]

This brings me to a crucial distinction which in the consideration I shall be giving to *Hamlet* I shall particularly need to sustain, between the version of the term 'subject' which my own approach produces, and individual internalised selfhood (of which the related term 'subjectivity' is symptomatic). The 'self' discovered amongst the traces of the past using the approach I am advocating is crucially an exterior one 'modified by local customs' – selfhood is read off the outside of the body, and is inseparable from that body. There are, as Clifford Geertz insists, no transhistorical 'real persons', separate from the artifacted incidents which give their 'embodied' behaviour meaning.[14] By contrast, the internalised (broadly psychoanalytical) version of selfhood and subjectivity separates a transhistorical 'self' from a historically located body, and produces the disparity between a universally understood selfhood and a historically specific body as problem or paradox.

In Stephen Greenblatt's pioneering work, the pursuit of the psychoanalytical subject via psychoanalytic theory coexists with the methodology of social anthropology.[15] The individual critic acknowledges the distance which separates him from the discoursing subject in past time; he (sic) attempts to 'speak with the dead'.[16] It follows that the terms of the dialogue he establishes are those which he can 'hear' as the textual trace of selfhood within his own discursive formation: desire and sexuality. By reaching back into texts which preserve desirous discourse in the early modern period, the new historicist critic retrieves those sign systems which he (from his own position in time and culture) can recognise; it is those shared discursive strategies which are, for him, all we can know of selfhood in past time.

The drawback in such an approach for the feminist historicist is that sexuality is explicitly assumed to code 'power' in ways which lead to the subjection of women (no longer *qua* women, but ostensibly as standing for something else) – even (ironically, and anachronistically) the subjection of Elizabeth I to her desirous male subjects.[17] But the main point to note is that, on this account of subjectivity, the 'actual' is coextensive with what discourses/cultural artifacts share – a matter of intertextual identity. This is, in my view, a fundamental difficulty for such a theory, and its methodology of power relation and subjectivity construction, when we are trying to deal with an inaccessible historical past, and particularly when we are trying to recover female agency/participation from the cultural traces of the past.[18]

It is precisely in the area of sexuality that the problem of 'feeling', and our access to it, arises in *Hamlet*. Hamlet's feelings towards his mother Gertrude were already described in recognisable terms of incestuous desire in the classic 1919 article on the play by T. S. Eliot:[19]

> The essential emotion of the play is the feeling of a son towards a guilty mother . . . Hamlet (the man) is dominated by an emotion which is inexpressible, because it is in excess of the facts as they appear. . . . Hamlet is up against the difficulty that his disgust is occasioned by his mother, but that his mother is not an adequate equivalent for it; his disgust envelops and exceeds her.[20]

This is an appropriate starting point, both because this idea of excess has been a feature of all *Hamlet* criticism since Eliot, and because it already makes clear that an account of Hamlet's 'excessive' feelings in terms of desire (inexpressible emotion) immediately makes concrete and specific his mother as focus of attention for her guilt – she is pronounced guilty not as a judgement on her actions, but as a condition of her presence in the play in relation to Hamlet (thus textual rather than historical in my sense). If Hamlet's feeling is excessive it is because his sense of his mother's guilt exceeds what could possibly fit the facts of the plot: the guilt of a mother who has stimulated sexual desire in her son.[21] Or, as a recent critic puts it, the problem for Eliot is that gap between 'Hamlet's vehement disgust and the Gertrude who is neither vehement nor disgusting'.[22]

Recently, critics have begun to notice that the recurrent use of the term 'incest' in *Hamlet* refers not to any putative or incipient relationship between Hamlet and his mother, but to Gertrude's remarriage to her dead husband's brother.[23] And the problem of Hamlet's excessive feeling and Gertrude's guilt has been reformulated as a gap between individual feelings and social perceptions – what Cedric Watts calls 'the strange case of invisible incest':

> In marrying Claudius, Gertrude was marrying her brother-in-law; and, according to [canon law], such a marriage was indeed incestuous and prohibited. . . . A peculiar anomaly in the play is, therefore, that while Hamlet and the ghost are well aware of this scandalous event, and though the remarriage of Gertrude was fully and ceremonially public, nobody in the court seems to have noticed any incest at all.[24]

Hamlet's excessive emotion is focused on Gertrude's sexual relations with Claudius. And the point about Claudius's marriage to Gertrude historically (as event) is (1) that it is 'unlawful', and (2) that it deprives Hamlet of his lawful succession. So for the remainder of this chapter I turn my attention to unlawful marriage in the early modern period, in order to show how the social relations of the play are altered if we put back the Gertrude/Claudius marriage in history – reinstate it as artifacted incident – and look closely at the nature of the offence that it causes to Hamlet.

Cases of 'unlawful marriage' – marriage within the prohibited degrees – in early modern England were a matter for the Ecclesiastical Courts. And the first thing to notice about the canons concerning unlawful marriage is that the 'unlawfulness' is couched in terms of a complaint – a charge of unlawful marriage arises when someone is offended by the union. As the 1603 canons put it:

> If any offend their Brethren, either by Adultery, Whoredome, Incest, or Drunkennesse, or by Swearing, Ribaldry, Usury, or any other unclean-nesse and wickednesse of life, the Church-wardens . . . shall faithfully present all, and every of the said offenders, to the intent that they may be punished by the severity of the Lawes, according to their deserts, and such notorious offenders shall not be admitted to the holy Communion till they be reformed.[25]

The crucial passage on incest itself in these canons runs:

> No person shall marry within the degrees prohibited by the lawe of God, and expressed in a table set forth by authority in the year of our lord 1563; and all marriages so made and contracted shall be adjudged

incestuous and unlawful, and consequently shall be dissolved as void from the beginning, and the parties so married shall by course of law be separated. And the aforesaid table shall be in every church publickly set up, at the charge of the parish.[26]

If we look at the residual tables of consanguinity and affinity drawn up in England under Henry VIII, we see how these already incorporate the idea of 'offence caused'.[27] 'Consanguinity' conforms broadly with what we might expect: a man may not marry his mother, his father's sister or his mother's sister, his sister, his daughter or the daughter of his own son or daughter.[28] The table of consanguinity prohibits marriages with close blood ties, in the generations in which it might plausibly occur (parent, sibling, offspring, grand-child). The table of affinity, by contrast, reflects unions which might produce conflicting inheritance claims.[29] A man may not marry his father's wife, his uncle's wife, his father's wife's daughter, his brother's wife or his wife's sister, his son's wife or his wife's daughter, nor the daughter of his wife's son or daughter. None of these are blood ties, but each creates complications over the line. In particular, the marriage of a widow to her dead husband's brother threatens the son's inheritance claim. The son is first in line, his father's brother second; the marriage of the dowager widow to the second in line threatens to overwhelm the claim of the legitimate heir.

Notoriously, Henry VIII's marriage to his dead brother Arthur's widow, Catherine of Aragon, was incestuous under the Levitican tables of affinity.[30] Slightly less notoriously, Henry's fifth marriage to Catherine Howard was also unlawful under affinity, since Catherine was Anne Boleyn's first cousin.[31]

Two depositions from the Durham Ecclesiastical Court Records concerning an 'unlawful marriage' (around 1560) give us some insight into how the idea of complaint or 'offence caused' has a bearing on individual cases brought to the notice of the church courts:

EDWARD WARD of Langton near Gainford husbandman, aged 40 years.
He saith that ther is dyvers writing hanginge upon the pillers of ther church of Gainford, but what they ar, or to what effect, he cannott deposse; saing that he and other parishioners doith gyve ther dewties to be taught such matters as he is examined upon, and is nott instruct of any such.
He saith, that he was married with the said Agnes in Gainford church by the curat S[r] Nicholas, about 14 daies next after Christenmas last past, but not contrary to the lawes of God, as he and she thought. And for the resydew of the article he thinks nowe to be trewe, but not then. Examined whither that he, this deponent dyd knowe at and before the tyme of their mariadg, that she the said Agnes was, and had bein, his uncle Christofore Ward's wyfe, ye or no, he saith that he knew that to be trew, for she had, and haith yet, fyve children of his the said Christofer's. Examined upon the danger of their soules, and evyll

example, he saith that both he and mayny honest men in that parish thinks that it were a good deid that thei two meght still lyve to gyther as they doo, and be no further trobled.

AGNES WARD, ALIAS SAMPTON, aged 40 years.

– all the Lordship and paroch of Gainford knew howe nighe hir first husband and last husband was of kyn, and yet never found fault with ther mariadg, neither when thei wer asked in the church 3 sondry sonday nor sence – they haith bein likned [linked?] to gither more and 2 yere, and yett never man nor woman found fault – but rather thinks good ther of, bicause she was his own uncle wyf.[32]

The directed or 'purposive' narrative of these depositions is not difficult to unravel: Edward Ward's marriage to his uncle Christopher Ward's widow, Agnes, is incest under ecclesiastical law, but 'mayny honest men in that parish thinks that it were a good deid that thei two meght still lyve to gyther as they doo, and be no further trobled', and, as Agnes testifies, everyone in the parish knew 'howe nighe hir first husband and last husband was of kyn', 'and yett never man nor woman found fault'. Not only did no one find fault; they 'rather thinks good ther of, bicause she was his own uncle wyf'.[33] Church law holds the marriage unlawful; christian charity suggests that no one is harmed by the marriage, and widow and children are appropriately cared for. The 'dyvers writing hanginge upon the pillers of ther church' that Edward Ward refers to are the 'table [to] be in every church publickly set up, at the charge of the parish', specified in the 1603 canons quoted above: the tables of consanguinity and affinity which specified who might legally marry whom (as Edward Ward clearly deposes, he himself is illiterate and unable to read the tables). And we may, I think, extend the idea of 'offence caused' one stage further. Someone had to draw the marriage to the attention of the courts; that person had to be someone to whom the 'unlawfulness' of the marriage gave some (material) offence.[34] This charge laid by another is what is referred to (but permanently uninterpretable without information now lost to us) in the sentence in Edward Ward's deposition: 'And for the resydew of the article he thinks nowe to be trewe, but not then.'[35]

Since, in *Hamlet*, Claudius's marriage to Gertrude is, like Henry VIII's, a marriage to a dead brother's widow, there is no doubt in the play of the incest, and Hamlet states the case directly:

> Let me not think on't – Frailty, thy name is woman –
> A little month, or ere those shoes were old
> With which she follow'd my poor father's body,
> Like Niobe, all tears – why, she –
> O God, a beast that wants discourse of reason
> Would have mourn'd longer – married with my uncle,
> My father's brother – but no more like my father
> Than I to Hercules. Within a month,

> Ere yet the salt of most unrighteous tears
> Had left the flushing in her galled eyes,
> She married – O most wicked speed! To post
> With such dexterity to incestuous sheets![36]

The ghost of Hamlet senior puts the case more forcefully still, but, unlike Hamlet, gives the active part in the incest entirely to Claudius:

> Ay, that incestuous, that adulterate beast,
> With witchcraft of his wit, with traitorous gifts –
> O wicked wit, and gifts that have the power
> So to seduce! – won to his shameful lust
> The will of my most seeming-virtuous queen. . . .
> O horrible! O horrible! most horrible!
> If thou has nature in thee, bear it not,
> Let not the royal bed of Denmark be
> A couch for luxury and damned incest.[37]

An offence – incest, marriage in a prohibited degree – but (as in the case from the court records) some anxiety as to who has been materially offended. In kinship terms there is a breach of the law. It goes unrecognised until it is decided who claims it as such, and against whom. Where, indeed, do the kinship claims lie in the text? As Cedric Watts perceptively puts it (in text critical terms): 'By accident or design, the play . . . exhibits an ideological disarray; a conflict within and between religious, political and dramatic conceptions of sexual order and transgression.'[38]

I think this problem is not specific to the play, *Hamlet*. As I believe often happens, I think the play literally dramatises the early modern narrative necessary (requiring to be recognised) for the apportioning of blame and establishing innocence wherever there is a 'cause'.[39] Indeed, this is, I think, why historians of the family have registered a discrepancy between general kinship rules (and legislation concerning lawful and unlawful unions in particular) and actual practice. The paucity of concrete evidence suggests that these codes rarely led to legal action.[40] A kinship grievance may, I suggest, be experienced as such without the specific offence having been identified. Once the offence is identified, however, 'due process of law' can transform 'emotional intensity' into action.[41]

Kinship and inheritance are remarkably strong themes in *Hamlet* from the outset.[42] Young Hamlet is heir to Old Hamlet, just as Young Fortinbras is heir to Old Fortinbras: he comes at the head of an army to reclaim his inheritance:

> our last King,
> Whose image [ghost] even but now appear'd to us,
> Was as you know by Fortinbras of Norway,
> Thereto prick'd on by a most emulate pride,

Dar'd to the combat; in which our valiant Hamlet
(For so this side of our known world esteem'd him)
Did slay this Fortinbras, who, by a seal'd compact
Well ratified by law and heraldry
Did forfeit, with his life, all those his lands
Which he stood seiz'd of to the conqueror;
Against the which a moiety competent
Was gaged by our King, which had return'd
To the inheritance of Fortinbras,
Had he been vanquisher; as, by the same cov'nant
And carriage of the article design'd,
His fell to Hamlet. Now, sir, young Fortinbras,
Of unimproved mettle, hot and full,
Hath in the skirts of Norway here and there
Shark'd up a list of lawless resolutes
For food and diet to some enterprise
That hath a stomach in 't, which is no other,
As it doth well appear unto our state,
But to recover of us by strong hand
And terms compulsatory those foresaid lands
So by his father lost.[43]

'Our last King', 'our King', 'the inheritance of Fortinbras, ... His fell to Hamlet', 'Now, ... young Fortinbras', prepares the audience for the entry of a 'young Hamlet' to match. Claudius's first entrance as King immediately emphasises the alienation of the Hamlet line. Indeed, what is striking about this first entrance is that it is entirely unexpected in revealing to the audience Claudius as King (referred to throughout the play simply as 'King', here only as 'Claudius King of Denmark'), sumptuously, with Hamlet in mourning black. The prolonged mourning (an interesting topic itself in early modern history) insistently keeps the direct line, Old Hamlet/Young Hamlet present. And Claudius's opening words fix for the audience the usurpation:

Though yet of Hamlet our dear brother's death
The memory be green, and that it us befitted
To bear our hearts in grief, and our whole kingdom
To be contracted in one brow of woe,
Yet so far hath discretion fought with nature
That we with wisest sorrow think on him
Together with remembrance of ourselves.
Therefore our sometime sister, now our queen,
Th'imperial jointress to this warlike state,
Have we ...
Taken to wife.[44]

The first exchange of words between Claudius and Hamlet (somewhat late in the scene – it follows the 'fatherly' exchange with Laertes) underlines the fact that the 'unlawful' marriage has strengthened the line in Claudius's favour, and to Hamlet's detriment:

> *King.* But now, my cousin Hamlet, and my son –
> *Hamlet.* A little more than kin, and less than kind.
> *King.* How is it that the clouds still hang on you?
> *Hamlet.* Not so, my lord, I am too much in the sun.[45]

If Hamlet is Claudius's cousin (simply, kin), Hamlet should be King; if Hamlet is Claudius's son, then he is confirmed as line-dependent on Claudius, who sits legitimately on the throne. Right here at the outset, the offence is Claudius's, committed against the Hamlet line. I suggest that Act 1 in its entirety dwells deliberately on incest as a specific material offence committed against young Hamlet.[46]

Why, then, does no one apparently respond? As Watts puts it:

> Nobody at the court seems to have noticed any incest at all. Further-more, the text vigorously precludes any assumption that this oblivious-ness is a symptom of a morally decadent or myopic court: one function of the exchanges between Laertes, Polonius and Ophelia in Act I, scene iii, and between Polonius and Reynaldo in Act II, scene i, is to emphasise that this court is concerned to maintain traditional moral proprieties in sexual conduct.[47]

The answer, I think, is that the moral taint is attached from the outset to a much more generalised and unspecific theme: the hasty remarriage of Hamlet's mother, which is the explicit focus for Hamlet's disgust, and which focuses on her all the guilt and blame.

Disgust gives way to clarity of thought when Hamlet correctly identifies the offence against himself as one regarding lineage and kin:

> *Hamlet.* Now mother, what's the matter?
> *Queen.* Hamlet, thou hast thy father much offended.[48]
> *Hamlet.* Mother, you have my father much offended. . . .[49]
> *Queen.* Have you forgot me?
> *Hamlet.*   No, by the rood, not so.
>   You are the Queen, your husband's brother's wife,
>   And, would it were not so, you are my mother. . . .[50]
> *Queen.* What have I done, that thou dar'st wag thy tongue
>   In noise so rude against me?
> *Hamlet.*   Such an act
>   That blurs the grace and blush of modesty.[51]

Offence against Old Hamlet ('my father'); offensive behaviour towards Clau-dius ('thy father', because Gertrude is '[her] husband's brother's wife',

and thus he her son's father). Hamlet is caught between the knowledge of
an unlawful marriage, a crime committed (perhaps two), to which the community turns a blind eye,[52] and a sense of personal outrage at a wrong
perpetrated against himself by his close kin, when to rectify that outrage
would be to commit petty treason.[53]

Claudius's unlawful marriage to Hamlet's mother, Gertrude, cuts Hamlet
out of the line.[54] The offence is against Hamlet; the offending party is
Claudius.[55] That within the narrative of the text this is importantly an offence
is supported by the very precise mirroring of the circumstances of that
offence in the *Murder of Gonzago* – the play-within-a-play with which Hamlet
hopes to catch Claudius's 'conscience'. 'King' Gonzago is murdered by his
nephew, who then claims the love of Gonzago's widow:

> *Hamlet.* This is one Lucianus, nephew to the King.
>
> . . .
>
> *Lucianus. Thoughts black, hands apt, drugs fit, and time agreeing,*
> *Confederate season, else no creature seeing,*
> *Thou mixture rank, of midnight weeds collected,*
> *With Hecate's ban thrice blasted, thrice infected,*
> *Thy natural magic and dire property*
> *On wholesome life usurp immediately.*
>
> Pours the poison into the sleeper's ears.
>
> *Hamlet.* A poisons him i' th' garden for his estate. His name's Gonzago.
> The story is extant, and written in choice Italian. You shall see anon how
> the murderer gets the love of Gonzago's wife.
> *Ophelia.* The king rises.
> *Hamlet.* What, frighted with false fire?[56]

Marriage to one's uncle's wife is also a marriage in a prohibited degree. In
other words, unlawful marriage is structured into the 'Mousetrap' play, exactly
as are murder by poisoning through the ear, and line-important woman's
second marriage. The difference between the two 'plays', however, is that
in the *Murder of Gonzago* no person is caused offence by the marriage in a
prohibited degree; no one stands in for Hamlet in that narrative, and therefore the play-within-a-play does not resolve the vital matter for Hamlet of
whether he has substantial cause to lodge a formal complaint (or to act as if
he did).

But in the *Murder of Gonzago*, just as in the Hamlet narrative, the moral taint
is on the woman (the Queen) rather than the unlawfulness of the match
which bears the emotional burden of the plot. In both narratives, that moral
taint is focused upon *second marriage* – indeed, that theme alone of all the
parallel themes clearly carries over from play-within-a-play to play narratives,
identifying the two queens:

Player King. Faith, I must leave thee, love, and shortly too:
   My operant powers their functions leave to do;
   And thou shalt live in this fair world behind,
   Honour'd, belov'd; and haply one as kind
   For husband shalt thou —
Player Queen.   *O, confound the rest.*
   Such love must needs be treason in my breast.
   In second husband let me be accurst;
   None wed the second but who kill'd the first.
Hamlet. [Aside] That's wormwood.
Player Queen. The instances that second marriage move
   Are base respects of thrift, but none of love.
   A second time I kill my husband dead,
   When second husband kisses me in bed.
Player King. I do believe you think what now you speak;
   But what we do determine oft we break.
   . . .

Player Queen. Nor earth to me give food, nor heaven light,
   Sport and repose lock from me day and night,
   To desperation turn my trust and hope,
   An anchor's cheer in prison be my scope,
   Each opposite, that blanks the face of joy,
   Meet what I would have well and it destroy,
   Both here and hence pursue me lasting strife,
   If, once a widow, ever I be a wife.
Hamlet. If she should break it now.
   . . .

   [To the Queen] Madam, how like you this play?
Queen. The lady doth protest too much, methinks.[57]

What is striking about this is that whereas marriage in a prohibited degree is unlawful, second marriage of widows is entirely within the law. But, of course, anyone working on the early modern English family knows that second marriage is the subject of an extensive and elaborate literature on the competing claims of the economic (kinship and inheritance) with the spiritual/moral (chaste love, constancy, fidelity).[58] In other words, the civil complexity of kin and inheritance obligations, under which Hamlet might claim a grievance (and proceed to law) against Claudius, is refocused as moral blame on the civically non-participating Gertrude.[59] And Hamlet responds fully to that cause for complaint as his own.

For a mother to connive in wronging her own blood-son (even if only by acquiescence) makes her an emotional focus for the blame.[60] She has indeed committed an unlawful act, yet it is on the *sinful* second marriage that Hamlet focuses. It is the remarriage which Hamlet dwells on, obsessively and offensively, as sexual. But once given discursive vitality, Gertrude's *sexuality* convinces even herself of her guilt ('O Hamlet, thou hast cleft my heart in twain').[61] We have not, then, exonerated Gertrude from blame (we have certainly not empowered her), but we have recovered a historically specific context for the guilt surrounding her, and identified it as a condition of her oppression. She is the focus of guilt not because of what she does, but because she embodies the contradictory claims of kinship on women important to the line.

What worries me, however, is the clarity, the unmistakable recognition, with which we (the twentieth-century cultural historians) can register Gertrude's culpability, while we have lost the ability to read the narrative which attributes blame to the initiator of an unlawful marriage. The former is (in the terms in which I began this chapter) a textual matter – a matter of cultural artifacts and the residual ideologies they perpetuate. The latter is cultural and historical – surely what the historicist should give attention to as she uses a knowledge and understanding of the past to allow her to 'speak with the dead' – to enter into a dialogue with interlocutors in past time.

3

CULTURAL CONFUSION AND SHAKESPEARE'S LEARNED HEROINES

'These are old paradoxes'

Desdemona. Come, how wouldst thou praise me?
Iago. I am about it, but indeed my invention
  Comes from my pate as birdlime does from frieze,
  It plucks out brain and all: but my Muse labours,
  And thus she is deliver'd:
  If she be fair and wise, fairness and wit;
  The one's for use, the other using it.
Desdemona. Well prais'd! How if she be black and witty?
Iago. If she be black, and thereto have a wit,
  She'll find a white, that shall her blackness hit.
Desdemona. Worse and worse.
Emilia. How if fair and foolish?
Iago. She never yet was foolish, that was fair,
  For even her folly help'd her, to an heir.
Desdemona. These are old paradoxes, to make fools laugh i' the alehouse.[1]

My title quotation for this chapter refers the reader to a familiar passage in *Othello* in which 'proper' and 'improper' uses of female initiative – proper and improper products of specifically female labour – are facetiously juxtaposed. Sexual knowingness – cannily getting a partner, astutely making a match – overwhelms all other possibilities for female wisdom and wit. Desdemona takes this as a familiar type of game, a familiar part of the contemporary culture ('These are old paradoxes'). The audience, however, easily hears the exchange as impugning Desdemona's own modesty (does her 'wit', then, betoken active sexuality?). Iago's muse labours and is delivered, metaphorically, of a healthy piece of witty repartee; Desdemona's female labour is, it seems, likely to recall all too readily sexual activity and reproduction. What provides a witty paradox for the jest-books is, it appears, a source of serious confusion when it comes to our scrutinising the activities of a particular woman.[2]

This chapter focuses on what I see as the source of Desdemona's difficulty, or, more accurately, perhaps, the source of our difficulty here with Desdemona. There is a confusion to be detected at the heart of early modern Europe's response to the humanist movement in education. That confusion was produced (I have argued elsewhere) by early pedagogic reformers failing to see the consequences of humanism's confident, and therefore unstated, assumption that its programme of learning in the liberal arts was designed specifically, but never explicitly, for young men of elevated social rank and good prospects. I have devoted a good deal of my recent work in intellectual history to analysing a body of epistolary exchanges between noble (or at least gentle) female humanists of quattrocento Italy and their male mentors, tutors and colleagues, in the course of which I found both sides ambivalent and evasive as to the propriety of imparting humanistic intellectual skills to women, however gifted.[3] In this chapter I propose to pursue further the pervasive ambivalence about 'woman's place' in Renaissance intellectual life by following the trace of the learned woman in some canonical literary texts of the early modern period – specifically, the texts of two of Shakespeare's plays.[4] Such an undertaking requires some preliminary explanation.

It is now twenty years since Natalie Zemon Davis's publications on women's place in the social and cultural history of early modern France signalled the arrival of a more sophisticated set of attitudes towards interpreting a peculiarly women's history, and the comparatively rich textual resources have at last begun to be thoroughly sifted and turned.[5] The result has been a wealth of new material to work with, and more familiar material freshly scrutinised, offering vigorous interpretation of the previously overlooked female presence in early modern society.[6]

It was predictable that this rich resource would be mined by scholars in other, associated disciplines, in which giving attention to the women might be expected to lead to revised assessments and interpretations. In particular, a number of literary critics have turned their attention to the textual residue of the period, and made a variety of cases for the relationship between the social history of women and the representations of women in Renaissance literature – a literature that is still held to play a crucially formative role within literary history.[7] But the literature of the early modern period in Europe (what literary historians confusingly call the Renaissance) is a treacherous source of insight into the 'woman question'.

For this latter kind of work turns out to raise problems which Davis's work does not foreground, dealing as it does with predominantly archival evidence concerning such matters as when women figured in records of public disturbances and what punishments the records show for female misdemeanour.[8] The attempt to unravel the women from Renaissance literary texts tends to begin with explicit position-taking on what are in fact the crucial areas of difficulty for interpreting the surviving social historical data. Linda Woodbridge, for example, states categorically at the outset of her investigation of Renaissance pamphlet controversies on the 'woman question':

A primary barrier to belief in sexual equality was Christian doctrine. The fabric of society was Christian, and the Renaissance typically (and not without reason) interpreted the Scriptures as endorsing male dominance.[9]

Juliet Dusinberre, in *Shakespeare and the Nature of Women*, opens her examination of 'women in literature' by asserting with equal confidence that reformed Christianity fostered equality between the sexes, on the grounds that it stressed mutuality in domestic dealings. In my own *Still Harping on Daughters* I opted for a kind of *via media* between these two strikingly opposed propositions: in its insistence on individual conscience and responsibility, I argued, reformed Christianity further burdened Renaissance women by making them responsible for the well-being of the domestic unit, within which they were explicitly not given any power.[10] What we each subsequently chose to read out of the literary texts that we considered depended rather strictly on this initial 'positioning' of our reading attention.

This is only one example of the pressure on the textual critic to embrace the fiction that there exists a reliable body of social and cultural historical 'fact', to be 'tested' somehow against the 'fiction' of the literary representation. It ignores the fact (as indeed the social historian frequently does) that in practice the social historian's evidence on which these studies draw – evidence concerning women's 'independence', 'assertiveness' and so forth – is as much in need of scrutiny and deconstruction as is the literary critic's.[11]

In this chapter I shall argue for a more complicated and involved relationship between 'women's history' and 'reading out the women', taking as my focus the educated (explicitly educated, that is) heroines in Shakespeare. I choose this particular focus for two reasons. In the first place, there are few such women: i.e. women of intellect capable of employing specialist knowledge customarily restricted to men.[12] In the second place, as a historical starting point from which to commence reading the literary texts, the 'documentary' residue of contemporary attitudes towards the education of women is gratifyingly rich and varied.

There were significant numbers of educated women amongst the gentry and nobility of Europe in the period, and the surviving texts that acknowledge them are split in their response to them (sometimes split within a single text). On the one hand, the view is expressed in pedagogic treatises that an education (by which is meant an education in the classics) will contribute to the pupil's moral fibre and fitness to be an active member of a social élite; this view is matched by the equally clearly expressed position that there is something intrinsically indecorous about a woman who (whether with the encouragement of her family or not) transgresses the social code which requires her to observe a modest silence and passivity in public. The cultural tension in which these two incompatible views result clouds contemporary celebrations of female intellectual accomplishment. One feels it, for example, as a pressure in one of Sir Thomas More's letters to his favourite (and intellectually gifted) daughter, Margaret Roper. More's pride in his daughter's mastery (just so) of the art of Latin letter writing is produced in a curiously negative form. It will be impossible, he writes, to prevent others from doubting that her letters are her own work; thus she will never gain the credit she deserves. And More takes it for granted that if her learning is to be compatible with the demands of decorum, then she must be clear that it is intended for no other audience than her husband and father:

> I cannot put down on paper, indeed I can hardly express in my own mind, the deep pleasure that I received from your most charming [Latin] letter, my dearest Margaret. As I read it there was with me a young man of the noblest rank and of the widest attainments in litera-ture. . . . He thought your letter nothing short of marvellous. . . . I could scarce make him believe that you had not been helped by a teacher until he learned truly that there was no teacher at our house, and that it would not be possible to find a man who would not need your help in composing letters rather than be able to give any assistance to you.
>
> Meanwhile, something I once said to you in joke came back to my mind, and I realized how true it was. It was to the effect that you were to be pitied, because the incredulity of men would rob you of the praise you so richly deserved for your laborious vigils, as they would never believe, when they read what you had written, that you had not often availed yourself of another's help: whereas of all the writers you least deserved to be thus suspected. Even when a tiny child you could never endure to be decked out in another's finery. But, my sweetest Margaret, you are all the more deserving of praise on this account. Although you cannot hope for an adequate reward for your labor, yet nevertheless you continue to unite to your singular love of virtue the pursuit of literature and art. Content with the profit and pleasure of your conscience, in your modesty you do not seek for the praise of the public, nor value it overmuch even if you receive it, but because of the great love you bear us, you regard us – your husband and myself – as a sufficiently large circle of readers for all that you write.[13]

I hardly need point out that whether or not Margaret Roper would have liked to 'seek for the praise of the public', that option was, in the interests of propriety, simply not open to her, and her father was bound to insist on the fact.

More's letter reconstructs Margaret Roper's (real) scholarly competence as appropriately unbelievable (because inevitably active and manly by contrast with her virtuous femininity) and insistently private (because chaste women are not to be produced as articulate before a public male audience). The strain (or perhaps anxiety) the reader detects is, I am arguing, not More's confusion alone, marking his choice of phrase and emphasis, but the result of an underlying cultural confusion. He strives to couch his admiration and approval in appropriate contemporary terms, in spite of the fact that there are competing and conflicting requirements for female propriety within the domestic and the intellectual spheres, and he needs to invoke both.

Research into attitudes towards learned women in the humanist texts of the Renaissance is left with these attitudes as insoluble paradox: on the one hand, texts on education encourage the training of girl children (by direct analogy with the acceptable occupations of spinning and embroidery, it will keep their 'idle hands' busy);[14] on the other, educated girls must display no more than that 'accomplishment' which fine needlepoint and musical competence also connoted.[15] On the one hand, the texts encourage female aspiration towards real learning; on the other, faced with female intellectual achievement, male writers consistently mythologise it into iconic chastity, or into a glorious emblem of the cultivatedness of the courts of Europe.

Women possessed of traditionally male learning – women who are not just witty, but are specifically practised intellectually, and (it turns out) able to make use of precise specialist knowledge in traditionally 'male' fields – figure prominently in the plots of two well-known Shakespeare plays: *The Merchant of Venice* and *All's Well That Ends Well*. In *All's Well That Ends Well*, Shakespeare introduces his heroine, Helena, with a comparably uneasy celebration of her cultivation. The specifically learned woman in history (whose real technical skill is viewed with incredulity) becomes the generally educated woman (trained as a gentlewoman), later to become the borrower/ appropriator of male knowledge, whose mastery will be more reassuringly temporary:

> *Lafew.* Was this gentlewoman the daughter of Gerard de Narbon?
>
> *Countess.* His sole child, my lord, and bequeathed to my overlooking. I have those hopes of her good that her education promises her dispositions [which] she inherits – which makes fair gifts fairer; for where an unclean mind carries virtuous qualities, there commendations go with pity; they are virtues and traitors too. In her they are the better for their simpleness: she derives her honesty and achieves her goodness.
>
> *Lafew.* Your commendations, madam, get from her tears.
>
> *Countess.* 'Tis the best brine a maiden can season her praise in.[16]

Helena is not presented here as explicitly learned in the liberal arts or classics as was the historical Margaret Roper. Rather, she is explicitly accomplished in a manner that is 'achieved' (i.e. taught) rather than 'derived' (i.e. innate). It is that upbringing (education) which subsequently makes it plausible for her to borrow/appropriate the male medical skills of her dead father. And the strain is again to be felt which indicates that 'skill' and 'accomplishment' are sustained as necessarily 'good' (virtuous) in a woman only with difficulty (Helena's iconic weeping is, the Countess observes, the safest feminine cover for the attention just drawn to her training).[17]

This point becomes clearer if we look at Castiglione's description of the ideally accomplished noblewoman in the third book of *Il Cortegiano*, in Thomas Hoby's sixteenth-century English translation (we are encouraged to do so by the fact that Helena's 'virtuous qualities' recall Hoby's version of the ideal courtier as 'learned, and of so many other vertuous qualities'):[18]

> And to make a briefe rehersall in few wordes of that is alreadie saide, I will that this woman have a sight in letters, in musicke, in drawing, or painting, and skilfull in dauncing, and in devising sports and pastimes, accompanying with that discrete sober moode, and with the giving a good opinion of her selfe, the other principles also that have beene taught the Courtier.
>
> And thus in conversation, in laughing, in sporting, in jesting, finally in everie thing she shal be had in great price, and shall entertaine accordingly both with jestes, and feate conceites meete for her, every person that commeth in her company.
>
> And albeit stayednesse, noblenesse of courage, temperance, strength of the minde, wisdome, and the other vertues, a man would thinke belonged not to entertaine, yet will I have her endowed with them all, not so much to entertaine (although notwithstanding they may serve thereto also) as to be vertuous: and these vertues to make her such a one, that she may deserve to bee esteemed, and all her doings framed by them.
>
> I wonder then quoth the Lorde Gasper smyling, since you give women both letters, and stayednesse, and nobleness of courage, and temperance, ye will not have them also to beare rule in cities, and to make lawes, and to leade armies, and men to stand spinning in the kitchin.[19]

The quintessentially accomplished gentlewoman is, as Gaspar Pallavicino facetiously observes, perilously close to a dangerously emasculating manliness. Helena, ideal gentlewoman, might all too readily force 'men to stand spinning in the kitchin'.

The plot of *All's Well That Ends Well* hinges on Helena's specialist knowledge, and on the power that knowledge gives her. The play is also organised around various iconic and folkloric modes of female transgression, by means of which 'woman on top' is presented as simultaneously a threat in both the social and the sexual sphere.[20] At the outset of the play, while the audience waits for the Countess of Rossillion to learn of Helena's love for her adoptive brother Bertram, the power of female sexuality to disrupt is introduced to the action by an exchange between the Countess and her clown which opens with man's sexual enslavement to woman ('Tell me thy reason why thou wilt marry.' / 'My poor body, madam, requires it' (1.3.25–6)) and ends with the disorder to be expected where women 'command' men:

> *Countess.* Sirrah, tell my gentlewoman I would speak with her – Helen I mean.
>
> *Clown.* *Was this fair face the cause, quoth she,*
>   *Why the Grecians sacked Troy?*
> *Fond done, done fond,*
>   *Was this King Priam's joy?*
> *With that she sighed as she stood,*
> *With that she sighed as she stood,*
>   *And gave this sentence then:*
> *Among nine bad if one be good,*
> *Among nine bad if one be good,*
>   *There's yet one good in ten.*
>
> *Countess.* What, one good in ten? You corrupt the song, sirrah.
>
> *Clown.* One good woman in ten, madam, which is a purifying a' th' song. Would God would serve the world so all the year! We'd find no fault with the tithewoman if I were the parson. One in ten, quoth'a! And we might have a good woman born but or every blazing star or at an earthquake, 'twould mend the lottery well; a man may draw his heart out ere 'a pluck one.
>
> *Countess.* You'll be gone, sir knave, and do as I command you?
>
> *Clown.* That man should be at woman's command and yet no hurt done![21]

When women like Helena's Greek namesake, the adulterous Helen,[22] govern male action (as the Countess commands her clown to do her bidding), then no good will come of it. And in reply to the Countess's charge that he is 'ever a foul-mouth'd and calumnious knave', the clown insists that he is, in fact, a prophet.[23] Within this play, to utter time-worn male fantasies about woman's capacity to deceive and disrupt is apparently to prophesy (while individual female characters are nevertheless represented as endeavouring strenuously to establish their integrity). Those sexually disruptive capabilities in (men's fantasy construction of) women have already been linked with the Helena of the play in the opening scene: when Helena is a match for Parolles in equivocating on virginity, she betrays herself textually as 'knowing' – too knowing for the innocent virgin she professes to be.[24] Here is woman's defining 'knowledge': private, domestic and sexual, requiring to be hidden from public view in the interests of decorum and modesty. Made public (here in response to Parolles's incitement, as Desdemona is similarly set on by Iago) it is 'impudent', unchaste; it mobilises expectations as it informs her actions. It is a small step from such verbal knowingness to Helena's manipulation of her other 'knowledge' to coerce Bertram unwillingly (and unwittingly) into marriage.

Before the end of Act 1, the confession extracted from Helena by the Countess confirms both the clown's premonition of the disturbing power that 'knowing' women wield, and the 'knowing' sexuality the audience has inferred from Helena's banter with Parolles. She confesses her love for Bertram to the Countess, his mother – a sexual desire whose goal is carnal union ('The hind that would be mated by the lion' (1.1.89)).[25] She then admits that this is her motive for proposing to go to Paris to cure the dying King, using the knowledge her father had bequeathed her:

> *Helena.* My lord your son made me to think of this;
>   Else Paris and the medicine and the king
>   Had from the conversation of my thoughts
>   Haply been absent then.[26]

The pun on 'Paris', as both the city and the adulterous lover of that other Helen, does not help. And one might add that in supporting her adoptive daughter's plan to win her son by subterfuge, the Countess's own behaviour supports the clown's claim that when women rule men should watch out for themselves.[27]

So one tendency of the plot of *All's Well That Ends Well* is towards realising the culturally vague folkloric threat of the woman who knows, in the tricking of Bertram into a marriage that offends him. No good can come from woman's knowingness. And in a cultural domain more historically precise than folk-tale, the force of knowing woman's manipulation of unknowing man is intensified if we notice that while the dowager Countess of Rossillion is party to Helena's scheme, the King of France (in whose wardship Bertram is) is not: by giving his word to Helena he is unwittingly made complicit in a marriage which disparages his ward – which marries him beneath his rank. Helena is explicit that she is petitioning for a marriage above her entitlement, but she is not explicit that it is the King's own ward whose 'disparagement' is at issue:

> *Helena.* Then shalt thou give me with thy kingly hand
>   What husband in thy power I will command:
>   Exempted be from me the arrogance
>   To choose from forth the royal blood of France
>   My low and humble name to propagate
>   With any branch or image of thy state;
>   But such a one, thy vassal, whom I know
>   Is free for me to ask, thee to bestow.[28]

('Exempted be from me the arrogance / To choose from forth the royal blood of France' is elaborately punning. It might read, 'May I be made free to marry above my rank' [made exempt from the charge of exceeding my right-ful demands in choosing a royal heir]; or it might read, 'As concerns my request, you need not worry about my arrogantly presuming to choose one above my station'; or it might read as some combination of the two. In its legalistic phrasing it is, I think, designedly imprecise enough to dupe the King). It is to this technical (politically and socially sensitive) disparagement that Bertram specifically objects:

> *King.* Thou know'st she has rais'd me from my sickly bed.
> *Bertram.* But follows it, my lord, to bring me down
> Must answer for your raising? I know her well:
> She had her breeding at my father's charge –
> A poor physician's daughter for my wife! Disdain
> Rather corrupt me ever![29]

Since a prime obligation on the owner of a wardship was to ensure a suitable match for his ward, Bertram is in fact right to protest at the mortgaging of his prospects to satisfy a promise made by the King.[30] Helena's learning has fulfilled its potential as a sexually and socially disruptive force.[31]

It was not Helena's knowingness that engineered Bertram's disgrace – it was her knowledge, her acquisition of an inheritance from her father in the form of the secret of medical cure. Nevertheless, the possibility of sliding from one to the other – of perceiving either as a disruptive force – is foreshadowed a speech or two earlier in Helena's oath uttered to convince the King of her good faith in maintaining that, however implausibly, her medical knowledge can cure him:

> *King.* Upon thy certainty and confidence
> What dar'st thou venture?
> *Helena.*   Tax of impudence,
> A strumpet's boldness, a divulged shame,
> Traduc'd by odious ballads; my maiden's name
> Sear'd otherwise.[32]

Helena the 'wise woman' (the woman within the community with knowledge of healing – always precariously placed), is allowed through her oath to become associated with the stereotypically lewd form of contemporary defamations of a woman's reputation – defamations which, as the depositions of the sixteenth-century Ecclesiastical Courts show, if allowed to stand, ostracise the knowing woman from the community, recasting her wisdom as witchcraft.[33] The very act of swearing is already damagingly close to woman's curse.[34]

But Helena's learning/knowledge, according to the paradoxical historical attitudes I spoke of earlier, is also a token of female accomplishment and female virtue. This produces a tension (or contrary movement), which the critics recognise, between Bertram's outraged reaction to the 'trick' that leads to his enforced marriage, and the view, expressed by Lafew, that Helena is chaste in her learned wisdom:

King.   What 'her' is this?
Lafew. Why, Doctor She! My lord, there's one arriv'd,
   If you will see her. Now by my faith and honour,
   If seriously I may convey my thoughts
   In this my light deliverance, I have spoke
   With one that in her sex, her years, profession,
   Wisdom and constancy, hath amaz'd me more
   Than I dare blame my weakness.[35]

(Even here, Lafew's 'serious' presentation of Helena's virtuous wisdom is juxtaposed with his preceding 'light deliverance' – a speech of pure bawdy, in which the 'cure' brought by Helena is clearly erotic.)[36]

It is the chaste, virtuous version of Helena to which both the King of France and the Countess of Rossillion subscribe, and that Helena herself displays in her direct dealings with her husband ('Sir, I can nothing say / But that I am your most obedient servant'; 'I am not worthy of the wealth I owe, / Nor dare I say 'tis mine'; 'I shall not break your bidding, good my lord' (2.5.71–2; 79–80; 87)). And accordingly, in the second half of the play, Helena acts out an atonement for her 'forwardness' which is at once ritual return to exemplary passivity, and fairy-tale 'performing of the task' set by Bertram's riddle. Together, atonement and performance effect the permanent transformation of the sexually active Helena of the first part of the play into the virtuously knowing, ideal wife who claims Bertram at the close of the play in a very different spirit from her original 'choosing a husband as her right'. She claims him dutifully, as loyal wife, in spite of the fact that the revelation of his 'ravishment' of Diana and his subsequent ungentlemanly denouncing of Diana as a loose wanton, have convinced Lafew (negotiating as marriage-broker with the King of France the marriage of Bertram and his own daughter) that Bertram is an unworthy match for a noble family:

Helena. O my good lord, when I was like this maid
   I found you wondrous kind. There is your ring,
   And, look you, here's your letter. This it says:
   When from my finger you can get this ring
   And is by me with child, &c. This is done;
   Will you be mine now you are doubly won?[37]

Bertram's 'wondrous kindness' recalls the ambiguity of Helena's knowingness in the early stages of the play – he was 'wondrous kind' in his lusty bedding of Helena when he believed her to be Diana:

Helena.   But, O strange men!
   That can such sweet use make of what they hate,
   When saucy trusting of the cozen'd thoughts
   Defiles the pitchy night; so lust doth play
   With what it loathes for that which is away.[38]

Helena's interpretation of Bertram's lustful and unchaste (debauched) passion for another woman as 'kindness' to herself, followed by her acceptance of Bertram's conveniently awakened love for the wife he claimed to hate, bear the hallmarks of patient Griselda's grateful acceptance, without reproach or recrimination, of Walter's reaffirmation of their marriage vows after his 'trial' of her virtue. All is well that ends well for the male world of the play in which Helena's initial transgression is redeemed into chaste service.

G. K. Hunter's Introduction to the Arden *All's Well That Ends Well* attributes to W. W. Lawrence the 'revolutionary' insight that the plot of the play is constructed out of two traditional episodes in folktale: 'the healing of the king' and 'the fulfilment of the tasks'.[39] Hunter himself maintains that these elements are to be interpreted (with difficulty, he admits) as contributing to the 'magical and romantic' heroism of Helena ('the magical and romantic actions of Helena are in strong contrast to the prosaic opportunism of Parolles' (p. xxxiii)). The difficulty, for Hunter, arises from the presence, in the 'fulfilment of the tasks' half of the play, of episodes in which Helena 'appears as a schemer'. The reading of the play I offer here suggests that this is no isolated difficulty, but is characteristic of Shakespeare's treatment of Helena. The 'knowing' woman is only precariously a force for moral good. Lurking behind that moral front is the female sensuality which is readily released into potential for harm (specifically, harm to men). In acting out the atonement of pilgrimage and the fairy-tale 'restoration to favour' of the solving of the riddle (bed trick, ring game and all), Helena is made a kind of wish-fulfilment solution to the paradox of the two-faced learned lady – a reconciliation of the opposed figurings of the educated woman as both symbol of civilisation and social stability, and 'impudent' (a sexually disruptive force for social disorder).

The Merchant of Venice is another play in which a woman with exemplary knowledge in a male sphere (this time the Law) provides the crux of the plot.[40] But this play does not resolve the actively knowing heroine into passively tolerant wife ('O my good lord, when I was like this maid / I found you wondrous kind'). Rather, the legal knowledge she deploys to save Antonio modulates Portia's initial obedient conformity with the patriarchal demands on her, in her position as female heir, into something close to unruliness. Portia's 'saving' intervention is followed by a piece of folk-tale misrule: in her disguise as the young lawyer Balthazar, she persuades Bassanio to give up to her the betrothal ring he promised never to part with,[41] while her maid Nerissa, disguised as a clerk, similarly dupes her husband Gratiano into giving up his ring.[42] Returning to Belmont, the two men find themselves severely compromised by the loss of their ring pledges, and the sorting out of the circulating rings fails to dislodge the two women convincingly from their position 'on top' (in a sexually dominant position).

When Portia seals her betrothal – her contractual undertaking to marry

Bassanio, according to the terms of her father's will – with the gift of a ring, she pledges:

> This house, these servants, and this same myself
> Are yours, – my lord's! – I give them with this ring,
> Which when you part from, lose, or give away,
> Let it presage the ruin of your love,
> And be my vantage to exclaim on you.[43]

If Bassanio parts with the pledge, she will be entitled to 'exclaim', to renounce her claim, to break the betrothal, to renounce the contract drawn up.[44] The formality of this pledge befits the fortune she brings to the marriage, which carries its own contractual obligations and undertakings. But in a piece of careful paralleling, her maid Nerissa's betrothal ring is a traditional love-token – a pledge of sexual fidelity, in another social class:

> . . . a hoop of gold, a paltry ring
> . . . whose posy was
> For all the world like cutler's poetry
> Upon a knife, 'Love me, and leave me not'.[45]

In freely bestowing their rings on the men who have successfully wooed them, Portia and Nerissa give a future promise to enter into a properly subordinate social and sexual relationship with their husbands. The terms of that bond, like those of Antonio's with Shylock, are called into question by a piece of sophistry, when the two betrothed men are prevailed upon to give up their rings to 'misrule' – to the very women who gave them, but now in breeches, unruly, free of speech.[46] Female 'knowledge' once again slides subtly into 'knowingness' – Portia's first words to Bassanio back in Belmont, back in her female role, equivocate on husbandly domination and female 'lightness' – sexual laxness:

> Let me give light, but let me not be light,
> For a light wife doth make a heavy husband,
> And never be Bassanio so for me.[47]

In the deliberately confused unravelling of the 'ring trick', Bassanio and Gratiano face the consequences of having parted with their betrothal rings. While the symbolic breach is for Portia contractual (she may default on the property agreement), it is produced dramatically as sexual misdemeanour by modulating the 'discovery' through the 'country' pledge given by Nerissa:

> *Portia.* A quarrel ho, already! what's the matter?
> *Gratiano.* About a hoop of gold, a paltry ring
>   That she did give me, whose posy was
>   For all the world like cutler's poetry
>   Upon a knife, 'Love me, and leave me not'.

Nerissa. What talk you of the posy or the value?
  You swore to me when I did give it you,
  That you would wear it till your hour of death,
  And that it should lie with you in your grave. . . .[48]

Portia and Nerissa solemnly announce themselves contracted as sexual partners to the doctor and his clerk; and when the rings are produced as renewed
pledges by Nerissa and Portia themselves, the two women repeat their threat
of sexual infidelity to their husbands (as yet husbands in name only) – this
time not as future possibility, but as achieved fact:

> *Bassanio.* By heaven [this ring] is the same I gave the doctor!
> *Portia.* I had it of him: pardon me Bassanio,
>   For by this ring the doctor lay with me.
> *Nerissa.* And pardon me my gentle Gratiano,
>   For that same scrubbed boy (the doctor's clerk)
>   In lieu of this, last night did lie with me.
> *Gratiano.* Why this is like the mending of highways
>   In summer where the ways are fair enough!
>   What, are we cuckolds ere we have deserv'd it?[49]

It is Portia who immediately resolves the enigma ('Speak not so grossly'), but
the play's ending is dense with sexual punning. Here, I suggest, we have a
reminder that Portia's learning/knowledge is always, potentially, culturally
translatable into 'knowingness' – into the sexual – and as such has to be
'bridled' by a vigilant husband (even if he depends upon her permanently for
financial support).

  The difference, in this play, is that Portia has in fact always been 'on top' –
and unlike the poor orphaned Helena, her active role has social justification.
She is the 'Lady', the woman of independent means, the heiress. In her
capacity as controller of wealth, and link-line in an inheritance, she 'takes the
man's part' in any case.[50] In her first participation in the play ('choosing
the casket') she makes explicit her tokenism: the extent to which she 'is' the
parental wealth, operating as mere passive intermediary in the selection of an
appropriate male perpetuator of the line:

> *Portia.* . . . but this reasoning is not in the fashion to choose me a husband,
>   – O me the word 'choose'! I may neither choose who I would, nor
>   refuse who I dislike, so is the will of a living daughter curb'd by the
>   will of a dead father: is it not hard Nerissa, that I cannot choose one,
>   nor refuse none?[51]

Although her father has placed unusually eccentric conditions upon her
choice of a husband, the situation is an entirely standard one for the
sixteenth-century woman of means: the line, not the woman's inclination,
dictates the match.[52]

Portia's first attempt at actively interceding to save her betrothed Bassanio's friend, Antonio, is made in the strictly financial terms appropriate to her 'wealthpower':

Bassanio.   Gentle lady
   When I did first impart my love to you,
   I freely told you all the wealth I had
   Ran in my veins, – I was a gentleman, –
   And then I told you true: and yet dear lady
   Rating myself at nothing, you shall see
   How much I was a braggart, – when I told you
   My state was nothing, I should then have told you
   That I was worse than nothing; for indeed
   I have engag'd myself to a dear friend,
   Engag'd my friend to his mere enemy
   To feed my means.
      . . .
Portia. What sum owes he the Jew?
Bassanio. For me three thousand ducats.
Portia.   What no more?
   Pay him six thousand, and deface the bond:
   Double six thousand, and then treble that,
   Before a friend of this description
   Shall lose a hair through Bassanio's fault.[53]

When this is ineffective, she takes it upon herself to intercede legally – independently, and without the knowledge or consent of her husband-to-be.

As in the case of Helena, this knowledge-intercession is strictly borrowed from the male sphere: the audience are reminded at the beginning of the lawcourt scene (4.1.153–9) that Portia's expertise comes from her cousin, the lawyer Bellario, although the 'greatness of learning' is her own:

Duke. [Reads.] . . . *I acquainted him with the cause in controversy between the Jew and Antonio the merchant, we turn'd o'er many books together, he is furnished with my opinion, which (bettered with his own learning, the greatness whereof I cannot enough commend), comes with him at my importunity, to fill up your grace's request in my stead.*

Portia's knowledge (like her male attire) is borrowed; her power is her rank-power over Bassanio (on his own admission, the penniless – powerless – suitor for her hand),[54] Antonio and Lorenzo, all of whom are her social and financial inferiors, despite their gender superiority.[55] For all of them her superior 'knowledge' proves the instrument of good fortune: she announces the recovery of Antonio's lost ships, restoring his lost fortune ('Sweet lady, you have given me life and living', exclaims Antonio (5.1.286)); while Nerissa presents to Lorenzo, who has eloped with Shylock's daughter,

Jessica, a deed of gift, entitling the couple to all Shylock's goods on his death (a deed that Portia negotiated as part of her legal settlement of the case) – 'Fair ladies, you drop manna in the way / Of starved people', exclaims Lorenzo.[56]

Yet in spite of her legitimate entitlement to rule, it is the sexual subordination of women (these women) that closes the play. Once again the sexual theme is conveniently produced by way of the Gratiano/Nerissa couple, with a reminder that now, finally, the two marriages are to be consummated, and a final lewd pun on the woman's 'ring':

> *Portia.*   Let us go in,
>   And charge us there upon inter'gatories,
>   And we will answer all things faithfully.
> *Gratiano.* Let it be so, – the first inter'gatory
>   That my Nerissa shall be sworn on, is
>   Whether till the next night she had rather stay,
>   Or go to bed now (being two hours to day):
>   But were the day come, I should wish it dark
>   Till I were couching with the doctor's clerk.
>   Well, while I live, I'll fear no other thing
>   So sore, as keeping safe Nerissa's ring.[57]

I am suggesting that Renaissance views on learned women, expressed with all their contradictory feelings about the 'value' of education and the 'forwardness' of female articulateness in the treatises and manuals of the period, are reproduced in the plot strategies of Shakespeare's learned women, whose 'noble' actions (curing the King, saving Antonio) also mobilise a set of expectations of 'knowingness', of sexual unruliness and ungovernability. It is typical of the ambivalent attitudes circulating in the play that the speech in *The Merchant of Venice* in which Portia offers herself entirely and whole-heartedly as 'vassal' to her new lord and master, the scholar-soldier Bassanio – the speech that culminates in the ring-gift and betrothal – is a speech whose inventory of Portia's womanly deficiencies contradicts everything that the rest of the play explicitly tells us about her:

> *Portia.* You see me Lord Bassanio where I stand,
>   Such as I am; though for myself alone
>   I would not be ambitious in my wish
>   To wish myself much better, yet for you,
>   I would be trebled twenty times myself,
>   A thousand times more fair, ten thousand times more rich,
>   That only to stand high in your account,
>   I might in virtues, beauties, livings, friends
>   Exceed account: but the full sum of me
>   Is sum of something: which to term in gross

> Is an unlesson'd girl, unschool'd, unpractised,
> Happy in this, she is not yet so old
> But she may learn: happier than this,
> She is not bred so dull but she can learn;
> Happiest of all, is that her gentle spirit
> Commits itself to yours to be directed,
> As from her lord, her governor, her king.
> Myself, and what is mine, to you and yours
> Is now converted. But now I was the lord
> Of this fair mansion, master of my servants,
> Queen o'er myself: and even now, but now.
> This house, these servants, and this same myself
> Are yours, – my lord's! – I give them with this ring,
> Which when you part from, lose, or give away,
> Let it presage the ruin of your love,
> And be my vantage to exclaim on you.[58]

Portia is not 'unschool'd', 'unlesson'd' (the plot hinges on her learning); she does not commit her 'gentle spirit' to Bassanio's direction (she continues to act with authority, and without his knowledge or permission); and as her accounting imagery reminds us, she retains full control of her financial affairs (even the servants continue to answer to her).

The play defuses the tensions this 'rule of woman' creates, in the carefully circumscribed, witty verbal play on the theme of potential cuckoldry of the play's close – the marriage-vow rings lost and then retrieved by the husbands-elect who are in their future wives' thrall until the true identities of the young lawyer and his clerk are revealed – compromised on the threshold of the consummation of their marriages.[59] The tale unfolded in order to unravel the mystery of the non-cuckoldry, however, is the tale that reinscribes the husbands in a position of servitude to the wives who are revealed to have rescued them from dishonour, yet it is the husband's ownership and control of his wife's 'ring' that closes the play.

I suggest that if we read out – unravel from the text – the figures of Helena in *All's Well That End's Well* and Portia in *The Merchant of Venice*, two versions of a confused cultural response to the learned woman emerge: the version of her as powerfully chaste and loyal in her emblematic capacity as woman *virilis animi* (of manly temperament/mind), circulating together with the version of her as threateningly unruly and disorderly in her indecorous articulateness and sexual 'knowingness' – in her wearing of the breeches. Humanist educators consistently promoted their programmes of classical learning as universally accessible – as available as means to moral and social 'worth' for any person of intelligence and ability. As they are silent on the class-specificness of their practice (concealed behind such problematic terms as 'worth'),[60] so they fail to distinguish gender-specific orbits for their linguistic and rhetorical skills. I suggest that insofar as this is the case, 'reading out the women' in the early modern canonical texts offers us a further gloss on the evasions and the silences in the pedagogic treatises and exposes a serious and deep-rooted ambivalence towards the educated woman.

4

TWINS AND TRAVESTIES
Gender, dependency and sexual availability in
Twelfth Night

Viola. He nam'd Sebastian. I my brother know
    Yet living in my glass; even such and so
    In favour was my brother, and he went
    Still in this fashion, colour, ornament,
    For him I imitate.[1]

(Ingling Pyander)
Walking the city, as my wonted use,
There was I subject to this foul abuse:
Troubled with many thoughts, pacing along,
It was my chance to shoulder in a throng;
Thrust to the channel I was, but crowding her,
I spied Pyander in a nymph's attire:
No nymph more fair than did Pyander seem,
Had not Pyander then Pyander been;
No lady with a fairer face more grac'd,
But that Pyander's self himself defac'd;
Never was boy so pleasing to the heart
As was Pyander for a woman's part;
Never did woman foster such another
As was Pyander, but Pyander's mother.
Fool that I was in my affection!
More happy I, had it been a vision;
So far entangled was my soul by love,
That force perforce I must Pyander prove:
The issue of which proof did testify
Ingling Pyander's damnèd villany.
. . .
O, so I was besotted with her words,
His words, that no part of a she affords!
For had he been a she, injurious boy,
I had not been so subject to annoy.[2]

65

Cross-dressing on the Renaissance stage has recently caused a considerable critical stir and aroused the interest of gender theorists. If by my choice of words here I deliberately suggest a measure of critical interest which is ever so slightly prurient, that is deliberate. We all of us, I think, respond one way or another to the erotic potential in concealed sexual identity, the prospect of being lured into desiring the androgynous desirable object – the object whose sex is problematic, or insufficiently clearly defined by the customary signs of dress and demeanour. The danger is, however, that such is our urge to emphasise 'the political necessity and the analytical utility of investigating sexuality as a relatively autonomous system of cultural meaning and site of social struggle', we lose sight of historical conditions which are necessarily part of the gender equation, however commendably politicised.[3]

This chapter tries to accommodate some of the apparently contradictory currents stirred by the two cross-dressing passages with which I began, to provide a single, coherent version of the erotic possibilities contained under a kind of rubric of transvestism in the early modern period. For, in the current text-critical literature, we seem to be being told both that these are texts of sexual fantasy, disturbing and transgressive, and that these texts record some 'actual' possibility for individualised, subversive affirmation of sexuality.[4] I do not myself believe we shall ever know how many cross-dressed youths and young women were to be found on the streets of London around 1600, but I do believe it is possible to show that the distinctive ways in which the textual imputation of their existence function in the various narratives which have come down to us can be resolved into a consistent positioning of dominant to dependent member of the early modern community.[5]

I have, of course, spoken about cross-dressing before, in *Still Harping on Daughters*.[6] But that was in the context of an argument specifically focused on the irrelevance of any detectable emotional intensity associated with the cross-dressed boy-player to any reconstruction, on the basis of the drama of the age of Shakespeare, of a peculiarly *female* early modern intensity of feeling. In the absence of women, the gendering of action is governed, I argued, by the attitudes of male members of the community, attitudes which crucially position women in relation to desire in ways which suit male (reproductive) requirements for female participation in alliance/marriage.[7]

Here my argument will be differently focused: upon the way in which, in the early modern period, erotic attention – an attention bound up with sexual availability and historically specific forms of economic dependency – is focused upon boys and women in the *same* way. Thus, crucially, sexuality signifies as *absence of difference* as it is inscribed upon the bodies of those equivalently 'mastered' within the early modern household, and who are placed homologously in relation to the household's domestic economy. Inside the household, I shall argue, dependent youths and dependent women are expected to 'submit', under the order of family authority, to those above them. And the strong ideological hold of the patriarchal household ensures that in the space outside the household – in the newer market economy whose values govern the street and public place – the tropes which produce structural dependency as vulnerability and availability are readily mobilised to police the circulation of young people.

Outside the household, the freely circulating woman is 'loose' (uncontained), is strictly 'out of place',[8] and her very comeliness in conjunction with her unprotectedness (no male kin with her) signifies her availability (as it continues, residually, to do today). And outside the household the dependent boy (the 'youth') is also constructed, via the patriarchal household, as 'at risk' – more legitimately in transit on 'business', but also, in his transactional availability, sexually vulnerable.[9] In the street, the bodies of the boy and the unmarried woman elide as they carry the message of equivalent sexual availability – male and female prostitution is represented textually (and probably fantasised communally) as transvestism. The boy dis-covered as a girl reveals her availability for public intercourse; the girl dis-covered as a boy reveals that intention to sodomy for financial gain.[10] The boy who walks the street cross-dressed as that comely girl (whether in reality or in fantasy/ grotesque fiction) does not, therefore, misrepresent himself: he conceals (and then reveals) the range of sexual possibilities available. The girl who enters the male preserve cross-dressed (ordinary, tavern or gaming-house) does not misrepresent herself, either. She is, in any case, 'loose', and eases the process of crossing the threshold into the male domain – and controls the manner of presenting herself in a suitable location for paid sex.[11]

I suggest that the way in which dependency functions in relation to representations of the sexual in early modern English culture is vital to a suitably historicised reading of cross-dressing and gender confusion in Elizabethan and Jacobean drama.[12] Here I shall try to show this set of relations in operation in the complex gender doubling and twinning of Shakespeare's *Twelfth Night*.

'The household was the classic form of patriarchy', writes Alan Bray.[13] In the period with which we are concerned, 'family' and 'household', as descriptions of the ordered unit for communal living, designate groupings which include both close and distant kin and a range of non-kin.[14] There was a constant 'drift of young persons' (as David Herlihy calls it), a flow of young well-to-do dependents into and out of the wealthier households – both of distant kin and of non-kin in 'service'.[15] And, in addition to the body of young well-to-do dependents in the wealthy household, there were numbers of adolescent servants: 'The great majority of the adolescent population probably entered some form of service or apprenticeship', writes Ralph Houlbrooke. In Ealing, in 1599, about a quarter of the total population of 427 was in service of some kind.[16] Of the eighty-five households in Ealing, 'a staggering 34.2 percent of them contained one or more servants'.[17] Finally, 'in the upper and middle ranks of society children were commonly sent away from home to another household' as part of their education.[18] While they resided in Calais, the Lisle family placed two of their daughters with French families of a wealth and status corresponding to their own.[19] 'The patriarchal household with its servants was an institution that touched the lives of an immense number of people' (to quote Alan Bray again); 'it was an institution that necessarily influenced the sexual lives of those who lived within it.'[20] That patriarchal household exercised its considerable authority and wielded its extensive economic power predominantly over young men and women between the ages of 14 and 24.

It is against this kind of background that Susan Amussen locates patriarchal authority at the most fundamental levels of consciousness-formation in the period:

> [The catechism] asserted that the family was the fundamental social institution, and that order in families was both necessary for and parallel to, order in the state. In the catechism, this idea is developed in the discussion of the Fifth Commandment, to 'honour thy father and mother'. The 1559 Prayer Book's catechism . . . summarized . . .
>
>> My duty towards my neighbour is to love him as myself, and to do to all men as I would they should do unto me: to love, honour, and succour my father and mother: to honour and obey the King and all that are put in authority under him: to submit myself to all my governors, teachers, spiritual pastors and masters: to order myself lowly and reverently to all my betters: . . . to learn and labour truly to get mine own living, and to do my duty in that state of life unto which it shall please God to call me.[21]

In the middle to upper ranks of society, deference and submissiveness were internalised in the form of 'good manners':

> In a society in which service was the most important avenue to advancement at all levels, one of the most essential skills was the ability to make oneself acceptable to superiors. . . . Marks of respect to be shown in conversation with superiors included baring the head, dropping the right knee, keeping silence till spoken to, listening carefully and answering sensibly and shortly. Compliance with commands was to be immediate, response to praise heartily grateful.[22]

For dependent youth, obedience was both a condition of their economic support and an internalised state.

Let us pause for a moment on this internalisation of codes of obedient conduct. One of its consequences is the *un*gendering of submissiveness and docility. Positioning within the household, rather than temperament or the characteristics of 'masculinity' or 'femininity', decides the relative positioning of individuals with regard to household 'service' of a wide variety of types. In fiction (particularly the drama) this is regularly represented in terms of the eroticisation of the dependent. In Ben Jonson's *Epicoene*, Clerimont's Boy says that at the mansion of the lady who is 'the argument' of the song taught him by Clerimont, he [Boy] 'is the welcom'st thing under a man that comes there':

> *Clerimont.* I think, and above a man too, if the truth were rack'd out of you.
> *Boy.* No, faith, I'll confess before, sir. The gentlewomen play with me, and throw me o' the bed, and carry me in to my lady, and she kisses me with her oiled face, and puts a peruke o' my head, and asks me an' I will wear her gown, and I say no; and then she hits me a blow o' the ear and calls me innocent, and lets me go.[23]

As far as Clerimont is concerned, this is why pages find it easier to gain access to noblewomen than the mature men who court them (just as in *Twelfth Night* Viola/Cesario succeeds with Olivia where Orsino has failed):

> No marvel if the door be kept shut against your master, when the entrance is so easy to you. – Well sir, you shall go there no more, lest I be fain to seek your voice in my lady's rushes a fortnight hence.

Within the household it is 'youth' which designates the individual as available to serve – 'youth', therefore, which signifies for the unscrupulous 'master' (or mistress) that a dependent is available for sexual as well as other domestic services.

In 1630, Meredith Davy of Minehead was prosecuted for sodomy at the Somerset Court of Quarter Sessions.

> According to the evidence of his master's apprentice, a boy 'aged twelve years or thereabouts' called John Vicary, with whom he shared a bed, Davy had been in the habit of having sexual relations with the boy on Sunday and holiday nights after he had been drinking; eventually the boy cried out and Davy ended up before the Justices.[24]

As Bray glosses this:

> The young apprentice would have had a lower standing in the household than Davy, who was an adult; and it was presumably this which encouraged him – wrongly as it turned out – to think that he could take advantage of the boy. It is an important point. In a household of any substantial size the distinction in their status would have been only one of a series of such distinctions; it was part of the nature of the household itself. The household was a hierarchical institution, in which each of its members had a clearly defined position. It was also a patriarchal institution, in which the pre-eminent position was that of the

master; and the distinction in status between master and servant was in some respects a model for distinctions between the servants themselves.[25]

My own gloss on this incident focuses more attention on the youth than on the defendant. Does the case suggest that young persons who were (inevitably) bedfellows to those of superior household status regarded bed overtures as commonplace – part of the obligations of a code of obedience and subservience intrinsic to household organisation? (It is, in any case, a curious case in the records, since it appears to have occurred while the actual master of the house was away from home – did the case come to public attention only because the substitute 'master' usurps powers considered unexceptionable under normal circumstances?) In any case, I think it is important, given our current interest in 'desire', to register the irrelevance here of any notion of 'consent' on the part of the dependent participant in the bed activities. Consent is an assumption built into the very nature of the relationship.

If we stay with this case just a little longer, once the alleged social transgression had taken place, the outcome of the discovery and prosecution seems to support the view that such activity was regarded as only slightly beyond the boundaries set on allowable demands for 'submission' from one considerably lower in the social hierarchy of the household.[26]

> Richard Bryant, the servant who slept in the room with Davy and the boy ... eventually took the matter to the mistress of the household, but it is striking as one reads his evidence how long it took him to realise what was going on and how reluctant he is likely to appear to us now to have been to draw the obvious conclusions.[27]

Finally, at the end of the boy John Vicary's, evidence, he notes: 'since which time [Davy] hath layn quietly with him.' In other words, household life continued unchanged – the boy continued to share a bed with (and hence, to be in a position of submission to) the alleged assaulter. Davy himself 'denieth that he ever used any unclean action with the said boy as they lay in bed together; and more he sayeth not'.[28]

We learn more from such cases than simply that 'consent' is a meaningless concept where a rigorous code of obedience to one's 'elders and betters' is in place. We begin to glimpse the possibility, I think, that dependency might be a socially defining category more symbolically compelling than gender. In other words, that individuals designated as obliged to comply without question with those above them in the household structure were perceived as both socially and sexually equivalent. And the possibility arises – as I think is suggested by the Davy case – that the young person experiences *themself* as bound by a code of sexual submission which we would describe as 'feminised', but which they complied with simply as a correlative to their status.

In the theatre these kinds of observations take on, I think, a yet more intriguing tinge. If (as I am supposing) it doesn't, in a sense, *matter* whether the dependent object of erotic attention is female or male, then might this be exploitable dramatically? Might the drama play on the very fact that gender is permanently problematic – that undressing the heroine is always, on the English Elizabethan/Jacobean stage, bound to be a disappointment (as Peter Stallybrass has pointed out)?[29]

Under these circumstances, the erotic promise (the pursuit of the unattainable, which culminates at the curtain call with the achievement of the desired object) is without gender, is almost literally textual – *en*gendered rhetorically and dramatically. As in the case of Middleton's deceiving ingle, the audience is seduced into believing their eyes (believing the gender disguise to be 'the' gender), by the rhetorical persuasion of the words:

> O, so I was besotted by her words,
> His words, that no part of a she affords!

In *Twelfth Night* the twin siblings, Viola and Sebastian, are of good family and fatherless.[30] They are therefore obliged to become dependent on households other than those of their own close kin. Indeed, one might argue that *finding a place* in the domestic economy of a household other than that of their family of birth is the initiation of the drama – they are shipwrecked on an unspecified voyage, and voyages are (in narrative) conventionally quests or searches. In addition to the careful specification of their being orphaned before the age of majority ('when Viola from her birth / Had numbered thirteen years'), the audience are persistently reminded of the extreme youth of *both* twins (since each resembles the other so completely):[31]

> *Olivia.* Of what personage and years is he?
> *Malvolio.* Not yet old enough for a man, nor young enough for a boy: as a squash is before 'tis a peascod, or a codling when 'tis almost an apple. 'Tis with him in standing water, between boy and man. He is very well-favoured, and he speaks very shrewishly. One would think his mother's milk were scarce out of him.[32]

After the shipwreck, the first objective of the siblings is to transform their state from vagrancy to service (or possibly, from wage-labour to service – Sebastian 'gets' Antonio's purse, while Viola's relationship with the captain is constructed as a cash transaction).[33] Both twins make immediately for the court of the Duke 'who governs here'. Both exchange their non-renewable cash assets (Viola's purse; Sebastian's borrowed purse) for the security of 'service' within a wealthy household ('I'll serve this duke' (1.3.55); 'I am bound to the Count Orsino's court' (2.1.41–2)). Viola's cross-dressing eases her way into Orsino's service.[34] Sebastian, mistaken for Cesario, believes Olivia to be spontaneously offering an invitation to enter her service – an invitation he accepts as the very 'dream' he wished for: 'Go with me to my house . . . would thou'dst be rul'd by me!' (4.1.53, 63).[35]

The eroticisation of Viola/Cesario and of Sebastian is dramatically constructed in terms of their relationship to the domestic economy, and the place they occupy in relation to the heads of their adopted households. In the case of both Cesario's and Sebastian's 'place', this is fraught with the possibility of demand for sexual favours in the very process of being established as 'service' (something which by now we might expect, in the light of the discussion of the early modern household with which this chapter began). The audience is entirely aware of the ambiguity in Sebastian's 'retention' by Olivia – he reads it as an invitation to enter her service, she offers it as a profession of passionate, sexual love and a marriage proposal. But Orsino's attachment to his new 'young gentleman', Cesario, is no less charged with erotic possibilities:

> *Valentino.* If the Duke continue these favours towards you, Cesario, you are like to be much advanced. . . .
>
> *Viola.* You either fear his humour, or my negligence, that you call in question the continuance of his love. Is he inconstant, sir, in his favours?[36]

'Love' here hovers dangerously between the mutual bond of service and passionate emotional attachment.[37] And the confusions possible in the Orsino/Viola service relationship are clinched shortly thereafter:

> *Duke.* O then unfold the passion of my love,
>   Surprise her with discourse of my dear faith;
>   It shall become thee well to act my woes:
>   She will attend it better in thy youth,
>   Than in a nuncio's of more grave aspect.
> *Viola.* I think not so, my lord.
> *Duke.*   Dear lad, believe it;
>   For they shall yet belie thy happy years,
>   That say thou art a man; Diana's lip
>   Is not more smooth and rubious: thy small pipe
>   Is as the maiden's organ, shrill and sound,
>   And all is semblative a woman's part.
>   I know thy constellation is right apt
>   For this affair. . . .
>   . . . Prosper well in this,
>   And thou shalt live as freely as thy lord,
>   To call his fortunes thine.
> *Viola.*   I'll do my best
>   To woo your lady: [*Aside*] yet, a barful strife!
>   Who'er I woo, myself would be his wife.[38]

As Orsino eroticises Viola in relation to Olivia he specifies the possibilities for sexualising his own attention to the 'small pipe' and the 'maiden's organ' of the preferred youth in his service. As 'pipe' and 'organ' are 'semblative a woman's part' they position Cesario as desired dependant of Orsino – as available for his own sexual pleasure.

Textually this delightful vulnerability is amplified for the audience by Viola – cross-dressed as Cesario, and the epitome of devoted youthful 'service' to her Lord – of woman's 'service' as one of pure passivity:

> *Duke.*   And what's her history?
> *Viola.* A blank, my lord: she never told her love,
>   But let concealment like a worm i' th' bud
>   Feed on her damask cheek: she pin'd in thought,
>   And with a green and yellow melancholy
>   She sat like Patience on a monument,
>   Smiling at grief. Was not this love indeed? [39]

This perfectly devoted and obedient 'love' which asks nothing for itself is a pure exemplar of household service – the very service 'Cesario' provides for her master Orsino. The elision here of kinds of loving allows for the sleight of hand in Act 5, whereby the passionate attachment of Cesario to her master can be transmuted into the heterosexual bond of marriage between Viola and Orsino, without interruption of feeling. That transformation begins when Viola/Cesario declares her total commitment to Orsino – rather than to Olivia – in terms which still fail to disturb the simulated maleness of her exterior persona:

> *Olivia.* Where goes Cesario?
> *Viola.*   After him I love
>   More than I love these eyes, more than my life,
>   More, by all mores, than e'er I shall love wife.
>   If I do feign, you witnesses above
>   Punish my life, for tainting of my love. [40]

'By all mores' – whether the customs of male/male service or of male/female marriage – Viola's 'love' for Orsino is of the most intense and admirable. And her 'feigning' in no way detracts from the sincerity of the declaration. So that when Orsino releases 'Cesario' from his bond of servitude, he effectively 'cashes in' that service as a prelude to the heterosexual lifelong liaison now on offer with Viola:

> *Duke.* Your master quits you; and for your service done him,
>   So much against the mettle of your sex,
>   So far beneath your soft and tender breeding,
>   And since you call'd me master for so long,

> Here is my hand; you shall from this time be
> Your master's mistress.[41]

If there is an echo here of sonnet 20, I think that only confirms the gender vacillations of this passage:

> A woman's face, with nature's own hand painted,
> Hast thou, the master mistress of my passion –
> A woman's gentle heart, but not acquainted
> With shifting change, as is false women's fashion.[42]

By declaring himself and Cesario 'quits' – equally dispatched of their mutual obligations under their old agreement – Orsino acknowledges an accumulated credit of dutiful service which can now be exchanged for an ideally dutiful (because ideally passive) bond of matrimony: 'Here is my hand.' In claiming Viola as his sexual partner he ratifies the terms of his original engagement with his 'young gentleman' – and consummates a relationship which was always available as promise of submission.[43]

This formal exchange actually regularises a more ambiguous hand-taking a scene earlier. There the 'discovery' of Viola's concealed sex prompts a betrothal – a mutual exchange of passionate vows and a hand-fasting:

> *Duke.* Boy, thou has said to me a thousand times
> Thou never should'st love woman like to me.
> *Viola.* And all those sayings will I over-swear,
> And all those swearings keep as true in soul
> As doth that orbed continent the fire
> That severs day from night.
> *Duke.*   Give me thy hand,
> And let me see thee in thy woman's weeds.[44]

The afterthought of 'let me see thee in thy woman's weeds' reminds the reader (as an audience does not need to be reminded) that this social rite of betrothal is performed by two 'men', and is thus, as ritual, unseemly and troubling.

If in the drama the bonds of youthful service do not depend on the sex of the youthful person, Sebastian's relationship with Antonio takes its place in the play appropriately historicised, rather than in the anachronistic form of a postulated homosexual relationship, as critics and directors of the play have recently tended to propose. Antonio's love for Sebastian, too, is constructed on the same social model as that intense commitment which characterises Cesario's for his lord. But Sebastian's rank makes Antonio the dependant, even though (presumably) his age suggests domination. The sea captain's profuse declarations of adoration for his juvenile charge do not, therefore, mirror the intensities of feeling in the Orsino/Cesario relationship. Antonio's 'love' appears as an inversion, and is thus, in the feelings it elicits from us, much closer to the Olivia/Cesario relationship. Olivia commands and

Cesario serves, but once the relationship becomes sexualised, Olivia's female-ness renders her erotic pursuit indecorous (like Venus's pursuit of Adonis in *Venus and Adonis*).

The Antonio/Sebastian relationship, cut off from the everyday context of the household, teeters between service and intense male friendship. Both contexts contain possibilities for interpreting passionate commitment as erotic interest.[45] In many ways Antonio and Sebastian conduct their friend-ship/service relationship in a more recognisably 'real' way than any of the other protagonists in the play. Ironically, it is the very fact that these absurdly travestied relationships are constructed as deliberately confused in their pro-fessions of 'love' that our ear is all too well attuned for equivalent overtones in Antonio's love for Sebastian.

Antonio is revealed as most vulnerable at the moment he believes himself betrayed: encountering Cesario and mistaking him for Sebastian, he takes Cesario's denial of knowing him as an utter breach of faith between them. Both in his mistakenness and in the intensity of his response, Antonio here uncannily resembles Olivia, when she too mistakes Cesario for Sebastian, and Viola/Cesario denies the marital bond so recently forged between them:

> *Olivia.* Ay me detested! how am I beguil'd![46]

For, of course, the final erotic twist in *Twelfth Night* is achieved by the irony that it is *Olivia* – the lady of significant independent means and a disinclina-tion to submit herself and her lands to any 'master'[47] – whose sexualised relationship of 'service' with Cesario is most socially and sexually transgress-ive. I think critics have been right in seeing this as Olivia's 'come-uppance' – patriarchy's retribution for mis-taking the conventions both of service and of marriage as a female head of household in an order explicitly designated male in its defining relationships.[48]

Twelfth Night steadily entangles the prospects for dependency in household service with those for sexual liaison – so steadily that it becomes possible to imagine that in the early modern world boys and women really are, to all intents and purposes, more alike than they are different. This is part of the conditions of the early modern stage in England – playboys, by their very profession, are both adept at standing in for girls and vulnerable to the sexual attentions of actors and playgoers (or so the polemical anti-stage propaganda would have us believe). It is therefore usefully corrective to consider one way in which Viola/Cesario and Sebastian are easily recognised as different; that is, the way failure to *fight* proves a more reliable diagnostic of Viola's sex than erotic attractiveness.

> A male person must pay attention to many things when he goes amongst people. He must think of the many virtues that he must allow to appear in him. But a woman has no need of this. She has only one virtue to which she need attend, namely, to modesty.[49]

In the wider social context of the world at large, maculinity is to femininity as active is to passive. It is, after all, only the relative positioning of dominant to dependent within the hierarchical household which ascribes dutiful passivity to the male youth. Beyond that structural docility, early modern constructions of masculinity include the expectation of potential for violence and disruption – the natural consequences of a man's active nature.

In a fascinating piece on early modern masculinity as a 'psychic phenomenon', Lyndal Roper comments on the ordinance above as follows:

> In this passage ... we seem to possess a clear statement of how sixteenth-century people understood the difference between men and women. Female virtue is understood in bodily terms and it ultimately means chastity; male virtue, by contrast, is plural and concerns a host of qualities which must be manifested in public, 'when he goes amongst people'.[50]

But this, according to Roper, is only a starting point for understanding 'manliness' in early modern society. Masculinity, she suggests, goes beyond a set of simple oppositions, or prescriptive rules of conduct policed by the community. Masculinity is an internalised state of preparedness for physical excess, restrained by individualised anxiety at the prospect of shamefully passing beyond the bounds of regularised behaviour:

> Sixteenth-century masculinity drew its psychic strength not from the dignity of the mean but from the rumbustious energy which such discipline was supposedly designed to check.[51]

The disruptive presence in Olivia's household of Sir Toby Belch and his companions is the manifestation of this uncontained masculinity, exceeding social bounds and unchecked by the female head of house. When challenged, Viola/Cesario literally *lacks* the ability to react with the physical violence the properly controlled (mastered) youth is expected to be able to release when circumstances require it. For

> ultimately, despite its disruptive nature, it was upon the citizens' preparedness physically to fight to defend the city that civic society and the power of the [city] council depended. ... The political community was akin to the military community: the citizen was also the weaponed man; the woman, who did not bear arms, was also never fully a political subject.[52]

Sebastian's preparedness to break heads in an unprovoked violent encounter with strangers confirms his masculine identity, and proves him the true master of Olivia's household he has just become in a marriage contract based on *mistaken* identity.

In the final unravelling of the plot of *Twelfth Night*, the easy deployment of the erotic possibilities of Viola's and Sebastian's service to the dynastic households of Orsino and Olivia, respectively, literally *resolves* the union of the two lines. At the end of the play, the marriages of the twin siblings to Olivia and Orsino effect what Orsino's courtship of Olivia was originally designed to achieve – the Orsino and Olivia households enter into a kin relationship with one another:

> *Olivia.* My lord, so please you, these things further thought on,
>   To think me as well a sister, as a wife,
>   One day shall crown th'alliance on't, so please you,
>   Here at my house, and at my proper cost.
> *Duke.* Madam, I am most apt t'embrace your offer.
>   [*To Viola*] Your master quits you; and for your service done him,
>   So much against the mettle of your sex,
>   So far beneath your soft and tender breeding,
>   And since you call'd me master for so long,
>   Here is my hand; you shall from this time be
>   Your master's mistress.
> *Olivia.*   A sister! you are she.[53]

The happy ending is one in which the erotic potential of service is appropriately contained within the admissible boundaries of the patriarchal household – dependent women 'mastered' by husbands or brothers; dependent boys elevated by marriage into masters and heads of households themselves (even desired dependent girls regulated into dependent younger sisters).

But, to return to my opening remarks, this is romance – a fictional resolution in which insuperable problems are superable, and convenient twinning can iron out the crumpled social fabric of early modern life. In the street the problem remains – the troubling possibility, 'in a throng', that those who appear to be available in the market-place, gender-wise, are not what they seem (either they are not available but in transit between households, or they are cross-dressed and marketing sodomy for female prostitution, female prostitution for boy-playing). In the market-place, the disreputable sexual favours sought from passing, available 'youth' blatantly fail to comply with the procreative requirements of reputable, marital intercourse. And the very confusion which hovers around desirability surely points to the historic specificity of early modern eroticism.

Eroticism, in the early modern period, is not gender-specific, is not grounded in the sex of the possibly 'submissive' partner, but is an expectation of that very submissiveness. As twentieth-century readers, we recognise the eroticism of gender *confusion*, and reintroduce that confusion as a feature of the dramatic narrative. Whereas, for the Elizabethan theatre audience, it may be the very clarity of the mistakenness – the very indifference to gendering – which is designed to elicit the pleasurable response from the audience.[54]

5

READING AND
THE TECHNOLOGY OF
TEXTUAL AFFECT

Erasmus's familiar letters and Shakespeare's
King Lear

A letter or epistle, is the thyng alone yᵗ maketh men present which are absent. For among those that are absent, what is so presente, as to heare and talke with those whom thou louest?

(Myles Coverdale)[1]

They were trained together in their childhoods, and there rooted betwixt them then such an affection which cannot choose but branch now. Since their more mature dignities and royal necessities made separation of their society, their encounters, though not personal, have been royally attorneyed with interchange of gifts, letters, loving embassies, that they have seemed to be together though absent.

(*The Winter's Tale*)[2]

My ambition in this chapter is an attempt at a particular kind of historicised reading which reveals the textual construction of feeling in the early modern period.[3] Historical approaches to Shakespeare's plays (including my own) have tended to concentrate on contextualising social and cultural practices. So, for example, we may revive the significance of a key plot point in a play like Othello's naming Desdemona 'whore' in front of Emilia, by retrieving the sixteenth-century social historical evidence on 'defamation'.[4] We have not, to date, tried in any systematic way to contextualise the pivotal affective moments: the point at which emotion is intensified so as to structure the audience's and the reader's allegiance, and gain our assent to the unravelling or resolving of the action.[5]

The body of writing chosen here to begin this historicising process is Desiderius Erasmus's *Epistolae*. At first sight such a choice appears perverse. Nothing could, apparently, be less contrived emotionally than Erasmus's *Letters*. Erasmus studies, indeed, are premised on the 'authenticity' and transparent truthfulness of those letters as *the* source of Erasmian biographical information.[6] It will be argued here, however, that Erasmus's letters are crucially affective, and that they are major contributions to the Renaissance's construction of letter writing and reading as emotionally charged events. Moreover, they were centrally influential in the pedagogic construction of a certain kind of reading: a version of emotionally compelling communication in the second half of the sixteenth century. So influential was this pedagogical model of reading that the exchange of familiar letters could come to stand for the efficiency with which humanistic text skills could be used to alter an individual's social position and prospects. As discussed in Erasmian handbooks on letter writing, the familiar letter structures and organises feeling so as to manipulate its intensity at a distance and, in the absence of the persons involved, enabling persuasion to a desired outcome.

The project of the present piece is to set *King Lear* within this contextualised version of the controlled production of feeling.[7] *King Lear* elicits our revulsion towards such efficiency by presenting us with the prospect of a world in which real affection is deprived of instrumentality (the ability to influence the outcome of actions and events) precisely to the extent that a cynically operated technology of affect – of warmth and intimacy generated by letters – debases the heart's expressive resources, leaving 'nothing' to be said.

Three key concepts structure early sixteenth-century, Erasmian thinking about familiar letters. These are friendship, effective transmission of feeling, and absence made present. All three are incorporated in the definition of the *epistola* which Erasmus gives in his *De conscribendis epistolis*. Letters should be 'intimate conversations between friends' ('amicorum inter ipsos confabulatione'):

> As the comedian Turpilius aptly wrote, the *epistola* is a kind of mutual exchange of speech between absent friends.

> [Est enim (quod scite scriptum est Turpilio comico) epistola absentium amicorum quasi mutuus sermo.][8]

This idea of a form of written work which crucially makes vivid the voice of the friend from whom one is separated, so as affectively to render that friend present, is a fascinating one, particularly since I don't think it tallies closely with our own understanding of the 'personal letter' (in other words, we have lost touch with this historicised version of letter writing).[9] It has its roots in pseudo-Libanius (a source in whom Erasmus had a considerable emotional investment, as I have discussed elsewhere). And it immediately notifies us of the importance for Erasmus of the affective dimension in epistolary writing – shared feeling, textually transmitted, substitutes for the individual who cannot be present, whose absence is a cause for regret and longing on the part of both parties in the textual transaction.

But the first thing to note, as we set about reconstructing a context for the pedagogic importance of 'familiar letters', is that Erasmus's clear indication of his source takes us not to Turpilius (for whom there are no surviving works), but rather to Saint Jerome. For the attribution of that precise definition of the function of the familiar letter is to be found in a key letter of Jerome's, included with a commentary in Erasmus's collected edition of Jerome's *Epistolae*. The letter opens as follows:

> Jerome to Nitias – In his treatment of the exchange of letters, Turpilius the comedian said: 'It is the unique way of making absent persons present'.

The familiar letter, in other words, constructs a fiction of the affective presence of an absent individual. Jerome indicates that in this case the deception of fiction is legitimate, because it achieves a morally laudable outcome:

> Nor, in so doing, does it deceive, although it achieves its purpose by means of what is not true. For what, if I may speak truly, is more present between those absent from one another, than to address and hear what you value by means of letters.

The feigned element in letter writing is legitimate, because it is needed to elicit the right degree of intensity of feeling in the recipient (by its simulation of overwrought feeling in the sender).[10] And he goes on to add historical and etymological material to support the fact that familiar letters have traditionally been the purveyors of humane understanding amongst men:

> Even before the use of paper and parchment, those primitive Italians, who Ennius calls 'Casci', who (according to Cicero, in his *Rhetorica*) wished to gain an understanding of themselves almost as a way of life, repeatedly sent one another mutual epistolary exhortations, either on writing tablets of smoothed and polished wood, or on the bark of trees. Whence those who carry letters are called 'tabellarii' [tablet carriers], and copyists are called 'librarii' from the bark [liber] of trees. How much the more, then, must we avoid overlooking what they themselves excelled in – whose milieu was raw and rustic, and who were ignorant of all 'humanitas' whatsoever?

Jerome now moves to exemplify the features of familiar letter writing which he has just identified. Notice how the tone changes:

> See how Chromatius, sacred Eusebius's brother by equality of morals as much as by nature, roused me to the task of letters. But you having departed from us, rend asunder our recently formed friendship rather than dissolving it, which Laelius most prudently prevented in Cicero. Unless perhaps the east is so hateful to you that you are afraid of your letters coming here also. Awake! Awake! wake from your sleep, produce a scrap of paper, for goodness' sake. Between the delights of your

native land and the journeys abroad we shared, breathe at least a word. If you love me, write I beseech you. If you have been angered, you are entitled to write angrily. I will have great solace, and that which I long for, if I receive my friend's letters, even if my friend is displeased.[11]

So Erasmus's definition of the familiar letter has already taken us to a fascinating source: a letter of Jerome's which bears all the marks of being itself 'exemplary' – illustrating the very features of letter writing which the writer identifies as those formally associated with the effective textual transmission of 'humanitas'. The letter is a textbook example of the genre, and indeed, following Erasmus's interest in it, it seems to have been used in northern classrooms on a regular basis to introduce students to letter writing.[12]

Actually in Jerome's letter to Nitias, 'Turpilius' does not say precisely what Erasmus attributes to him. For 'Turpilius' (or should we say, Jerome?) the familiar letter 'is the unique way of making absent persons present'. Here, the familiar letter renders absence present, its written text substituting for the affective presence of a physical speaker, without the extra component of *amicitia*. The letter in its entirety, however, adds the crucial dimension of 'friendship' and intimacy performatively – the absence for which the letter itself seeks to compensate is that of a beloved friend: 'you having departed from us, rend asunder our recently formed friendship'. As Erasmus explicitly adds *amicitia* to 'Turpilius's' definition, he apparently regards the friendship aspect of epistolary communication as particularly important.

Since Erasmus himself chooses to direct us to Jerome for an understanding of the fundamental features of the familiar letters, it is appropriate to turn for further insight to the commented edition of Jerome's letters which Erasmus contributed to the Froben complete Jerome of 1516. There he summarises Jerome's 'Letter to Heliodorus' (the opening letter in his collection) as follows:

When St. Jerome had gone to the desert he tried to keep with him his dearest friend Heliodorus, who out of a sense of duty had accompanied him, as he testifies elsewhere. Failing in this endeavour he wrote him a letter urging him to join him in the solitary life. He refutes several considerations which could either keep him from the desert or detain him in a city. And he shows him how it is not safe to undertake the office of bishop and how it is not easy to keep that office once undertaken. Then as a peroration he sings over and over the joys of the hermit life, and he portrays for him the terror of the Last Judgment. He mentions this letter by name in the catalogue of his works and calls it a hortatory letter. He wrote this when quite young, little more than a boy, as he testifies in the next letter, adding that in this letter he had played with the flowery language of the schools, still fired with enthusiasm for rhetorical studies, youth that he was. Accordingly it abounds with metaphors, allegories, even fictitious in origin, and with the oratorical ornaments of exclamation, dilemma, and other figures of that sort. His efforts show the kind of artistry in which one can recognize a beginner, but a beginner of the highest promise. The subject-matter belongs to the hortatory genre, which we will discuss a little later.[13]

The letter itself begins as follows:

> So conscious are you of the affection that exists between us that you cannot but recognize the love and passion with which I strove to pro-long our common sojourn in the desert. This very letter – blotted with tears – gives evidence of the lamentation and weeping with which I accompanied your departure. With the pretty ways of a child you then softened your refusal by soothing words, and I, being off my guard, knew not what to do. Was I to hold my peace? I could not conceal my eagerness by a show of indifference. Or was I to entreat you yet more earnestly? You would have refused to listen, for your love was not like mine. Despised affection has taken the one course open to it. Unable to keep you when present, it goes in search of you when absent. You asked me yourself, when you were going away, to invite you to the desert when I took up my quarters there, and I for my part promised to do so. Accordingly I invite you now; come, and come quickly. . . . But what is this, and why do I foolishly importune you again? Away with entreaties, an end to coaxing words. Offended love does well to be angry. You have spurned my petition; perhaps you will listen to my remonstrance. . . .[14]

What is striking is the intensely affective tone of the Jerome letter which Erasmus (unlike other editors) selects to put first in his collection, and to which, exceptionally, he attaches two separate commentaries – a more or less standard commentary on unusual words, allusions and doctrinal points, and an *annotatio artis*, which explicates the structural and rhetorical devices which produce the letter's emotional impact.[15] This *annotatio artis* is remarkable in a sixteenth-century scholarly commentary on a leading Father of Church and, in particular, one whose *vita* contained a well-known episode in which (in a dream) he was summoned before God's tribunal to answer the charge of paying too much attention to secular literary excellence, in particular to Cicero. Here, at the very beginning of his *renovatio* of Jerome's oeuvre and reputation, Erasmus foregrounds the rhetorical and affective in Jerome's letter writing.[16]

In fact the *annotatio artis* confirms what is already thematically clear in Erasmus's first commentary (as in commentaries to subsequent letters in the volume) – that the key criterion according to which Erasmus judges the effectiveness of Jerome's epistolary writing is its emotional intensity. As Jacques Chomarat puts it:

> L'émotion est le critère esthétique décisif.[17]

[Emotion is the decisive measure of aesthetic success]

Erasmus justifies the provision of the *annotatio artis* itself on the grounds that 'St Jerome ... confesses that in this [letter] he played with an ornate rhetoric.'[18] The following are typical passages from the 'rhetorical annotation':

> When [Jerome] tells how Heliodorus had accompanied him on his journey into the desert and how in vain he had asked him to remain with him there is a narration, so to speak. Then when he says that it was the object of his letter to have Heliodorus leave the cities and come to the desert there is the proposition. And yet St Jerome does not give us a lifeless account of these details, but he is always on fire, a man, it appears, of a vigorous disposition and vehement in both praise and blame. For he ardently praises those he loves, and he vigorously attacks those who have aroused his hostility.[19]

> *What keeps you in your father's house?* Such rhetorical figures as questions, repetitions, and short clauses make the discourse more impassioned. Metaphor or rather allegory elevates it to an even loftier and more pleasing level. Indeed he uses a well-nigh continuous metaphor. It is almost the constant practice of Jerome, however, to place at the beginning passages that are especially attractive and delightful by which to entice the reader through pleasure and induce him to read on more eagerly. For no one is inattentive to what gives him delight.[20]

This commentary is of a kind with Erasmus's discussion of the rhetorical structure of the familiar letter in his textbook, *De conscribendis epistolis*. There, too, Erasmus cites this very letter as a model example of an emphatically persuasive letter (*exhortatio*):

> Amongst Jerome's letters there is an *exhortatio* addressed to Heliodorus, which is an absolute classic of this genre.

> [Est et inter Hieronymianas epistolas, exhortatoria ad Heliodorum, quae vniuersum eius generis artificium vna complectitur.][21]

Note that this letter conforms fully to Erasmus's preferred definition: it is an 'intimate conversation' between separated friends, which vividly produces the one to the other. Notice something else. The classic of the form is a piece of highly specific writing from the *vita* of St Jerome – a letter in which he implores his close friend to join him in a life of asceticism and study. And (according to the commentary which Erasmus provides for his edition) the affective power of the letter impinges with equal force on the reader who is neither the original recipient of the letter nor its author. Erasmus has something further to say on this score in his *annotatio artis*:

> Writings of this kind are nothing else than Christian declamations. For when Christians saw that eloquence was something at the same

time most beautiful and most useful and did not think it fittng to be occupied as the profane rhetoricians were with trifling subjects . . . they made the whole theory of declamation subservient to moral instruction.[22]

The intimate conversation between separated friends makes any suggested (closely argued) proposal vividly compelling by its emotional 'presence'. The patristic familiar letter is therefore the preferred genre for exhortation to moral rectitude, which makes church teaching on behaviour vividly present to the sixteenth-century Christian reader.[23]

For the second stage in this historical contextualising of the way Erasmian epistolary instruction develops a technology of affect to 'fabricate intimacy' I turn to the pedagogic context – not to the *De conscribendis epistolis* (Erasmus's manual on letter writing), but to the *De copia* (his general textbook on Latin textual production). There are a number of indications in the *De copia* that Erasmus has in mind familiar letter writing as the generalised model for textual production which deploys ornament and amplification persuasively in order to have some desired compelling emotional impact on the reader. The most obvious signal is Erasmus's choices of phrase for virtuoso variation in Book one (*de copia verborum*) – one hundred and fifty alternative ways of expressing the sentiment:

> Your letter pleased me mightily
> [tuae litterae me magnopere delectarunt]

Two hundred versions of:

> As long as I live, I shall preserve the memory of you
> [semper dum vivam tui meminero][24]

The first of these is obviously epistolary. The second is an intense expression of friendship, and of presence evoked affectively, and as Erasmus specifies his own and Thomas More's names in the course of the variations ('as long as Erasmus lives, the name of More will never perish') the phrase involves absence across geographical distance (Erasmus in the Low Countries, More in England).[25]

    The compelling reason for choosing the *De copia* to contextualise the pedagogy of affective epistolary writing is, however, a more local and specific one. It has to do (as elsewhere in my recent work on Erasmus) with a particular published volume, and one which was not a first edition. The volume in question, I shall argue, in its capacity as friendship gift in a particular geographical location, for a particular occasion, offers us the chance to respond to the texts it contains in something like the spirit in which Erasmus offered them, and (I believe) contemporary readers in northern Europe – for our purposes, in England – received them.

In 1514 Erasmus gave the second, emended edition of the *De copia* to the printer Matthias Schürer at Strasbourg, to publish together with the first edition of his *Parabolae*, or book of comparisons. Between the two pedagogic texts are printed two letters, exchanged between Erasmus and Jakob Wimpfeling – spokesman for the *sodalitas literaria* (literary society) at Strasbourg, and a collection of verses. In addition, the *De copia* carries a prefatory letter to Schürer, the printer, and the *Parabolae* carries a prefatory letter to Erasmus's close friend in Antwerp, Pieter Gilles. These four letters frame the pedagogic contents of the two treatises in a particularly interesting way. In essence, they construct a quite elaborate affective scenario – a sequence of *epistolae* which do two different jobs simultaneously. They specify the 'occasion' for the volume (providing it with a vivid biographical Erasmian setting); and they carefully exemplify and animate the pedagogic precepts in the *De copia* and the *Parabolae* manuals.[26]

P. S. Allen includes Wimpfeling's brief letter to Erasmus, and Erasmus's lengthy reply in their chronological place, in his *Opus epistolarum Erasmi*, as a genuine exchange of letters. The internal evidence of the letters, however, makes it quite clear that the second is a highly contrived, virtuoso rhetorical exercise, elicited at the request of Wimpfeling's *sodalitas literaria* following a visit to the literary society by Erasmus as he was passing through Strasbourg on his way to Basle. The presence of the Wimpfeling letter, unlike the prefatory letters, is announced on the title-page of the volume itself. The Erasmus letter should therefore, I think, be treated as a worked example of a familiar letter, clearly offered to the reader of the volume as such.[27]

The rhetorical techniques used in Erasmus's letter to Wimpfeling consistently follow closely the rhetorical methods of amplification inventoried in the *De copia* (and metaphors from the *Parabolae*).[28] The letter, in other words, is a full exemplum of the kind provided throughout the *De conscribendis epistolis*. It has the added advantage, however, over those compressed, generalised examples, of being clearly addressed to specified, known individuals at a specified, known location. Given that the invitation to write, and Erasmus's reply itself, specify that the 'familiarity' of those addressed is more courtesy than reality the tone of the affect can be very precisely placed as warm but not intimate.[29]

Beyond the detail of its rhetorical structure – the technology of its affect – the Wimpfeling letter does something further. It stages the entire volume as a textual gift, an *amicitia* or friendship transaction with the intellectual community at Strasbourg. It comes complete with verse offerings to individual members of the group, one of whom (Thomas Vogler) has previously sent laudatory verses to Erasmus:

Johann Witz, since I saw that he could hardly be torn away from me, I have consoled with a quatrain; and to make the keepsake of more value to my admirer, or more truly to one who is head over heals in love with me, I have written it out in my own hand. Here it is. I send you also what I had written on the journey to that incomparable man Sebastian Brant; for I have changed a few words in it of no importance. I have added the nonsense I scribbled rather than wrote to Vogler.[30]

All these items are printed in the physical volume following the Wimpfeling letter, so that the material gift is as nearly as possible present to the reader.[31] The device of the 'keepsake' which Erasmus has 'written out in [his] own hand' (meis digitis scripsi') is a favourite of his, which teases the reader with the discrepancy between the original, and its print 'copy', deceptively 'the same'. And just as these poems are friendship offerings, so the texts themselves – the *De copia* and the *Parabolae* – are gifts to the Strasbourg printer, Schürer.

Matthias Schürer is named as a worthy member of the Strasbourg *sodalitas literaria* in the letter to Wimpfeling:

> Besides, there is Matthias Schürer, a man to whom I am much attached on many other grounds, but still more as a son of Sélestat, that town so fertile in learned and gifted men to which I owe also Beatus Rhenanus and Johann Witz and Wimpfeling himself. And so, were I not deeply attached to Matthias, I should rightly be accused of having iron and adamant where my heart should be, such was his initiative in offering by acts of kindness to become my friend. Nor will I so act as to fall short in spirit at least and in readiness, although it was he who began it; one day I will repay what he has done for me, if only my spirit is matched by my capacity.[32]

The 'acts of kindness' Schürer has performed are editions of Erasmus's works; the suggestion is that they were no less acts of friendship for the fact that Schürer's relationship is a professional one. Erasmus's prefatory letter to the *De copia* text specifies that text and the text of the *Parabolae* as gift-offerings to a printer personally worthy of Erasmus's admiration, a man of humane learning, as emanating from a circle with whom he has (in the Wimpfeling letter) publicly associated himself in *amicitia*.

The prefatory letter to Schürer effectively refers us back to the letter to Wimpfeling. For there Erasmus offers a *narratio* in which he gives a vivid account of his movements since he left Strasbourg ('And now, since you want to know how the rest of my journey went, here is the story in few words'). That *narratio* establishes Basle – Erasmus's settled location, and the publishing centre for his major works of the next three years, the Seneca, the expanded *Adagia*, the *Novum Instrumentum*, Jerome – as crucially situated both geographically and intellectually in relation to neighbouring Sélestat and Strasbourg (Wimpfeling's native town, and the place where he now resides). The intellectual centrality of Basle is skilfully conveyed through Erasmus's vivid account of the physical convergence of scholars from these locations upon Basle (Witz accompanying Erasmus on his journey; Beatus Rhenanus, native of Sélestat, meeting him there to take on the job as trusted editor), coupled with his equally vivid picture of a constant exchange of letters and verses between those physically separated and remaining at the three locations. All of this finally allows Erasmus to lay claim to Basle as 'his' native town – Germany as his intellectual motherland 'mea Germania'.

If we turn, finally, to the prefatory letter to the *Parabolae*, addressed to Pieter Gilles, it makes compellingly explicit the scenario I have been teasing out of the volume's structure and physical presentation. The letter opens on the theme of true *amicitia* (intimate friendship), and with a series of *parabolae* or emotionally stimulating comparisons, fully worthy of the textbook it proffers:

> Friends of the commonplace and homespun sort, my open-hearted Pieter, have their idea of relationship, like their whole lives, attached to material things; and if ever they have to face a separation, they favour a frequent exchange of rings, knives, caps, and other tokens of the kind, for fear that their affection may cool when intercourse is interrupted or actually die away through the interposition of long tracts of time and space. But you and I, whose idea of friendship rests wholly in a meeting of minds and the enjoyment of studies in common, might well greet one another from time to time with presents for the mind and keepsakes of a literary description. Not that there is any risk that when our life together is interrupted we may slowly grow cold, or that the great distance which separates our bodies may loosen the close tie between our minds. Minds can develop an even closer link, the greater the space that comes between them. Our aim would be that any loss due to separation in the actual enjoyment of our friendship should be made good, not without interest, by tokens of this literary kind. And so I send a present – no common present, for you are no common friend, but many jewels in one small book.[33]

Here the *Parabolae* is offered as a gift (a jewel, a token) to an intimate friend, and the tone of the letter is equivalently more intense and affectively compelling.[34] Following the opening contrast between commonplace friendship, and friendship of minds, Erasmus produces a variant on a favourite *topos* – truly intellectual friendship is not cooled by separation; minds sustain their ardour even when apart.[35] Written texts are the ideal tokens for such enduring friendships.

Erasmus produces a worked example of personalised and intimate letter writing, in which *parabolae* heighten the affective force of the (otherwise formulaic) sentiments, and in which he once again foregrounds the exemplary nature of the writing by self-consciously alluding to the effectiveness of the devices he incorporates in the very act of employing them ('Deprive the orators of their arsenal of metaphor, and all will be thin and dull'; 'this man has a pretty knack of making his work sound important'; 'Would this win no credit as an ingenious application of the parallel?').[36]

I think it is absolutely essential that we register the 'staging' of Erasmus's epistolary technology of affect in the Schürer volume if we are to historicise appropriately the ways in which feeling is textually provoked and manipulated in writing of the period.[37] The Schürer *De copia/Parabolae* volume does much more than provide an inventory of techniques of rhetorical amplification, and itemise comparisons drawn from classical works of literature. Yet we have the greatest difficulty in seeing beyond the apparently unstructured compilation of textual material, because we tend to ignore all the physical apparatus of the book itself which provides the instructions for its reading. It is the self-conscious framing in terms of geographical place of publication (prominent on the book's title-page), the prefatory material to the publisher (selected on grounds of friendship and past gift exchanges), the letters from and to Wimpfeling, locating the publishing 'event' in relation to Erasmus's pedagogic and publishing activities as a whole, the letter of friendship to Gilles, transforming the *Parabolae* from textbook into intellectual gift cementing *amicitia*, which together provide the school reader (teacher or student) with instructions on how to read. They frame instruction so as to convey the efficacy of the precepts compellingly by producing them in a vivid scenario of 'real life' textual transaction.

I have been arguing that Erasmus's is an extremely sophisticated version of the ability of the familiar letter to capture and communicate highly wrought emotion from absent friend to reader. At the heart of Erasmus's thinking lies some idea of *authenticity*. Whereas a textual version of a Cicero oration lacks the gesture and intonation which made it compelling in its original form, a letter written by Jerome survives in precisely its original state – every element in it preserved and available to the sixteenth-century reader. And I have been arguing that we miss the care with which, in his pedagogic treatises, Erasmus reconstructs a textual milieu within which the richness of possibility for letter writing is 'staged' for the novice reader. Renaissance readers of the *De copia*, I am suggesting, composed their own 'occasional' letters in the engaged and rhetorically stringent way exemplified by Erasmus in the letter to Wimpfeling. It remains to show that such possibilities were recognised by Shakespeare's contemporaries in England, in particular – that those who passed through early modern English classrooms expected 'familiar letters' to convey passionate feeling, to create bonds of friendship, and to make the absent loved one (or intellectual kindred spirit) vividly present. That they, like their continental contemporaries regarded the familiar letter as a highly crafted form of communication which could act as intermediary between separated individuals linked by bonds of shared feeling and an emerging trans-European intellectual ideal of *humanitas*.

We know that Erasmian works like the *De copia* were the staple of European schoolteaching throughout the second half of the sixteenth century, and that the persuasive potential of the Erasmian familiar letter was well understood. Erasmus's 'epistle to perswade a young gentleman to marriage' was included in Thomas Wilson's popular *Arte of Rhetorique*, as a model of the kind of discourse which could combine the affective transmission of warmth of feeling, friendship and emotional sincerity with conventional techniques of logical persuasion to produce a compelling case for a particular course of action.[38] To reassure ourselves further that such continental subtleties may realistically be associated with an English setting, a 1564 publication of Myles Coverdale provides us with a vivid context for such feelingful epistolary communication. Coverdale's *Certain most godly, fruitful, and comfortable letters of such true Saintes and holy Martyrs of God, as in the late bloodye persecution here within this Realme, gaue their lyues for the defence of Christes holy gospel* is a compilation of letters 'written in the tyme of theyr affliction and cruell imprysonment' by Protestant Englishmen persecuted under Mary.[39] Coverdale recommends to the devout reader the careful reading of the letters of those who suffered punishment and death for their faith. And he draws directly upon Erasmus to make a double case for letters as the primary resource for spiritual truth and Christian feeling:

[I]t doth vs good to read and heare, not the lying legendes of fayned, false, counterfayted, and popish canonized saincts, neither ye triflyng toyes & forged fables of corrupted writers: but such true, holy, & approued histories, monuments, orations, epistles & letters, as do set forth vnto vs y^t blessed behauiour of gods deare seruau*n*tes. It doth vs good (I say) by such comfortable reme*m*braunce, conceaued by their notable writinges, to be conuersaunt with them, at the least in spirite.

S. Hierome, writing to one Nitia, and hauyng occasion to speake of letters or epystles, maketh mention of a certain Authour named Turpilius, whose woordes (sayeth he) are these: a letter or epistle, is the thyng alone ye maketh men present which are absent. For among those that are absent, what is so presente, as to heare and talke with those whom thou louest? Also, that noble Clarke Erasmus Roterodame, commendyng the booke of the Epistles or letters which S. Augustine dyd write, sayeth thus: by some of Augustines bokes we may perceaue, what maner of man he was being an infant in Christ. By other some, we may knowe what maner a one he was being a young man, and what he was being an olde man. But by thys onely booke (meaning the booke of the Epistles or letters) thou shalt knowe whole Augustyne altogether. And why doth S. Hierome or Erasmus saye thus? No doubt, euen because that in such writynges, as in a cleare glasse, we maye see and beholde, not onely what plentifull furniture and store of heauenly grace, wisedome, knowledge, vnderstanding, fayth, loue, hope, zeale, pacience, mekenes, obedience, with the worthy fruites thereof, almighty god had bestowed vpon the same his most deare children: but also what a fatherlye care he euer hadde vnto them.[40]

The first idea here – that saints' letters are a more valuable source of spirituality and insight into sanctity than legend and fiction – is taken from Erasmus's *Vita Hieronymi*, which prefaces his edition of Jerome's letters.[41] The second, that letters provide the affective presence of the absent loved one, complete with its reference to Turpilius and Nitias, comes, as we saw, from the beginning of Erasmus's *De conscribendis epistolis*, referenced to the first Jerome letter in Erasmus's collection of the saint's letters.

Erasmus's subtle and doctrinally complex version of affective Christian feeling, transmitted through the familiar letter, is here invoked as definitive, at the pulse-point of Elizabethan Protestantism. And the easy way in which Coverdale makes the assumption that the reader will take the Erasmian point allows us, I think, to infer that the familiar letter, for the Christian Englishman, carried a freight of Erasmianism concerning its capacity to transmit feeling – to make the absent friend present, and to make the effects of intimacy and friendship work at the level of persuasion.

In Act 4, scene 3 of *King Lear*, a gentleman describes to Kent the effect upon Cordelia of letters he brought her:

> *Kent.* Did your letters pierce the queen to any demonstration of grief?
> *Gentleman.* Ay, sir; she took them, read them in my presence;
> And now and then an ample tear trill'd down
> Her delicate cheek; it seem'd she was a queen
> Over her passion; who, most rebel-like,
> Sought to be king o'er her.
> *Kent.*   O! then it mov'd her.[42]

The gentleman goes on, prompted by Kent, to specify the intense way in which Cordelia responded:

> *Kent.*   Made she no verbal question?
> *Gentleman.* Faith, once or twice she heav'd the name of 'father'
> Pantingly forth, as if it press'd her heart;
> Cried 'Sisters! sisters! Shame of ladies! sisters!
> Kent! father! sisters! What? i' th' storm! i' th' night?
> Let pity not believe it!' There she shook
> The holy water from her heavenly eyes,
> And clamour moisten'd, then away she started
> To deal with grief alone.[43]

This passage is often used as the most intensely affective presentation of Cordelia in the play. Indeed, I have argued myself that this portrayal of Cordelia, iconically grieving, passively suffering on behalf of her father, provides the moral justification for her active participation in warfare a scene later. It now strikes me somewhat differently. The gentleman recounts an exemplary response to a familiar letter – a textbook example of the production at a distance of intense emotion and passionate feeling. The letters in question are, surely, from Kent: in Act 2, scene 2, Kent, in the stocks, comforted himself with a letter from Cordelia;[44] in Act 3, scene 1, Kent sends a gentleman to Dover with letters and a token for Cordelia.[45] Now the gentleman tells Kent how Cordelia received 'his letters' – letters of *amicitia*, vividly making absence present ('Kent! father! sisters! What? i' th' storm! i' th' night?'), transmitting passionate feeling ('O! then it mov'd her').[46]

But most of the many epistolary transactions in *Lear* are not so securely morally admirable. Feeling and attendant action are manipulated by letters not to connote the bonds of intense personal commitment, but rather to mislead and distort. The most obvious examples of this are the forged letter Edmund uses to persuade Gloucester that his son Edgar is treacherous, and the adulterous letter from Goneril to Edmund, whose interception brings about hers and Edmund's downfall. In between, letters which Gloucester receives secretly from France, the existence of which Edmund betrays to Cornwall, lead to Gloucester's mutilation. Clearly something un-Erasmian, or possibly anti-Erasmian is at stake here.

Let us look first at the two letters which are sent in haste towards the end of Act 1, the receipt of which provides a plot crux in Act 2. 'I'll write straight to my sister / To hold my very course', resolves Goneril in Act 1, scene 4, as she determines to insist on Lear's reducing the number of his followers and curbing their riotousness. At the end of the scene, after her confrontation with Lear and his precipitate departure, Goneril dispatches her letter at the hands of her household servant Oswald:

> *Goneril.* What he hath utter'd I have writ my sister;
>
>   . . .
>
>   How, now, Oswald!
> What, have you writ that letter to my sister?
> *Oswald.* Ay, madam.
> *Goneril.* Take you some company, and away to horse:
>   Inform her full of my particular fear;
>   And thereto add such reasons of your own
>   As may compact it more.[47]

Oswald is here involved with the letter, not simply as trusted messenger but as rhetorically expert co-author of the text – should the persuasive technology prove inadequate he is authorised to 'add such reasons of [his] own / As may compact it more'. By contrast, Lear too resolves to send letters to Regan, informing her of his ill-treatment at Goneril's hands, and requesting lodging at her house. His messenger is the disguised Kent, who has specified his suitability for such message-carrying as part of his recommendation for Lear's service:

> *Lear.* What services canst thou do?
>
> *Kent.* I can keep honest counsel, ride, run, mar a curious tale in telling it, and deliver a plain message bluntly; that which ordinary men are fit for, I am qualified in, and the best of me is diligence.[48]

Kent, in other words, is not the kind of servant to employ fancy rhetoric and pen his master's letters, nor add to their arguments if they fall short.[49] When Lear sends his letters he specifies that Kent will be the mere carrier of his message:

> *Lear.* Go you before to Gloucester [i.e. the place] with these letters. Acquaint my daughter no further with any thing you know than comes from her demand out of the letter. If your diligence be not speedy I shall be there afore you.
>
> *Kent.* I will not sleep, my Lord, till I have delivered your letter.[50]

For Lear, letters are mere messages, sent by the fastest carrier to anticipate his own arrival. Or, put rather more closely in Erasmian terms, Lear does not trust the letter to convey the arguments of his love and authority, persuading for him in his absence; he simply dispatches it to herald his imminent arrival in person, which he assumes will be an argument irresistible in itself.

What happens to the letter sent, and to its messenger, conforms to the spirit in which it was dispatched: Lear's 'blunt' missive is repelled, its carrier clapped in the stocks; Goneril's messenger and message insinuate themselves into favour. As Kent describes it, after the event, to Lear:

> *Kent.*   My Lord, when at their home
>   I did commend your Highness' letters to them,
>   Ere I was risen from the place that show'd
>   My duty kneeling, came there a reeking post,
>   Stew'd in his haste, half breathless, panting forth
>   From Goneril his mistress salutations;
>   Deliver'd letters, spite of intermission,
>   Which presently they read: on whose contents
>   They summon'd up their meiny, straight took horse;
>   Commanded me to follow, and attend
>   The leisure of their answer.[51]

Because the contents of the letters are never revealed to the audience (they are never 'read aloud'), their dramatised reception stands in for the contrast between their epistolary techniques.

On her arrival at Gloucester's castle, Regan describes the way in which her sister's letter has prompted Cornwall's and her removal from their home to seek Gloucester's advice. They have come:

> *Regan.* Thus out of season, threading dark-ey'd night:
>   Occasions, noble Gloucester, of some prize,

Wherein we must have use of your advice.
Our father he hath writ, so hath our sister,
Of differences, which I best thought it fit
To answer [away] from our home; the several messengers
From hence attend dispatch.[52]

Effectively, this is a contest for affective impact between the two letters, a contest which apparently Goneril and the persuasive technology of Oswald's crafted letter win: Kent is clapped in the stocks, his message unanswered; Gloucester is persuaded to give shelter to Goneril, Cornwall and their cause, allowing Lear, on his arrival, to be turned out into the storm. Dramatically, the contest is displaced on to the messengers – their brawl physically reproduces the differing terms of the communications they bear. The insults Kent heaps upon Oswald all characterise him as a manipulator of language and forms, 'a lily-livered, action-taking, whoreson, glass-gazing, super-serviceable, finical rogue'; 'you come with letters against the King, and take Vanity the puppet's part against the royalty of her father'.[53] As for Kent himself, on the contrary, ''tis my occupation to be plain'. Or, as Cornwall puts it:

Cornwall.   This is some fellow,
   Who, having been prais'd for bluntness, doth affect
   A saucy roughness, and constrains the garb
   Quite from his nature: he cannot flatter, he,
   An honest mind and plain, he must speak truth:
   And they will take it, so; if not, he's plain.[54]

It is this plain truth which (as in the morality plays) ends up in the stocks. It is the smooth-tongued rhetorician who carries the day.[55]

What we seem to have here is the demonisation of the persuasive technology of affect. We recall that the rhetorical 'feigning' of the epistolary transaction, though sanctioned by Jerome (and Erasmus) nevertheless implies an 'insincerity' to which some commentators drew attention.[56] In this play, bastard sons and unnatural daughters conduct epistolary transactions which convince; plain folk and close kin are misled by letters, or betrayed by them.[57] The most striking contrast here is that between the intimate letters which are exchanged between Kent and Cordelia in private (through the trusted intermediary of the gentleman), and the mirroring exchanges of letters which bring about Gloucester's downfall. In the first scene of Act 3, Kent sends letters to the French camp; in the third scene, Gloucester tells Edmund he has received letters thence:

Gloucester. Go to; say you nothing. There is division between the Dukes, and
   a worse matter than that. I have receiv'd a letter this night; 'tis
   dangerous to be spoken; I have lock'd the letter in my closet.[58]

Challenged by Cornwall – 'Come, sir, what letters had you late from France?' – Gloucester tries to establish that these are familiar letters, not espionage:

Gloucester. I have a letter guessingly set down,
    Which came from one that's of a neutral heart,
    And not from one oppos'd.[59]

But in the economy of this play, letters are written and received to incite mendaciously to action and to pervert the truth.[60]

The two most vital exchanges of letter for the plot, however, are of course those which involve the treachery and duplicity of Edmund. At the beginning of the play, it is the forged letter, supposedly from Edgar to his brother Edmund, which convinces Gloucester that his legitimate son is a traitor to him. In the final act, the intercepted letter from Goneril to Edmund, reminding him of their 'reciprocal vows' and inciting him to murder her husband, leads to the discovery of Edmund's general treachery. These are also the only two letters whose contents are divulged to us – both are banally instructive, without any kind of rhetorical embellishment. For Shakespeare's dramatic purposes, persuasive affect is located elsewhere. It is in the mouths of Regan and Goneril, contradicting their marriage vows in order to swear total love and duty to their father, and the mouth of Edmund, assuring his father of his trust at the moment he betrays him.

In the final section of this chapter I want to argue that this is significant: that *Lear* severs affect from its epistolary setting where it could be controlled, and leaves it circulating at large – on the Heath. Affect, let loose from its civilised setting in the familiar letter, is demonised as the trigger for social disruption and disturbance.

Cordelia. Unhappy that I am, I cannot heave
    My heart into my mouth: I love your Majesty
    According to my bond; no more nor less.
Lear. How, how, Cordelia! Mend your speech a little,
    Lest you may mar your fortunes.[61]

True blood kin, in *Lear*, are distinguished by their reluctance to commit their feelings of obligation and love to any contrived form of words. Cordelia loves 'according to [her] bond', but refuses to enhance that bond's immediate value by giving it rhetorical expression.

Neither Cordelia nor Edgar is prepared to manipulate expressions of feeling within the setting of court and household to match the complex version of 'service', as technical command of language transactions, manifested by Regan, Goneril and Edmund.[62] These latter, unlike the 'natural kin', held in place by innate, unexpressed emotional bonds, are problematically placed in relation, in particular, to first-born sons. Rather than being held in place by locally specific bonds of emotional and economic dependency, they become threateningly mobile as a result of their capacity to 'study' to create affection and compel belief.[63]

Exchanges of letters in *Lear* seem to draw attention to their disturbing efficiency as instruments for effecting social mobility. Just those features of the familiar letter which Erasmus values for their ability to create intense feeling at will, to concoct *amicitia* and its associated binding emotional intensity are shown to be capable of loosening existing bonds of affection and creating new alliances where expedient. Letters transform old affections, persuade friends to new courses of action, and finally make the reader of the printed text (the audience) morally complicit. With each alteration in the configuration of alliances in *Lear*, fresh letters redefine the bonds of affection amongst the remaining protagonists. The news of Cornwall's death, putting out Gloucester's eyes, is brought to Goneril and Albany accompanied by urgent letters for Goneril from her sister:

> *Messenger.* This letter, Madam, craves a speedy answer;
> 'Tis from your sister.   [*Presents a letter*]
> *Goneril.*   ... I'll read, and answer.[64]

In Act 4, scene 5, Regan knows that there is some reorganisation of the bonds of affection as soon as she hears that Oswald carries a letter from Goneril to Edmund:

> *Regan.* Why should she write to Edmund? Might not you
> Transport her purposes by word? Belike,
> Some things – I know not what. I'll love thee much,
> Let me unseal the letter.[65]

Her remedy is herself to send a note, by the same bearer, to Edmund, to persuade him to turn his affections towards her.

Which brings us, finally, to that almost intolerably powerful emotional effect which we as audience experience on the Heath with Lear, and on Dover cliffs with Gloucester and Edgar. For if the persuasive technology of familiar letters has been demonised in this play, where does that leave the true *amicitia* between friends and close kin and its possibilities for expression? Cordelia's consternation at the play's opening already answers the question:

> *Lear.*   what can you say to draw
> A third more opulent than your sisters? Speak.
> *Cordelia.* Nothing, my lord.
> *Lear.* Nothing?
> *Cordelia.* Nothing.[66]

Equally unjustly accused of unfilial conduct, Gloucester's 'true' son Edgar also finds himself incapable of confecting the kind of plausible utterance which would restore him to his father's favour:

> *Edgar.*   Edgar I nothing am.[67]

So strong is their resistance to 'feigned' sentiment of the kind so adeptly marshalled in the play's familiar letters that each child is reduced to inarticulateness and verbal helplessness before the spectacle of their father's misfortune in the last two Acts of the play. There is, within the play's ambit, no scope for 'true expression' to set against the sentimental contrivedness of Edmund and Oswald, Goneril and Regan.

For Erasmus, the beauty of the familiar letter lay in its structuring and controlling emotional transactions, so that their moral value is enhanced. In *Lear* such controlled expression of feeling is apparently not available – it has been banished from the scene, and replaced by a version of epistolary artifice which distorts and misleads because it is in the wrong hands (always a risk the rhetorician is aware of). In consequence, I suggest, the only emotional transactions to which true kin have access are uncontrolled and unstructured – are technically out of control. Cordelia cannot 'heave her heart into her mouth' to order for her father; she can only pant out verbal ejaculations of distress to represent her true feelings:

> *Gentleman.* Faith, once or twice she heav'd the name of 'father'
> Pantingly forth, as if it press'd her heart.[68]

Throughout his companionship with Lear on the Heath and his compassionate guiding of his blinded father, Edgar utters not one word of comfort or consolation to either. Instead he contributes a sense of surreal dislocation of speech and action, which produces an almost intolerably emotionally meaningless commentary on the events as they unfold.

Such emotional dyslexia is meant, I think, to be a terrifying prospect. Lear and his party on the Heath, and Gloucester and the disguised Edgar at Dover Cliffs, are offered as appalling manifestations of helplessly uncontrolled feeling, damagingly circulating without motive or purpose, its moral efficacy terribly out of focus. When unnatural sons and daughters have taken control of the technology of affect for their own manipulative purposes, there is, it seems, no possibility of articulation left for the naturally caring members of the family. This is the play's catastrophe – its darkly nihilistic message, not its resolution.

Once we historicise the networks of feeling which form and reform the bonds of duty and friendship in *Lear* around the persuasive technology of letter writing and reading, we are bound, I think, to recognise that the 'natural' and uncontained versions of passionate emotion in the play are not available as a solution to the problems raised by Lear misconstruing his daughters' declarations of love. Raw emotion is not an attractive prospect for an audience which had placed its trust in Erasmus's promise that mastery of the familiar letter would enable humane individuals to persuade one another affectively to collaborate for a better, more Christian Europe. The spectacle of such 'civilised' technical skill working successfully on the side of deception and self-interest is disturbing and deeply pessimistic. Yet it is to precisely this vividly dramatised scenario that we, the modern audience, respond positively and intensely emotionally, because it is, of its essence, a representation of emotion unmediated by historicised social forms. The combination of horror and embarrassment with which we experience the spectacle of Edgar deluding the desperate Gloucester into casting himself down from a non-existent cliff owes nothing to Erasmus, or to humanist rhetoric, or to Renaissance philosophy. Like Gloucester and Edgar, we experience with immediacy that raw emotional intensity in a moral, social and historical void.

6

ALIEN INTELLIGENCE

Mercantile exchange and knowledge transactions in Marlowe's *The Jew of Malta*

Shylock. Three thousand ducats for three months, and Antonio bound.
Bassanio. Your answer to that.
Shylock. Antonio is a good man.
Bassanio. Have you heard any imputation to the contrary?
Shylock. Ho no, no, no, no: my meaning in saying he is a good man, is to have you understand me that he is sufficient, – yet his means are in supposition: he hath an argosy bound to Tripolis, another to the Indies, I understand moreover upon the Rialto, he hath a third at Mexico, a fourth for England, and other ventures he hath squand'red abroad, – but ships are but boards, sailors but men, there be land-rats, and water-rats, water-thieves, and land-thieves, (I mean pirates), and then there is the peril of waters, winds, and rocks: the man is notwithstanding sufficient, – three thousand ducats, – I think I may take his bond.
Bassanio. Be assur'd you may.[1]

Throughout this volume, I have been arguing that a historicised reading of Shakespeare proposes a dialogue which consistently registers and problematises the temporal chasm across which critic and play-text attempt to converse. The familiar voice of the Shakespearean text does not come to us evenly across the passage of time – it rises and falls in volume as it resonates (or fails to resonate) with our late twentieth-century beliefs and preoccupations. We pick up a strand in the conversation, recognise its relevance to us, formulate our response and watch for the illumination – the luminosity of the page we scrutinise – which convinces us that the recognition was mutual.[2] The question which remains from my introduction, however, is: is there something about the way in which *Shakespeare*'s works are located within the literary canon which eases this dialogue across history?

This chapter explores the proposition that there is, indeed, a fundamental difference between our discursive relationship with Shakespeare's plays and our relationship with other contemporary, or near-contemporary drama. I choose to test this proposition against a play which readily suggests itself for comparison with the Shakespearean treatment of an enduringly problematic topic: Christopher Marlowe's *The Jew of Malta* – a play which invites comparison with Shakespeare's *The Merchant of Venice*.

The two main adversaries in Shakespeare's *The Merchant of Venice* – Antonio and Shylock – are vividly part of the commercial world of Venice, the community of merchant adventurers, traders and money-changers and lenders (what we would regard as 'bankers' in a pre-banking age). The plot turns on transactions which form a crucial part in Venice's economic activity – risk on overseas venture, lending and borrowing under contract, penalty clauses for defaulting on a loan. Yet I shall suggest that Shakespeare's plot, unlike Marlowe's, does not depend upon an understanding of Renaissance trading conventions. To this extent it is historically more transposable – more culturally accessible across time – than Marlowe's precisely topical plot-version of mercantile greed, overseas trade and anti-Semitism. But for that very reason, I shall suggest, Shakespeare's play more dangerously persuades us that its prejudices are transhistorical or ahistorical.[3] The plot of *The Merchant of Venice* uses the audience's emotional engagement with the characters to elicit our consent as to the justice of the plot's outcome – to confuse our reasoned sense of the temporal specificness of early modern conventions governing ideas of justice, contract and obligation.[4]

I am going to argue here that in Marlowe's *The Jew of Malta* a series of historically precise market-related concepts – 'jew', 'merchant', 'commerce', established trade routes – structure the plot explicitly, and shape the outcome of events. As a consequence, the questions of value and belief which Marlowe raises via his plot can be clearly perceived to be fundamentally early modern questions concerning the transition from old to early modern commercial worlds.

Let's begin with a striking passage from early in Marlowe's play, which locates Barabas's sphere of operations in Malta with great precision:

> *Merchant.* Barabas, thy ships are safe,
>   Riding in Malta road; and all the merchants
>   With all their merchandise are safe arrived,
>   And have sent me to know whether yourself
>   Will come and custom them.
> *Barabas.* The ships are safe, thou say'st, and richly fraught?
> *Merchant.* They are.
> *Barabas.*   Why then, go bid them come ashore
>   And bring with them their bills of entry;
>   I hope our credit in the custom-house
>   Will serve as well as I were present there.
>   Go send 'em threescore camels, thirty mules,
>   And twenty waggons to bring up the ware.

> But art thou master in a ship of mine,
> And is thy credit not enough for that?
> *Merchant.* The very custom barely comes to more
> Than many merchants of the town are worth,
> And therefore far exceeds my credit, sir.[5]

Barabas's ships have come from Cairo; within fifty lines, a second successful maritime venture has returned from Alexandria:

> *Second Merchant.* Thine argosy from Alexandria,
> Know, Barabas, doth ride in Malta road,
> Laden with riches, and exceeding store
> Of Persian silks, of gold, and orient pearl.[6]

If you look at a map of the Mediterranean you will see how accurate this 'placing' of Barabas's wealth-generating is.[7] Barabas trades from Malta with the key outlets for exotic goods in the region. And in Act 2 his commercial activities are further specified so as to convey clearly the extent and importance of his merchant ventures:

> *Lodovico.* O, Barabas, well met;
> Where is the diamond you told me of?
> *Barabas.* I have it for you, sir; please you walk in with me.
> What ho, Abigail; open the door, I say.
> *Enter Abigail [with letters].*
> *Abigail.* In good time, father; here are letters come
> From Ormus, and the post stays here within.
> *Barabas.* . . .
> Nay, on my life it is my factor's hand.
> . . .
> My factor sends me word a merchant's fled
> That owes me for a hundred tun of wine.
> I weigh it thus much: I have wealth enough.[8]

Hormuz, at the mouth of the Persian gulf, was an important centre for gem trading, but at the limits of risky ventures (the pioneering London merchant John Newbery was imprisoned there while on an exploratory trading venture in 1583).[9] Barabas keeps a factor there – a trusted servant responsible for administering his financial affairs.[10] In this instance the factor is unable to collect the gems (or coin) in exchange for a shipment of wine dispatched from Malta, a loss which Barabas shrugs off because he is in the process of 'trading' his daughter Abigail as a 'diamond' with a more highly prized reward – revenge on the nobles of Malta who confiscated his wealth.[11]

Barabas's primary occupation, then, is as a prestigious merchant-trader (in this, of course, he differs from Shakespeare's Shylock). Insofar as he is a source of hard currency, precious metals and stones, it is because these are the 'tools' of his trade. He is a money-lender only in the sense that his surplus profits can be temporarily loaned to those who do not generate cash as a by-product of their daily activities (notably the gentry). As Lawrence Stone puts it in *The Crisis of the Aristocracy*:

> None of [these London merchants] were specialists in the money-lending field. Money-lending was merely a temporary investment of wealth which had been earned and was still partly employed in foreign trade and retailing in the home market.[12]

On the other hand, his position gives him a formidable ability to intervene outside the immediate sphere of business, to influence public affairs, and even policy (shades of the recurrent uproar over business funding of the Tory party). In 1519 a substantial cash loan from the Fugger merchant family in Augsburg had been directly responsible for Charles V's success in gaining election as Holy Roman Emperor.[13] Thus Barabas is accurately placed by Marlowe in contemporary terms at the intersection of commerce and power.

Like Jacob Fugger, Barabas functions structurally as more than a mere merchant. Barabas is the centre of a network of exchanges which, at the beginning of the play, mesh with the social and political fabric of Malta to make that 'economy' on which the nation depends.[14] In addition to his trading links and his ready access to hard currency, gold and precious stones essential for state business, Barabas also occupies a crucial position as information gatherer. In the course of the play we learn that Barabas's knowledge networking extends to knowledge of fortifications, insider insight into policy decisions, possessing advance warning of international decision making (like the Turks' rescinding of the suspension of Malta's tribute), and participation in academic instruction and book-lending.[15] And apparently crucial to this position is Barabas's alienness – his being a specific kind of transactor of international business outside the bounds of the nation state. The financial implications of this insider/outsider status in terms of levies, customs duties and taxation, are bluntly stated by the Knights Templar as they seize Barabas's wealth:

> *Barabas.* Are strangers with your tribute to be taxed?
> *Second Knight.* Have strangers leave with us to get their wealth?
>   Then let them with us contribute.
> *Barabas.* How, equally?
> *Ferneze.*   No, Jew, like infidels.[16]

Barabas's position as alien merchant places him to one side of the customary levies which return a percentage of merchant profit to the state.[17] English trade had wrestled with the problem of alien versus denizen (home) merchants since the German Hanse merchants cornered the market in English cloth in the mid-sixteenth century.[18] The usefulness of foreign merchants with overseas connections and the particular skills and knowledges of another culture were always offset by a suspicion that their loyalty ultimately lay elsewhere.[19]

Although Barabas plays such a prominent role in the affairs of Malta, he is, from early on in the play, consistently subject to hostility on the part of both high- and low-born nationals of Malta. I suggest that it is tautologous to suggest (as critics customarily do) that this is the standard early modern response to Jewishness; for as Barabas himself points out, it is his success in finance in conjunction with his outsider status which attracts such negative feeling:

> *Barabas.* Thus trolls our fortune in by land and sea,
>   And thus are we on every side enriched;
>   These are the blessings promised to the Jews,
>   And herein was old Abram's happiness.
>   What more may heaven do for earthly men
>   Than thus to pour out plenty in their laps,
>   Ripping the bowels of the earth for them,
>   Making the sea their servant, and the winds
>   To drive their substance with successful blasts?
>   Who hateth me but for my happiness?
>   Or who is honoured now but for his wealth?
>   Rather had I, a Jew, be hated thus,
>   Than pitied in a Christian poverty.[20]

What the play in fact seems to show us is a regular pattern of fascination for Barabas's ability to generate wealth with apparent effortlessness, leading to a kind of intimacy based on dependency upon access to that wealth. Although ultimately this inevitably gives way to dislike and bad faith, it briefly simulates the kind of 'friendship' which was the basis for peer bonding and service of a more customary kind. At the point of dissolution of such a bond, both parties experience the breakdown as betrayal. While Barabas is the catalyst for corruption and malicious dealing, his own extreme (and absurd) villainous acts repay (on an 'eye for an eye and tooth for a tooth' balance sheet) negative acts perpetrated against himself and his own good faith. It is the uneasy balance between fascination for Barabas and triumphalism at his downfall that I want to look at more closely in the course of this chapter.

Behind the ambivalent relationship between the merchant and what for convenience I shall call the 'ruling élite' (the state) lies the ambiguity about what the merchant *does* which produces his handsome surpluses in wealth. He profits from exchanges of commodities – but not commodities he has manufactured. His profit derives from his knowledge and understanding of markets, his ability to anticipate rise and fall in demands, his judgement as to what goods are valued more highly in one location than another. His transactions do, therefore, conform more to the pattern of intellectual service than to the simple supply model of manufacture. I think it is important to recognise that mercantile transactions, like knowledge transactions, were 'strange' in early modern England.

The theme of this chapter, then, is an early modern anxiety about private transactions for deferred profit, upon which interest accrues. I am going to argue that in a period of consolidation of mercantile habits and practices, evasive strategies relating to the prohibition on usury – advancing money and charging interest on it – spill over into the sphere of what I call 'knowledge transactions'. The figure in the drama of the diabolical merchant-usurer-intelligencer is, I shall suggest, a consolidated cultural manifestation of such an unease concerning mercantilism and deferred profit.

Early in 1591, Henry Wotton wrote from Vienna to his patron/employer Lord Zouche, then at Altdorf, confirming the execution of a commission for him:

> Your Honour's books which I delivered very safely, trussed up to the merchant, upon conference with him, I thought convenient to stay a while, till his next sending of certain wares upon the river towards Nuremburg. . . . *The sum is not great, and if your Honour would allow me leave to be so bold, I would crave the employing of it in a better use for me there, because here (I thank God) I want no money for as far as my affairs go.* At my being in Altorph, I remember myself to have dealt with Glasianus [Professor of Oratory at Altdorf] for a Polybius in Greek, which he signified unto me he could well help me unto: if by his means I might procure me a copy of that author ancienter than MDXXX (because I have Perot's edition of that year already), I should be very glad and most earnestly entreat your Honour at his visiting of you, to motion it unto him in my behalf. I desire the bare Greek without the Latin version, if it be possible [my emphasis].[21]

Wotton's purpose, in this correspondence, is to recommend himself to Zouche in the role of retained information gatherer and professional reader – as 'intelligencer'. He eventually obtained such a post with the Earl of Essex five years later. What interests me here is the financial arrangements he discreetly makes with Zouche. He has purchased books for Zouche at Vienna; he requests repayment in Altdorf in the form of specified volumes for his own use. Such an arrangement elegantly avoids two sources of contemporary difficulty associated with this kind of transaction: the association of any notion of 'hire' with services rendered by one highly educated élite man to another; and the awkwardnesses of early modern understanding of loans, debts and, above all, repayments with interest.

Wotton goes on to propose further possible arrangements facilitating the exchange of knowledge between himself and Lord Zouche, which he considers might prove mutually profitable:

> We have here in his Majesty's [Imperial] library notable discourses of

military matters, and in that sort a book of especial estimation, written in Italian, having many experiences of fortification and the like. If your Honour have a fancy to it, I will cause it to be written out, which I desire to hear in the next, because the book is in quarto and of a reasonable quantity. If in any other particular state-point you crave the like, no doubt whatsoever the argument be, amongst 9,000 volumes (whereof the most part are manuscript) we shall find some author to please your Honour. For my part my chief care and charges are be-stowed in Greek and Dutch writers and secret letters of the Empire, of which, in my profession, *I have some that might make a great man beholding to me.* . . . . *Whatsoever it be, or can become unto by exchange of those I have, or gain otherwise, shall ever be, and most worthily are, only at your Honour's commandment* [my emphasis].[22]

Once again here, Wotton takes care both to offer services which are 'only at your Honour's commandment' in a form which at once recognises the trans-actional nature of the service ('Whatever it be, or can become unto by ex-change of those I have, or gain otherwise'), and at the same time avoids casting that formally as a financial indebtedness. Instead, steady use is made of a language of moral indebtedness which shadows the 'fealty' feudal service relations, at the very moment when a young man is bidding vigorously for employment.

A number of recent studies have drawn attention to the ways in which, in the 1590s, private forms of service associated with information gathering and processing (broadly called 'intelligence') produced public uneasiness. Lorna Hutson's *The Usurer's Daughter* looks at the relationship set up textually be-tween service and indebtedness.[23] Alan Stewart has described the way in which the private secretary's close but invisible contractual relationship with his employer is publicly perceived as a kind of dubious intimacy. As he puts it:

The role of the secretary is twofold: firstly, to maintain secrecy in the collation and processing of information with which to provide counsel to the prince, and secondly, to maintain an outward show which pub-licly signals secrecy and privacy. The price paid for this impossible twofold operation is that the publicly-signalled secrecy and privacy is available to be read as sexually compromising, the intimacy of lovers.[24]

Bill Sherman has recently written extensively about the ways in which John Dee rendered such knowledge transaction services for noble employers like Sir Edward Dyer, on behalf of Essex. He has pointed out the way in which the evasions concerning the employment basis (particularly its finances) have been responsible for Dee's reputation as some kind of mysterious 'magus'. A relationship is perceived between the knowledge gatherer and his patron which apparently gives the former some kind of hold over the latter. Since

Dee is a mere intellectual, the indebtedness (in fact a deferred promise of payment or reward) is construed as supernatural.

> Dee's studies led him, as a matter of course, to theories and practices which were less than orthodox. . . . To Dee's irrepressible chagrin, [his areas of study] attracted suspicion from all quarters: time and again he felt the need to pen *apologiae* against 'the scornefull, the malicious, the proud, and the rash [with] their vntrue reports, opinions, and fables of my studies, or exercises Philosophicall.' To package Dee – or Prospero – as magi is not only to be reductive, but to fail to see behind (and therefore to reproduce) the 'fables' which plagued Dee during his life. Knowledge was magical, and sometimes even entailed magic. But the attacks on libraries, the condemnations for conjuring, and the polemical complaints betray a deeper and more significant phenomenon: there were in early modern England dramatic uncertainties about the power of information and those who possessed it.[25]

The Wotton/Zouche correspondence suggests that some of this difficulty in construing the status of private knowledge transactions in the public domain is intrinsic to the relationships themselves – the participants are not comfortable with the available possibilities for formalising intimate service between those of comparable social status, particularly the financial aspects (both the outlay of money by the professional information gatherer on behalf of his client, and the form that reward for services rendered should take).

When Barabas and the Christian Don Mathias are surprised in consultation together by Mathias's mother, the 'private transaction' they spontaneously invent is a knowledge transaction:

> *Barabas.* As for the comment on the Maccabees,
> I have it, sir, and 'tis at your command.
> *Mathias.* Yes, madam, and my talk with him was but
> About the borrowing of a book or two. . . .
> Sirrah, Jew, remember the book.
> *Barabas.* Marry will I, sir.[26]

Within the plot, this matches symmetrically the mercantile excuse for private commerce between Jew and Christian which Barabas has concocted to account for precisely the same private transaction between himself and Lodowick (Barabas is in fact betrothing his daughter twice over, to both Lodowick and Mathias):

> *Mathias.* What makes the Jew and Lodowick so private?
> I fear me 'tis about fair Abigail. . . .
> But wherefore talked Don Lodowick with you?
> *Barabas.* Tush, man, we talked of diamonds, not of Abigail.[27]

Procurement of knowledge is here homologous with purchase of precious stones, reminding us that financial reward is at stake in both cases, since both transactions are with an alien whose company would not be kept for friendship's sake. In other words, Marlowe here seems to support explicitly the relationship implicit in the surviving records of 'real' knowledge transactions, namely some kind of contractual undertaking to supply desired commodities in exchange for deferred and generally imprecisely specified gain for the supplier.[28]

Wotton also appears to think of knowledge transactions in established mercantile terms, which extend to trading techniques for circumventing conceptual and moral awkwardnesses associated with certain kinds of exchanges which involve cash rather than kind. The Wotton proposal that he be repaid for his outlay of ready money in Vienna with equivalent purchases in Altdorf mimics the kind of transaction refined by merchants trading abroad which enabled them to minimise the risks involved in foreign currency dealing, in the absence of fixed exchange rate mechanisms or public banking. The transaction is a financial 'deal': books in Altdorf to compensate for the outlay of cash for books in Vienna. But Wotton constructs it as a bond of obligation or 'amity': 'I should be very glad and most earnestly entreat your Honour at his visiting of you, to motion it unto him in my behalf'. So there is at once acknowledgement of the knowledge transaction as such, and evasiveness about its consequences for the relationship it establishes.

I am moving towards the suggestion that Barabas in *The Jew of Malta* concentrates compellingly within the single figure of the cash-rich alien a vacillating set of cultural attitudes towards exchange for profit of commodities which somehow fail to match a simple model of payment for services rendered (or manufacture provided). The situation is further complicated by the fact that the circulation of commodities is not tidily matched by the movement of ready money – it does not correspond to goods being transferred to points where wealth has accumulated in the form of coin or precious metals. Rather, the expanding market is accompanied by a rapidly spreading credit network – bills of exchange, bills obligatory, bills of debt or bond being transacted and passed between the parties in any transaction as a substitute for 'real' money:

> In the period 1538–1660 the ratio of money (coins) to debts by bond bill obligatory and book was on average 1:9; among merchants, shipowners, merchant tailors and others of similar rank, 1:26; among farmers and cultivators, 1:6; among graziers, drapers, ironmongers, haberdashers, mercers, grocers and high-class shop-keepers, 1:7; among textile manufacturers, clothiers, bonelacemen, silkweavers, threadtwisters, yarnmasters, market spinners, maltsters, brewers, millers, tanners, whittawers, saddlers, fellmongers, wheelwrights and upholsterers, 1:5; among labourers, manual workers in textile trades, cutting butchers,

106

bakers, small retailers, blacksmiths, locksmiths, curriers, tailors, shoe-makers, cooks, sailors, mariners, glovers, domestic servants, servants in husbandry, petty chapmen, innholders and innkeepers, 1:3; among the lower landed gentry, 1:2. . . . Were [the bigger of the London merchants (whose records perished in the Great Fire)] included, we guess the general ratio would change to about 1:12. If we were then to add the moneylenders, usurers and bankers, who were an integral part of the financial structure, the ratio might be 1:15.[29]

The consequent lack of clarity over who has the right to make money on a transaction is, I suggest, significant. 'It is against Nature, for *Money* to beget *Money*', as Francis Bacon puts it in his essay 'Of usurie' (a fascinating docu-ment on the pros and cons of commercial lending).[30] The barrenness of money was a fundamental tenet of early modern Christianity – so the vividly literal idea of 'making money' is fraught with difficulty. As a result, there hovers around early modern profitable commercial transactions in England a suspicion of the illicit or forbidden. Usury is defined as profit made on money lent, where the borrower (like Antonio in *The Merchant of Venice*) bears all the risk.[31] The question seems to be: how far from usurious gain are the profits accumulated by those whose trading ventures are apparently conducted out of surplus, and without apparent personal risk?

To illustrate how the taint of usury constrained mercantile activities in the period I choose a single example which still excites the interest of economic historians for its complexity and ingenuity – 'dry exchange'.[32]

The regulation of foreign trade was based on a simple model of exchange of one commodity for another. Cloth, plentifully produced in England and shipped to the Levant, could be exchanged for spices, gems, silks, etc. How much cloth it took depended on how desirable that commodity was at the point of exchange (actually the Levant was never interested in English cloth as western Europe had been, but that's another story). Since spices, gems and silks were less desirable in Hormuz than in London, they could be sold for more on return than had been laid out for them; hence profit was assured. So the coin resulting from sale of goods on return would be more than the coin laid out by the merchant to purchase the cloth at the outset of the voyage.

In fact, of course, things were never that simple. In particular, the financer of the purchase of cloth in London might not be paid until the ship had returned with its cargo. Meanwhile, the financer risked his capital outlay, and therefore expected additional profit (interest on the advance) to reflect that risk. These additional sums were built into the costings of the goods by the merchant, in order that they not appear as interest, but as profit at the point of sale (since that was not subject to the same doctrinal and legal prohibitions as usury).[33] Interest charged could also be concealed within notional exchange rates by valuing the pound differentially in London and abroad.

In 'dry exchange' no goods at all passed from one country to another, but the conventions of international exchange were reproduced in paper transactions, enabling large loans of cash in London arranged between merchants with trading activities at two geographically separate locations (London and Antwerp, say) for substantial interest. For example, if Jones in London needs a loan of £100, he approaches merchant Smith, who lends him the money in exchange for a bill of exchange for the £100, issued at the prevailing rate for the pound sterling in Antwerp (22s 6d gr per pound st). Smith's factor in Antwerp collects the cash one month later from Jones's factor. Smith's factor, acting for Smith, seeks out another potential borrower, and lends the Jones repayment money to Adams in Antwerp. Adams issues another note for collection in London at the prevailing rate (22s 2d gr per pound st). One month later Smith collects his loan again in London from the factor in London acting for Adams, now with the addition of the increase in value due to the differential rate of the pound in London and Antwerp, which (according to Raymond de Roover's calculations) might result in a repayment of £101 10s 1d, equivalent to an interest rate of 9 per cent a year.

This formal arrangement is perhaps made more vivid if, once again, we relate it to a 'real life' event in the financial world:

> Beginning in 1551, Thomas Gresham's famous plan for restoring royal financial and monetary stability [in England] was implemented. Acting as the Crown's financial agent [factor], Gresham required the Merchant Adventurers to hand over to him in Antwerp a large part of the proceeds in foreign currency from the sale of their cloths. This would be repaid in sterling in London at a fixed rate of exchange, with Gresham making sure to value the pound at appreciably more than it was quoted in Antwerp. This mechanism allowed the Crown to assure itself, on a continuing basis, of a massive source of short-term loans. It also allowed Gresham, acting for the Crown, to control the supply of sterling at Antwerp and, in this way, to force up the price of English currency on the international market. This system remained in effect for some two decades.[34]

Here the scale of Gresham's fictional exchanging is such as actually to alter the prevailing exchange rate, and thus decrease the interest the Crown paid on its short-term loans. But the principal is the same, as is the reliance on fictional trading of goods to make money-lending and money-borrowing respectably 'material'.

My point in describing 'dry exchange' is that it provides a vivid example of elaborate arrangements for exchange of paper (bonds, bills, etc.) which stand in for overseas trading transactions in order to conceal institutionalised cash lending for gain. Such transactions have to be produced as a kind of textualised version of classic trading, to satisfy the desire for 'real' exchange of goods, when for many people – and particularly those in powerful positions in the state – ready money was more valuable than any precious commodity. For behind the persistently exotic images of cloth exchanged for precious metals and gems, or wine exchanged for alum and currants, lurks the 'sordid' reality of the pressing political need for ready money, increasingly becoming the unique asset which can transform power blocs and revise policy, without recourse to the complex systems of alliance, fealty and friendship which notionally determine the political map.[35]

I suppose my last section was a kind of digression, in an attempt to try to capture the way profit taking and interest charging are mystified deliberately in the paper transactions between individuals, so that mere borrowing and usurious gain can be glamorised as trade in precious commodities. Barabas, in *The Jew of Malta*, stands for the bad faith elision of glamour and excessive profit. I think it is Marlowe's genius to locate contemporary unease with such devastating accuracy within the figure of the merchant Jew. So let's see how Marlowe's Barabas focuses some of the issues.

Whenever Barabas talks of his activities involving shipping and trade, which produce his immense wealth, it is in the orientalist, exotic terms of Hakluyt and the travellers' tales:

> *Barabas.* Cellars of wine, and sollars full of wheat,
>   Warehouses stuffed with spices and with drugs,
>   Whole chests of gold, in bullion and in coin,
>   Besides I know not how much weight in pearl,
>   Orient and round, have I within my house;
>   At Alexandria, merchandise unsold:
>   But yesterday two ships went from this town,
>   Their voyage will be worth ten thousand crowns;
>   In Florence, Venice, Antwerp, London, Seville,
>   Frankfurt, Lubeck, Moscow, and where not,
>   Have I debts owing; and in most of these,
>   Great sums of money lying in the banco.[36]

Wherever we encounter mercantile transactions within the action of the play, however, they are of an explicitly corrupt, sordid and morally dubious kind. Ithamore, to whom Barabas has pledged all his wealth after his daughter's departure, sends a series of formal bills of exchange to Barabas:

> *Ithamore.* 'Sirrah Barabas, send me a hundred crowns.'
>   . . .
>   'I charge thee send me three hundred by this bearer, and this shall be your warrant; if you do not, no more but so.'[37]

But Ithamore wants the money to please a whore, and behind the bills of exchange is an implicit threat of blackmail. Similarly, the seizure of Barabas's and his fellow Jews' wealth to pay the Turkish tribute is a crude version of an unsecured loan, and is in fact not all that far from actual seizures of surplus under the guise of 'lending' in the same period:

> In the autumn of 1640, the Crown raised £50,000 from some 140 leading London citizens. Although this was technically termed a loan, it seems that London's wealthiest citizens were more or less obliged to lend in proportion to their estates. The Crown had used this method for its loan of 1617, and it appears that the loan of 1640 fits the same pattern (as does the comparable citizens' loan of £100,000 to the king in the spring of 1641). Among these wealthy contributors there were twenty-one Merchant Adventurers, whose average payment was £155, in comparison with thirty-one Levant Company traders, whose average payment was £275.[38]

The 'loan', in other words, was actually a levy. And this is exactly the kind of 'necessity' which Ferneze and his knights appeal to to justify their levy from Malta's Jews:

> *First Knight.* Thou art a merchant, and a moneyed man,
>   And 'tis thy money, Barabas, we seek.
> *Barabas.* How, my lord, my money?
> *Ferneze.*   Thine and the rest.
>   For to be short, amongst you 't must be had.[39]

At the centre of the plot, indeed, is a paradox, whereby the Knights Templar of Malta are forced by the Turks to raise impossible quantities of gold as back-payment of tribute money, in order to sustain a treaty which enables them to trade with the Levant for precious stones and metals.[40] In other words, the tribute secures the conditions to raise the wealth required to pay the tribute (and Barabas does indeed continue to create wealth as fast as it is taken away from him):

> *First Knight.* This truce we have is but in hope of gold,
>   And with that sum he craves might we wage war.
> *Bosco.* Will Knights of Malta be in league with Turks,
>   And buy it basely, too, for sums of gold?[41]

Once again, the glamour of riches is reduced to the expediency of bought alliance, the possibility of buying off the enemy, bribery and bought military strength.

But the symbolic centre of the corruption of financial dealing in the play is the matter-of-fact buying and selling of human bodies:

> *Bosco.* Our fraught is Grecians, Turks, and Afric Moors;
>   For late upon the coast of Corsica,
>   Because we vailed not to the Turkish fleet,
>   Their creeping galleys had us in the chase:

But suddenly the wind began to rise,
And then we luffed, and tacked, and fought at ease.
Some have we fired, and many have we sunk,
But one amongst the rest became our prize:
The captain's slain, the rest remain our slaves,
Of whom we would make sale in Malta here.[42]

Here, and in the following scene, in which the captives are produced 'Every one's price ... written on his back', and bargained for as merchandise, the images of courageous seafaring, stout ships battling against the elements and outrunning enemy ships, voyages of discovery in search of rare and exotic foreign commodities, and trade with foreigners which yields unimaginable private wealth, are collapsed into a market in which the victors literally buy the losers. Whereas in reality English merchant adventurers shamelessly seized cargoes from other nation's vessels on the high seas, here the foreign nationals are themselves seized as 'wealth' to be traded.[43]

Just as the slave-market collapses commercial trade into trade in men, the final scenes of the play reduce to parody the play's key themes of policy control through access to surplus wealth. A classic knowledge transaction allows Barabas to hand Malta over to the Turks – as an 'intelligencer' or spy, he knows the layout of the town's sewers, which will allow the enemy to enter the fortified citadel.[44] His appointment as Governor of Malta replicates the meteoric rise to high position in government of a number of merchant adventurers whose funds had supported the Crown; he then literally sells his post back to the old Governor and lures the Turks back to be ambushed, with the promise of a banquet (in spite of the sack of the city) funded with the price of a single pearl from his personal wealth. As these parodies of the relationship between power and commerce accelerate, Barabas, their perpetrator and Machiavellian orchestrator falls victim to his own plots, into a vat of boiling oil, in an icon of the downfall of the morally doomed.

Marlowe's Barabas unites in one culturally recognisable figure a collection of late sixteenth-century commercial activities in which transactions involving knowledge for future promise of private gain (with interest payable upon the investment) give rise to public unease. I have suggested that these represent a real, and ultimately unresolved problem in late sixteenth-century economic and social thought. Marlowe's play both focuses and underlines the problems, and brilliantly provides a pastiche, comic-book resolution. The downfall of Barabas resolves absolutely nothing but, like Faustus's morality-play demise in *Faustus*, it gives audience satisfaction with its pat finality.

That finale, however, is pure dramatic illusion. For Marlowe's subtle mental mapping of merchant on to international networker, on to intellectual knowledge gatherer, on to political intelligencer, on to alien, on to Jew, has produced a figure at once entirely overdetermined and undecipherable. To decipher Barabas, and thus resolve the play's outcome satisfactorily, would be to crack the mercantile code – to understand the as-yet incomprehensible relationship between knowledge transaction and financial gain. I'm not sure we've managed to do that even now, four hundred years after Marlowe.

So where does this leave *The Merchant of Venice*? We undoubtedly experience Shakespeare's Shylock as a more emotionally three-dimensional figure than Barabas, and our involvedness with his fortunes is correspondingly the greater. We believe that in following the trajectory of Shakespeare's plot we recognise some fundamentally flawed predisposition in the Jew which leads him from the initial loan to the inhumanity of the courtroom scene. I think myself that this belief ought thoroughly to alarm us.

Because we have thoroughly internalised the culturally constructed anti-Semitism which makes money-lending a moral abomination and all money-lenders Jews, we engage approvingly with a play which does not entirely allow us to side with the merchants against the money-lender. What has been lost, however, is the precisely historically located detail of Marlowe's play, which ensures that we understand that antipathy to the Jew is a cultural construct – the outcome of a set of contingent circumstances surrounding trade, mercantilism, money, usury, in which the Semitic alien is accidentally enmeshed. As a consequence, he carries the burden of the conceptual difficulties raised by new mores and unfamiliar codes of conduct.

In *The Merchant of Venice*, the relationship between trade as an activity and the personality of the merchant is internalised and pathologised. The very opening of the play represents the merchant Antonio as inextricably bound up existentially with his argosies. Their fortune (his financial fortunes) is his state of mind and body:

> *Antonio.* In sooth I know not why I am so sad . . .
> *Salerio.* Your mind is tossing on the ocean,
>   There where your argosies with portly sail
>   Like signiors and rich burghers on the flood,
>   Or as it were the pageants of the sea,
>   Do overpeer the petty traffickers . . .
> *Solanio.* Believe me sir, had I such venture forth,
>   The better part of my affections would
>   Be with my hopes abroad. I should be still
>   Plucking the grass to know where sits the wind,
>   Piring in maps for ports, and piers and roads:
>   And every object that might make me fear
>   Misfortune to my ventures, out of doubt
>   Would make me sad.
> *Salerio.*   My wind cooling my broth,
>   Would blow me to an ague when I thought
>   What harm a wind too great might do at sea.[45]

Antonio's reply to this is to deny that his current mercantile projects are of the kind to generate such 'sadness' – not to deny that the moods of merchants *are* dependent upon their ventures. 'Sadness', 'kindness', 'friendship',[46] 'mercy', 'justice' are detached from the transactions which define them in context, and attached to the individuals caught up in them.

Thus naturalised and rendered deceptively familiar as 'types' of individual, we as the audience cease to concentrate on the precise terms of the plot, and instead accept decision as governed, in effect, by humour. It is a short step from this to anti-Semitism – Shylock's decisions are determined by his innate Jewish character, not by the technicalities of bonds or the conventions of markets. I leave as an open question the matter of Shakespeare's part in this shift in dramatic sensibility in relation to Jews, wealth and European trade. For whether or not the dramatist shapes Shylock as pathologically greedy, deceitful, vengeful and inhumane *because* that is dramatically the most effective strategy for engaging the audience against him, engage us against him they inevitably do. Not against his historically localised practices, but against his generalised person, his alienness and his creed.

7

COMPANIONATE MARRIAGE VERSUS MALE FRIENDSHIP

Anxiety for the lineal family in
Jacobean drama

[A good wife] is a man's best movable, a scion incorporate with the stock, bringing sweet fruit; one that to her husband is more than a friend, less than trouble; an equal with him in the yoke. Calamities and troubles she shares alike, nothing pleaseth her that doth not him. She is relative in all, and he without her but half himself. She is his absent hands, eyes, ears and mouth; his present and absent all.[1]

The companionate marriage, characterised here by Thomas Overbury in 1614, is treated as something of a milestone in household development by early modern social historians.[2] For Keith Wrightson and others it is the reformed church's contribution to progressive household management: 'In the domestic economy, decision-making, conflict resolution and sexual behaviour, mutuality in marriage, within the context of ultimate male authority, may well have been not only the conjugal ideal, but also the common practice among the English people as a whole.'[3] Historians have tended to see partnership based on free choice, intellectual and educational equality, self-regulation in personal behaviour and shared responsibility as self-evidently desirable as the model for the contracted reproductive household unit. Arranged marriage, strenuous dependency in all household management decision making, and subordination of wife to husband as his 'chattel' (subject to his will in all matters) seem clearly inferior as the organising principles within the domestic unit.[4] Here, however, I shall argue that the new model raised problems in relation to the contemporary understanding of the structural coherence of 'family', and in particular, produces anxieties concerning the agency of women within it. As a further stage in my argument I shall suggest that the perceived possibilities for conflict, or at least inconsistency of goal, between the long-term objectives of the lineal family and the short-term agreements made between consensual marriage partners closely resembled another area of contestation – that between the bonds of kinship and the contracted undertakings between non-kin male 'friends'. In both cases the consenting parties were motivated by the desire to optimise the social and economic possibilities for their own 'domestic' unit. In both cases the resulting inter-ference with lineal prospects and planning takes place in the private rather than the public domain. And in both cases any value attached to a modern type of 'intimacy' had to be offset against the dangers of secrecy, and of binding relationships invisible to (and impervious to) regulation by the admin-istrative systems of the state.[5]

The problems these issues raise are vividly dramatised in the theatre of the early seventeenth century. They are central and structural to the plots of the plays of an early seventeenth-century dramatist like Thomas Middleton. Here I shall use Middleton's best-known play *The Changeling* (now attributed to Middleton and Rowley) as the basis for an exploration of some of the underly-ing features of intimate relationship which created dynastic anxiety. I shall argue that the source of anxiety is less the instrumentality of women them-selves than the way the new marriage model is in contest with traditional social organisation. I shall suggest that the *frisson* caused by the prospect that emotional closeness might prove socially effective charges the relationship erotically – it is intense, secret and powerful. In the same way, the close relationship between men of similar social standing which emerges in the late sixteenth and early seventeenth centuries as the model for household service gains an erotic charge from the way it manages to intervene in family mat-ters.[6] In drama, these two forms of socially disturbing intimacy collide against a backdrop of traditional dynastic and lineal aspiration.

We can already detect a cultural difficulty in the language of the period associated with alliance and duty. The term 'love' modulates during the period we are looking at from a formally acknowledged designation of duty and affection towards the authority figure who governs one's life to a more self-centred, freely willed directing of emotion generated by a bond of unofficial obligation and indebtedness.[7] The former version of 'love' is vividly captured in Shakespeare's *King Lear*, in Cordelia's description of the nature of her commitment to her father:

> Good my Lord,
> You have begot me, bred me, lov'd me: I
> Return those duties back as are right fit,
> Obey you, love you, and most honour you.
> Why have my sisters husbands, if they say
> They love you all? Happily, when I shall wed,
> That lord whose hand must take my plight shall carry
> Half my love with him, half my care and duty:
> Sure I shall never marry like my sisters,
> To love my father all.[8]

Since the obedience and dutiful dependency expected of female kin is desig-nated 'love', regardless of whether it is directed towards father, brother or uncle (in the absence of father), or husband, a moment of representational crisis arises at the point of transfer. As the father 'gives away' his daughter in marriage, her 'love' passes instantaneously from him to her new husband – a transfer which is represented symbolically by the pause of the wedding cortège at the church porch. On the threshold between the woman's belonging to one household and another, the husband specifies the terms of partition of lands and property between himself and his wife (the jointure), as she passes (as currency, but not as agent) from one contractual undertaking to another; she continues passively to 'love', but reactively redirects her emotional attention.[9] Cordelia's two sisters, who do voice their total and permanent love for their father at the beginning of *King Lear* in spite of the fact that they are married and have left the paternal household, turn out, inevitably, to be adulterous wives, as well as feignedly loving daughters.[10]

This structural and formalised version of love has its corresponding type in the male/male relationship between feudal master and his servant – the kind of loyal, no-nonsense relationship Kent describes at the beginning of *King Lear*:

> Royal Lear,
> Whom I have ever honour'd as my King,
> Lov'd as my father, as my master follow'd,
> As my great patron thought on in my prayers.[11]

Even Lear's dismissal and banishment of Kent (for giving him advice he did not wish to hear) does not sever the relationship – it is not within Kent's 'nature' to do other than continue to 'love' and serve, and he merely disguises himself and re-enters his master's service.

David Starkey has represented the shift from this kind of 'loving' relationship between master and servant as an inflection towards intimacy as the basis for trust and service.[12] And whereas 'alliance' and its contractual undertakings rested squarely in the public domain (its negotiations formally recorded and witnessed), 'affection' and individualised emotional attachment establish private and invisible bonds which escape the terms of recognised kinship relationships: in such cases mutual obligation and indebtedness – on which might rest undertakings to further each other's causes, for instance, or to deal financially on each other's behalf – might be entirely undetectable in the public domain. I shall argue that Jacobean theatre dramatises the way in which developing strategies for male private service within the noble household came into conflict with the equally vital strategies for assuring lineage continuity through marriage alliance, and for consolidating resources in land and monies on the basis of family unions – strategies which necessarily focused on women, and on reproduction as the most valued manifestation of sexuality. In so doing, I shall argue, the theatre preserves the textual trace of anxiety or uncertainty about the consequences of gradual shifts in acceptable social practice which are not clearly articulated in other kinds of 'documentary' historical evidence. In other words, new kinds of liaisons between men, formally unacknowledged in the public sphere, came into competition with the more traditional forms of liaison, or bond-forming, between dynastic houses, with their feudal accoutrements (including lineal retainers). And a play like *The Changeling* allows us to recapture contemporary cultural strategies for responding to such submerged conflict.[13]

The move towards intimacy in male service is vividly captured in Shakespeare's sonnet 29:

> When in disgrace with Fortune and men's eyes,
> I all alone beweep my outcast state,
> And trouble deaf heaven with my bootless cries,
> And look upon myself, and curse my fate,
> Wishing me like to one more rich in hope,
> Featur'd like him, like him with friends possess'd,
> Desiring this man's art, and that man's scope,
> With what I most enjoy contented least;
> Yet in these thoughts myself almost despising,
> Haply I think on thee, and then my state,
> Like to the lark at break of day arising
> From sullen earth, sings hymns at heaven's gate;
>> For thy sweet love rememb'red such wealth brings
>> That then I scorn to change my state for kings.[14]

Some years ago John Barrell drew attention to this sonnet as exemplifying and deftly manipulating a 'discourse of patronage'.[15] Here, 'love' designates a relationship of dependency of the author to the addressee which is at once passionate and dutiful: a relationship of serving (or, more accurately, service), loyalty, *fides* or good faith, a homosocial bonding on which, by the 1580s, apparently, the smooth and effective running of the households of noblemen depended. Although the tone of this sonnet suggests the kind of intensity of feeling which we associate with courtship of a woman, what is at issue here is an attempt to gain the attention of, and enter a relationship of trust with (in other words, the courtship of) a male patron.

Traces of the intimacy which characterises the new type of relationship amongst men are to be found in letters exchanged between lord and member of his private household close to his person, in which the terms of passionate commitment are virtually indistinguishable from those in a contemporary love sonnet. Here is an exchange of letters between Anthony Bacon and his employer, the Earl of Essex:

> My singular good Lord, If God had not sent me the other day so special a defensive of the honour and comfort of your Lordship's presence to fortify my spirits beforehand, they could never have resisted such cruel enemies as have since assailed me without giving me any respite or breathing till this morning.
>
> (*Anthony Bacon to the Earl of Essex*)

Farewell, worthy Master Bacon, and know that, though I entertain you here with short letters, yet I will send you from sea papers that shall remain as tables of my honest designs and pledges of my love to you from your true and best wishing friend Essex.

(*Essex to Anthony Bacon*)[16]

The professions of intense feeling in exchanges like these use 'love' to code a kind of mutuality of obligation and indebtedness within which the responsibilities of employer and employed form part of a private undertaking. As in sonnet 29, Anthony Bacon recommends himself as ideally equipped to serve, and Essex responds by valuing that service in personal (intimate) terms. What seems to be at issue here is the kind of access which personable young men can gain to prominent persons in the public sphere via their personal accomplishments including both congeniality as a companion and competence in producing and processing knowledge – expertise in information gathering and in self-presentation using the discursive skills associated with a humanistic training in letters. The 'secretary' and the 'intelligencer' offer a new kind of service to the nobleman, fit for the world of international diplomacy and embassy.[17] The relationships established are, I think, felt to be disturbingly volatile – a far cry from the steady commitment of the feudal retainer.

There is a recognisable emotional affinity between the intensified, private relationship of noble master to gently born intimate servant and the newly mutual and personalised love between partners in a marriage love-match. The similarity is recorded, I suggest, in cultural productions which appear to waver in indecision between a male and a female lover as addressee. In other words, it is a comparatively short step, from the sorts of sentiment exchanged in familiar letters between Essex and Anthony Bacon to the following:

> A woman's face, with Nature's own hand painted,
> Hast thou, the Master Mistress of my passion;
> A woman's gentle heart, but not acquainted
> With shifting change, as is false woman's fashion;
> An eye more bright than theirs, less false in rolling,
> Gilding the object whereupon it gazeth;
> A man in hue all hues in his controlling,
> Which steals men's eyes and women's souls amazeth.
> And for a woman wert thou first created;
> Till Nature, as she made thee, fell a-doting,
> And by addition me of thee defeated
> By adding one thing to my purpose nothing.
> > But since she prick'd thee out for women's pleasure,
> > Mine be thy love, and thy love's use their treasure.[18]

Since the groundbreaking work of Alan Bray, these kinds of texts have been identified as homoerotic, and used to argue that sodomitical relationships were not clearly censured in the period (although Bray also argues that they were not clearly defined either).[19] Here, however, what I am interested in is the tension sustained between love towards a man and love towards a woman, ambiguously evoked through the term 'love'. The important passage for us is the final two lines:

> But since she prick'd thee out for women's pleasure,
> Mine be thy love, and thy love's use their treasure.

Until the final couplet, the ambivalence of the 'love' has turned on its subject: the 'master–mistress' of the poet's passion, who, in his seductive power towards both men and women is of confused or indeterminate gender. Thus far the sonnet supports my suggestion that the two *were* readily confused, that 'masters' increasingly demanded attentions of an intimate kind, thereby modulating 'favour' towards them from public courtship towards feminised seduction. The clinching couplet, however, turns upon the love actively offered by the sonnet's addressee: directed towards the poet it is 'love'; towards a woman it is 'love's use'. Constructive (intense) mutual commitment between men is here finally contrasted with the merely sexual and reproductive heterosexual activity – love's use.[20] Since this is the 'turn' in the sonnet, it apparently resolves the struggle between the (certainly erotic) interest aroused by the addressee in the author, and the addressee's availability ('prick'd out') for 'women's pleasure'. That resolution takes the form of a preference declared for male bonding ('mine be thy love'), over procreative sex ('thy love's use their treasure').

It would be easy to jump to the conclusion that the import of this (and a significant number of others amongst Shakespeare's sonnets) is that male friendship is socially acknowledged as a superior kind of alliance to courtship of a woman.[21] I am suggesting precisely the opposite: that we should read the tendency of poems of this kind to elide professional male friendship and sodomy as part of the period's mistrust of concealed, irregular networks of cooperation amongst men which interfered with the recognised, public forms.[22]

When the Earl of Essex's secretary, the future Lord Chancellor, Francis Bacon, was given the job of 'minding' the Spanish defector Antonio Pérez in 1593, his mother, Lady Anne Bacon, who disapproved of her son's consorting with a Catholic informer, levelled the accusation that this was a sexual, rather than a professional relationship:

> He keepeth that bloody Pérez, as a coach-companion and bed-companion, a proud, prophane, costly fellow, whose being about him I verily fear the Lord God doth mislike and doth less bless him in credit and otherwise in his health.[23]

It was a charge readily levelled at any man who apparently neglected bond-forming with women (with a view to marriage) in favour of intelligence-networking with men. In a recent book on the Elizabethan spy network, Alan Haynes offers the following explanation for why Anthony Bacon came to be charged for sodomy in France:

> There is substantial evidence that [the source of the accusation against Anthony] was Charlotte Arbaleste, Madame du Plessis, the wife of the chief advisor to Henri of Navarre. . . . Bacon had . . . declined to marry one of the daughters of Madame du Plessis, although it might have provided him with an advantageous cover. His error was to have allowed the notion of marriage to arise.[24]

Where intimacy between men was a feature of the network of relationships on which an activity depended (in this case spying or 'intelligence'), an aggrieved or politically motivated adversary might apparently readily mobilise the slur of sodomy (and in this case, more damagingly, the court charge). Although this gets us no further in deciding whether in fact sodomy *was* a customary practice in such households, it does, given the deeply illicit nature of any such relationship, suggest generalised anxiety concerning the difficulty in deciding upon the real nature (and effectiveness) of these kinds of 'privy' loyalties and dependencies.

What happens if we now turn our attention to women, and specifically to marriage in which the woman chooses her partner, rather than complying with an alliance contrived to enhance the prospects of her family or line? Curiously enough, I think the version of 'love' produced by the 'choice' model of marriage tends in the direction of intensifying the problem we are looking at (rather than clarifying or resolving it). Because this model stresses the active participation of the woman in the liaison, it makes her 'love' equivalently more active. No longer a simple reflection of duty, stimulated by context (love's object to be father or husband depending on whose household she inhabits), she now directs her love according to her own will. Hence, ironically, the potential unruliness not only of Cordelia (as I quoted her above), but of Desdemona:

> My noble father,
> I do perceive here a divided duty:
> To you I am bound for life and education,
> My life and education both do learn me
> How to respect you, you are lord of all my duty,
> I am hitherto your daughter: but here's my husband:
> And so much duty as my mother show'd
> To you, preferring you before her father,
> So much I challenge, that I may profess,
> Due to the Moor my lord.[25]

Desdemona's admission that 'she did love the Moor, to live with him', is an admission of her own, wilful choice, which animates that shift of 'duty' from father to husband with a kind of dangerous energy which Cordelia's avowal of duty lacked (however short of the mark it came for her father).

Where the plot involves a conventional courtship, the drama of the period frequently turns on a tension (still residually resonant for us today) between the 'love' of male bonding and the 'love' of heterosexual emotional attraction – can the commitment between the men survive the absorption of one of them with a woman? In Shakespeare's *Much Ado About Nothing* this tension produces a telling moment of confusion in the play. Returning from the wars in the service of Don Pedro, Prince of Aragon, the young nobleman Claudio falls headlong in love – at first sight – with Hero, the daughter of their host Leonato, Governor of Messina. He confesses his love to his master, who offers to gain permission for the match from Leonato, and to woo Hero on Claudio's behalf.

Don Pedro's relationship with Claudio is represented as an *amicitia* or friendship relationship, one in which the authority of the one and the service of the other are sustained by mutual respect, personal indebtedness and obligation, and above all, intimacy and warmth of feeling. Within the play, this produces a curious elision of dynastic and consensual models of marriage: Don Pedro correctly intercedes for Claudio with Leonato, since his rank (and Claudio's dependent relationship with him) will make Leonato's consent to the match more likely. Don Pedro effectively acts as Claudio's social and financial guarantor. His proposal to woo Hero (disguised as Claudio) to gain her *love*, however, confuses his role in the match.[26] By the time the plan reaches the ears of the troublemaker Don John it has become one for Don Pedro to win Hero's love for himself, and then to make gift of her to Claudio:

> I whipped me behind the arras, and there heard it agreed upon that the Prince should woo Hero for himself, and having obtained her, give her to Count Claudio.[27]

This is a fair version of the plan. Don Pedro has apparently elided old and new forms of alliance formation: negotiation of a dynastic alliance, and personal courtship aimed at a love-match. A suit to establish lineage is transitive (Don Pedro sues on Claudio's behalf with Leonato). A courtship to gain an individual's 'love' is not – there is a reciprocal service bond of 'love' between Don Pedro and Claudio, and there is Claudio's 'love' for Hero which he hopes to make reciprocal, but these are independent of one another, and possibly in competition.[28] Hence when Claudio sees Don Pedro successfully gaining Hero's 'love', he reads it as a competitive bid for *her* love, in the face of the challenge offered by the heterosexual relationship to the 'love' between lord and young man in his service. Claudio's close friend Benedict also interprets Don Pedro's wooing as self-interested, counselling Claudio to affect the pose of the forsaken lover 'for the Prince hath got your Hero'.[29] Don John's mischievous insinuations only have the effect of intensifying Claudio's jealousy.

In *Much Ado About Nothing* the confusion caused by the elision of line-match and love-match is short-lived. The puzzlement it causes us does, I think, serve to remind us that we have lost the intensity of emotion potentially to be associated with the tension generated between male/male and male/female 'love' bonds. In Middleton and Rowley's *The Changeling*, by contrast, such tension is woven into the play's very fabric. Unpicking the threads allows us access to insights withheld from us by the passage of time in more 'documentary' evidence.

The dramatic power of Middleton and Rowley's *The Changeling* has fascinated generations of critics. The play's obsessive preoccupation with emotional intrigue, female betrayal, murder and corruption has a vividness which has tempted commentators to link the plot with actual contemporary sensational cases of female interference in dynastic affairs, like the Thomas Overbury/Frances Howard scandal.[30] It is not, however, necessary to propose links of this kind – the play's aura of 'reality' is equally plausibly attributable to skilled writing on the part of the play's two authors. Sub-plot and main plot are unusually closely integrated for a play of the period, with the sub-plot comically highlighting key themes and commenting ironically on some of the play's main preoccupations, and the two parts of the plot are drawn together at the conclusion of the play. Such structural integrity in a jointly authored play tends to bear out the current critical view that Middleton and Rowley took responsibility for writing designated characters, rather than individual scenes (as earlier criticism was inclined to assume).[31]

The Changeling dramatises tensions created by the competing demands of noble lineage and contracted obligation, duty to family and self-advancement. As elsewhere in Middleton's drama (notably in *Women Beware Women*), the social imperative for hierarchical organisation of family and inheritance is endangered by the self-centred plans of a well-born fortune hunter (and Middleton's sympathies appear to be on the adventurer's side). The continued prosperity and social standing of Vermandero's line depends upon his making an advantageous marriage match for his daughter. Alonzo de Piracquo is Vermandero's social superior: an alliance with him will enhance the fortunes of the Vermanderos. By thwarting that choice and giving rein to her own desires, Beatrice-Joanna intervenes in the public world of courtly position and lineage connections. Her own choice, Alsemero, is a self-made man (though of good birth and background), and in local terms an interloper and adventurer.[32]

The Changeling's plot highlights the potentially damaging effect on Alicante's social order of Alsemero's bid to secure his own fortune in marriage. His inclination becomes Beatrice-Joanna's burning desire. The direct outcome of her arranging for Alonzo de Piracquo to be disposed of is that the union she actually achieves – the forced union with the household servant, De Flores –

is one well beneath her socially, with a 'mere' gentleman (his unsuitability is highlighted dramatically by the fact that he is physically repulsive), thus underlining the socially disruptive consequences of Beatrice-Joanna's meddling with lineage.

The dramatic demonisation of the woman who, like Beatrice-Joanna, intervenes on her own behalf in the social process of contracting a lineal marriage is closely linked to the perceived structural importance of traditionally arranged marriage to a family's long-term economic calculations in early modern England. Strategic improvement of the family's fortunes was a significant criterion used in parental choice of a marriage partner, particularly where the only heir was a daughter:

> A suitable marriage, especially among the propertied classes, was one which gave the individual and those closest to him potentially useful new kinsmen, and increased the number of people through whom favours might be sought and advancement achieved. 'Good lordship' and help in recovering lands were among the possible advantages accruing from matches considered by the Paston family, while Alice Wandesford's match with a man of very different religious and political sympathies from her own was made after the civil war in order to free the family's lands from sequestration. The need to use marriage to gain useful allies made for the choice of partners from within one's own region.

Material substance was always a very important consideration.[33]

Whether an advantageous marriage was effected by traditional contracting amongst established families, or by the new-style bargain-making of a more straightforwardly material kind which Houlbrooke describes, the central need for a woman's consent also made it possible to transfer on to her the blame for any failure in the outcome. In *The Changeling* Middleton and Rowley have convincingly designed a plot which shifts the epicentre of blame for the disruption of traditional family alliance from the fortune-seeking man who is ultimately the cause to the woman whose fortune he seeks.

When, in the final Act of *The Changeling*, Beatrice-Joanna confesses to her father that she has engineered a murder and dishonoured her marriage bed, the metaphor she chooses is one which draws attention to the fact that family inheritance depends on the guaranteed integrity of shared blood, or blood-relatedness:

> *Beatrice.* I am that of your blood was taken from you
> For your better health; look no more upon't,
> But cast it to the ground regardlessly:
> Let the common sewer take it from distinction.[34]

Vermandero's closest blood relation – his only living daughter – represents herself as blood which must be purged from a congested body, a tainted issue of the family's head, to be discarded and wiped from the record (deprived of its 'distinction' or the privilege of its rank). Here Middleton powerfully draws together the positive and negative associations of the hereditary and sexual senses of 'blood'. As a result of Beatrice-Joanna's determined pursuit of her own desires in love, against her father's wishes for the posterity of his family, lineage (blood) and the 'hot blood' of the pursuit of carnal gratification have converged and been run together – issue has become corruption, and death is the punishment.

The chastity test to which Alsemero proposes to subject his bride on her wedding night (in Act 4) highlights the importance of pure reproductive descent for the play's male protagonists. Alsemero, the shrewd seaman-adventurer, has been converted by his encounter with Beatrice-Joanna into a lovesick suitor. But the pragmatic Alsemero remains alert to the possibility that the woman who freely returns his love may be fundamentally unreliable as a participant in what is essentially a man's world of contractual undertakings – unlike the courtly Alonzo de Piracquo, whose infatuation clouded his masculine judgement ('Why, here is love's tame madness', comments his brother Tomazo[35]). Although Beatrice-Joanna's successful counterfeiting of the symptoms of chastity after the test absolves her temporarily from suspicion, those symptoms themselves remind us of precisely what is at stake in woman's sexual purity: the 'gaping', sneezing, and helpless laughter which are Diaphanta's involuntary bodily responses to the potion represent purity as a state of uncontrolled foolishness, entirely available for shaping masculine control. By simulating that state herself, and then by substituting a 'true' virgin for herself in Alsemero's wedding bed, Beatrice-Joanna demonstrates her own ability to manipulate the tokens (and guarantees) of chastity, and thus how vulnerable the marriage bond is to female interference.

Beatrice-Joanna's choice of Alsemero as partner is guided by personal inclination, and the belief that his choice of his closest companions is made with discretion and judgement. She confidently believes that these form a proper basis for a marriage alliance:

> Then I appear in nothing more approv'd
> Than making choice of him;
> For 'tis a principle, he that can choose
> That bosom well, who of his thoughts partakes,
> Proves most discreet in every choice he makes.
> Methinks I love now with the eyes of judgment,
> And see the way to merit, clearly see it.[36]

Beatrice-Joanna's admiration for Alsemero's judgement relates specifically to his choice of a friend of the utmost discretion in whom to confide – Jasperino. Her assumption that she too can build such intimacy in the form of a friendship-marriage turns out, however, to underestimate the gendered nature of such relationships.

According to Beatrice-Joanna, her own marriage to Alsemero will be a liaison based on emotional and intellectual compatibility. These would be ideal grounds for close personal friendship between men – amity or *amicitia* – the social bond by which men of good birth set considerable store. But such a basis for an alliance between a man and a woman seems regularly in the drama to be suspect (compare the relationship between the Frankfords in Heywood's *A Woman Killed with Kindness*). The liaison which involves the active consent of both parties, and some kind of equal participation, makes female 'love' equivalently more active.

Once marriage is determined on the model of mutual affection and shared preference, it appears to come into direct conflict with the socially acceptable form of close partnership (friendship between adult men of good birth), quite as much as with traditional, parentally sponsored marriage alliance. Like male friendship, its outcome is no longer confined to the continuation of the line, but becomes much more likely to produce networks of relationships and profitable dependencies within and between households. In the case of male friendship, these are the invisible networks of credit and profit around which early modern society built a system of obligation and indebtedness. But where women become involved there is no recognised code of conduct to ensure a socially responsible outcome.

The bargain of mutual obligation which Beatrice-Joanna enters into with De Flores travesties her freely chosen relationship with Alsemero (just as Antonio's 'mad' courtship of Isabella in the sub-plot apes and ironises the main plot). As soon as Beatrice-Joanna hits on the plan to use De Flores to get rid of Alonzo de Piracquo, the attention she bestows upon him is readily confused with sexual attention: 'Her fingers touch'd me! / She smells all amber';[37] ''Tis half an act of pleasure / To hear her talk thus to me'.[38] De Flores is quite clear, from the instant the compact is made between himself and Beatrice-Joanna, that the request by a desirable woman that he provide her with 'service' will yield carnal intercourse as its reward (he is also clear that such a contract serves the blatant self-interest of the participants):

> *Beatrice.* As thou art forward and thy service dangerous,
>   Thy reward shall be precious.
> *De Flores.*   That I have thought on;
>   I have assur'd myself of that beforehand,
>   And know it will be precious, the thought ravishes.[39]

Alsemero's intimate servant, Jasperino, is equally convinced that freely chosen intimacy of any kind between a woman and a man is suspect, when he alerts his master to the possibility that Beatrice-Joanna and De Flores are secretly 'allied':

> I heard your bride's voice in the next room to me;
> And lending more attention, found De Flores
> Louder than she. . . .

> Then fell we both to listen, and words pass'd
> Like those that challenge interest in a woman.[40]

A woman's 'interest' – where she invests her affections and duty – is compromised by attention to a man other than her husband-to-be, without the need to prove any suspicious details.

As she embarks on her scheme to do away with the man chosen by her father to be her husband, Beatrice-Joanna is oblivious to the fact that the move she makes actually means that she has freely chosen De Flores, rather than Alsemero, as her alternative sexual match. But it should be stressed that she alone is unaware of the inevitable consequences of her refusing Alsemero's (honourable) proposal that he fight a duel with Alonzo, in favour of De Flores. When Beatrice-Joanna (still operating under the conventional marriage model) protests her elevated birth as an impediment to De Flores's proposal of sexual union, he confidently declares such observations to be irrelevant:

> *Beatrice.* Think but upon the distance that creation
>   Set 'twixt thy blood and mine, and keep thee there.
> *De Flores.* Look but into your conscience, read me there,
>   'Tis a true book, you'll find me there your equal:
>   Push, fly not to your birth, but settle you
>   In what the act has made you, y'are no more now;
>   You must forget your parentage to me:
>   Y'are the deed's creature.[41]

De Flores, like Bosola in Webster's *Duchess of Malfi*, is a household servant of the new model, who offers service for material reward, and whose prospects depend precariously on a balance sheet of obligations and indebtednesses for services rendered.[42] In this world Beatrice-Joanna's appeal to rank has no relevance: the 'true book' is the account book in which service is costed, and where the 'rate' for disposing of a suitor is sexual intimacy with Beatrice-Joanna.

The moment in the play which most vividly conveys the way Beatrice-Joanna's active choice impinges upon the world of men's affairs is the scene in which her adulterous union with De Flores is formally discovered in Act 5. Immediately Alsemero has pronounced his wife 'whore' and she has confessed to having instigated murder, he locks her in his closet: 'Enter my closet; / I'll be your keeper yet.'[43] Twenty lines later, he thrusts De Flores in to join her.

The man of property's 'closet' was the physical place of his greatest privacy.[44] His closet was adjacent to his sleeping quarters, and contained his books, his correspondence and his most private possessions. It was generally locked, and inaccessible to anyone but himself and his most intimate personal servants. The woman of the household might have her own closet or 'cabinet',[45] which might contain her personal effects and toiletries, but she would not have access to her husband's. For a woman to cross the threshold from the general house into the husband's closet is to intrude on the man's most personal and private space. Beatrice-Joanna thus infringes Alsemero's privacy twice in the play, and in both cases the intrusion is sexually fraught.

When Beatrice-Joanna finds Mizaldus's medical treatise, and stumbles upon the concoctions Alsemero has prepared from it for testing her virginity, they are in Alsemero's locked closet, in whose door he has inadvertently left the key. What she discovers is a secret practice, his medical experimenting, the kind of pursuit of knowledge a gentleman might well have been expected to engage in discreetly in private:

> Here's his closet,
> The key left in't, and he abroad i'th' park:
> Sure 'twas forgot; I'll be so bold as look in't. [*Opens closet*]
> Bless me! A right physician's closet 'tis,
> Set round with vials, every one her mark too.
> Sure he does practice physic for his own use,
> Which may be safely call'd your great man's wisdom.[46]

By gaining access to the private space and the secrets which it contains, she is enabled temporarily to dupe Alsemero into believing her chaste when she is already deflowered. Entirely fittingly, then, it is within that same space – the space of intimacy she has already betrayed and violated – that Alsemero confines her when he discovers her guilt. He will be her 'keeper' (jailer), even if he could not guard her virtue. His decision to confine De Flores with her intensifies the sense of violation of his own innermost enclosure, and does, I think (as Marjorie Garber has argued) load the screams which the audience hears issuing from there with sexual overtones:[47]

> Beatrice. (*within*)   Oh, Oh!
> Vermandero. What horrid sounds are these?
> Alsemero. [*unlocking closet*] Come forth, you twins of mischief!

> *Enter De Flores, bringing in Beatrice, [wounded].*[48]

The adulterous couple, confined within Alsemero's most intimate chamber, are heard violating its secrecy. The space of a man's private knowledge is violently entered, and it becomes witness to illicit carnality and unspeakable acts – copulation and murder.

It is against this fundamental violation of male intimacy that we need to set the sub-plot, with its obsessive echoing of enclosure and intrusion. The elderly Alibius confines his young wife and his domestic charges – the madmen and fools of his private asylum – under a single roof. Though notionally a 'secret' enclosure, its confines are breached on a daily basis by 'daily visitors, that come to see [the] brainsick patients'.[49] These are 'gallants

... of quick enticing eyes, rich in habits, / Of stature and proportion very comely'.[50] This arrangement makes for dangerous proximity within Alibius's household between his officially chaste wife and a large number of men who are not 'kin'. Easily violated by counterfeiting madmen, this renders his wife vulnerable to amorous attentions in his absence ('Alibius' means 'elsewhere'), including those of his personal servant cum keeper, Lollio. Alibius himself is therefore totally gullible, his family virtue entirely open to external penetration. The secret and unsupervised exchanges between the gentleman-intruder Antonio and Alibius's wife, deep in the inner space of his household, raise the immediate possibility that Isabella will be easily unfaithful to this, the first man successfully to breach its defences. That these exchanges are observed and spied upon reminds us (as in the main plot) that privacy within the domestic space is a theoretical concept rather than a reality – individual privacy is almost unthinkable in a space filled with minor family members (here supplemented by the 'family' of fools and madmen) and servants going about their business within the household enclosure (as Alice Friedman has vividly shown in her work on Elizabethan domestic architecture).[51]

The integrity of Alibius's marriage in *The Changeling* is only upheld because of a conscious choice by Isabella herself. Isabella is no less wilful, then, than Beatrice-Joanna – faced with the temptation to arbitrary sexual infidelity she merely makes the socially acceptable choice and declines Antonio's advances. This makes her a 'good' wife (a foil for the 'bad' wife Beatrice-Joanna), but without any suggestion that her choice was any more reasonable. She shows no emotional interest in her actual husband, she is easily disobedient when presented with the opportunity to consort with strange men (albeit supposed madmen), and Alibius's intention at the outset to confine Isabella forcibly – to lock her away – underlines the fact that she can be assumed to be fundamentally untrustworthy, simply by being a woman.

In *The Changeling*, the main plot insists on the inevitable downfall of the woman who acts on her own behalf to choose her destination as wife . She is doomed to bring about her own destruction as soon as she woos for herself. Even in the sub-plot, Isabella becomes temporarily threatening when she herself feigns madness, and physically 'touches' Antonio – the man who is trying to force his attentions upon *her*:

> *Isabella.* [*Touching him*] Let me suck out those billows in thy belly;
> Hark how they roar and rumble in the straits!
> Bless thee from the pirates.
> *Antonio.* [*Pulling free*] Pox upon you, let me alone![52]

In spite of this moment of horror (mirroring Alsemero's disgust at discovering his wife's 'active choice' of him over his rival by engineering that rival's death), Antonio's desire revives as soon as Isabella reverts to a socially acceptable passivity before his advances. Any woman, the play suggests, may swerve from desirable acquiescence to disruptive initiative-taking, at any moment, and without warning.

> De Flores. I see in all bouts, both of sport and wit,
>   Always a woman strives for the last hit.[53]

The strongest lines imputing dangerously disruptive motives to the active woman are all put into the mouth of the arch-villain, De Flores. The fact remains, however, that the final message the audience carries strongly away from *The Changeling* is that when a woman freely chooses her sexual partner she moves beyond restraint:

> De Flores. I have watch'd this meeting, and do wonder much
>   What shall become of t'other [suitor]; I'm sure both
>   Cannot be serv'd unless she transgress; happily
>   Then I'll put in for one: for if a woman
>   Fly from one point, from him she makes a husband,
>   She spreads and mounts then like arithmetic,
>   One, ten, a hundred, a thousand, ten thousand,
>   Proves in time sutler to an army royal.[54]

The outcome is inevitably spiralling disorder and disaster for those around her. The only remedy, as Isabella insists to her husband, is perpetual male vigilance: 'You were best lock me up.'[55]

When Beatrice-Joanna's father welcomes Alonzo de Piracquo, the man he has selected to marry his only daughter, into his house, he describes his choice in terms of 'love' – a lineage bond between the male representatives of two important families:

> [*To Alonzo and his brother*]   Y'are both welcome,
>   But an especial one belongs to you, sir,
>   To whose most noble name our love presents
>   The addition of a son, our son Alonzo.[56]

The transforming power of love between men of equal rank intensifies the union by marriage into one of blood: 'our son Alonzo.' When the torrid plot of *The Changeling* has run its course, it is this bond which survives Beatrice-Joanna's treachery and restores social order and harmony. As Vermandero bewails the loss of his family's good name, his son-in-law Alsemero counsels him to wipe the memory of his daughter from the record. By this expedient, 'innocence is quit / By proclamation'.[57] Alsemero offers himself as dutiful son (surviving son-in-law) to fill the gap left by the absent and forgotten daughter:

> Alsemero. Sir, you have yet a son's duty living,
>   Please you, accept it.[58]

His epilogue reaffirms the male line as the bedrock of early modern society, its reassuringly indestructible basis:

> *Alsemero.* All we can do to comfort one another,
>   To stay a brother's sorrow for a brother,
>   To dry a child from the kind father's eyes,
>   Is to no purpose, it rather multiplies;
>   Your only smiles have power to cause re-live
>   The dead again, or in their rooms to give
>   Brother a new brother, father a child;
>   If these appear, all griefs are reconcil'd.[59]

The plot of *The Changeling* pivots around a struggle for control of lineage between a network of interested men and a woman set upon her own heart's desire. That plot, I have been suggesting, corresponds to a perceived conflict of interests within contemporary society between the traditionally structuring forms of family alliance and two separately developing versions of 'love' – the bond of mutuality in marriage, and the conduit to service–relationship between men within the household. What, then, does *The Changeling* offer us as a contribution to understanding that conflict?

In *The Changeling* the dynastic alliance which Vermandero has formally negotiated for his daughter is threatened by the 'love' (at first sight) of a less suitable but well-networked and supported man, by the gaining of control over the daughter by a mere household servant, and by that daughter's own amorous desires. Yet of the three, it is the daughter's actions which are made dramatically appalling, and for which the punishments are ritually devastating – a humiliating enforced sexual union with the physically repellant servant she despises, abuse and rejection by the man for love of whom she acted, and violent death. Alsemero's intervention in family matters on his own terms, by contrast, is only temporarily disruptive – he takes his place at the close of the play as successor in the family line.

The personal negotiation and internal flexibility which the reformed Church apparently offered in its marriage-model (mutual consent; free choice; partnership) made it readily comparable with intimate male friendship – a type of liaison whose goal was not reproduction (the continuation of the line) but unspecified (and publicly untraceable) networks of relationships and profitable dependencies within and between households. In practical terms, the impact of hidden undertakings between men (between, say, the Earl of Essex and the numerous gentlemen of his extended household who acted as his intelligence gatherers and secretaries) might have real political consequences – was indeed always potentially in conflict with court and ministerial control.[60] Given the constraints on women's behaviour in general, female autonomy in choice of marriage partner was likely to be less really socially and politically disruptive. Yet *The Changeling* shows us this as more psychologically and emotionally disturbing. Beatrice-Joanna's pursuit of her own sexual desires may not initially be technically 'illicit', but her action readily arouses the anxiety associated with illicitness. Non-conforming sexual conduct is apparently always culturally disturbing and symbolically disruptive, then as now.[61] In the final analysis the drama vividly captures collisions between domestic and public interests which might otherwise be lost to us. It does so, however, in a sensationalised form in which, as ever, in the matter of blame we are asked to 'look to the woman'.

In the context of the present book on historicising Shakespeare, the implicaations of my argument are troubling. I have suggested throughout that because of the cultural centrality of Shakespeare's works on both sides of the Atlantic, it is peculiarly easy to provoke a dialogue between late twentieth-century issues and the Shakespearean text. A Shakespeare play seems to respond all too readily to the probing pressure of the critic's interrogation, voiced in contemporary terms and resonated back across time from the formative work of the seventeenth-century playwright.

But here I have suggested that all the drama of this period is a distorting glass. That, in particular, it uses the figure of the woman as part of a cultural act of transference. The woman is made to bear the burden of an irresolvable conflict between competing social models in early modern life – because she is perceived as quintessentially a social construct (her manners and mores shaped by consumer demand and the precise requirements of contemporary 'taste') she carries society's problems with its own practices, and then is driven out into the wilderness like the proverbial scapegoat. Perhaps this is particularly the tactic of drama because, in the early modern period in England, there are no women present on the stage – 'woman' is, precisely, a set of learned social codes and mannerisms, executed by a boy.

If this is the case, we may in fact be conserving ancient prejudices when we take up the dialogue with the play-text of Shakespeare as if it were innocent in its relationship to early modern society, and as if all that is needed is to learn to respond to those points in the text which excite our critical attention. I have already hinted at such a possibility in relation to *The Merchant of Venice* and its particular version of the Jew.[62] Here I believe we see, in the less reassuringly familiar forms of Middleton's and Rowley's drama, aspects of the much-loved – and supposedly intensely 'real' – faces of Shakespeare's heroines which ought to give us pause.

8

UNPICKING THE TAPESTRY

The scholar of women's history as Penelope among her suitors

The final question I will raise concerns how [ethnographic] narratives, or models, change. If the narrative is transformed with each retelling, then how much transformation can occur before the story is no longer acknowledged as being the same? And where do new stories come from? In part, this is a question of perspective, for we can look back over the various tellings and stress either continuity or discontinuity: continuity, or incremental change, in which the old story is continually modified; or discontinuity, or structural change, in which a new story emerges. The first is experienced as evolutionary change and the second as revolutionary, as a rupture in the social fabric.

In the first process, stressing continuity, the telling takes account of the context, previous tellings, and the relationship between narrator and audience; thus, the story is modified incrementally. Each retelling starts from the old story and encompasses new conditions, but it is recognized as being the same story. In structural change a new narrative is seen, as in the change from assimilation to resistance, because the old narrative can no longer be stretched to encompass the new events. The key to structural change is a radical shift in the social context. New stories arise when there is a new reality to be explained, when the social arrangements are so different that the old narrative no longer seems adequate. . . .

Because of its new role in discourse, the new narrative can be forcefully articulated. It is eventually accepted, not piecemeal, bit-by-bit, but whole, all at once, as a story. It takes time, however, for a new narrative to become dominant. For such change to occur there must be a breakdown of previously accepted understandings, a perception that a once familiar event no longer makes sense, a penetration of the previously taken-for-granted. Stories operate not simply in the realm of the mind, as ideas; to be convincing they also must have a base in experience or social practice. It is the perceived discrepancy between the previously accepted story and the new situation which leads us to discard or question the old narrative; and it is the perceived relevance of the new story to our own life situation that leads to its acceptance.[1]

This chapter is about the weaving, unweaving and reweaving of historical narratives, the telling and retelling of women's tales, about historical narratives which rupture the social fabric, and the changing life situations to which these are addressed and by which they gain acceptance.[2] For, as the passage from Edward Bruner suggests, I believe that much more is at stake in 'attending to women' in the early modern period than simply an incremental growth in the volume of learned articles on women's history. I believe that the emerging narrative of women's history *does* indicate 'a radical shift in the social context', that (to quote Bruner again) 'the old narrative can no longer be stretched to encompass the new events'.[3]

I begin with a comparatively recent incident in past time – an incident in women's history. In June 1988, an article appeared in the *American Historical Review (AHR)*, the journal of the American Historical Association, entitled 'The refashioning of Martin Guerre'. This piece was a long and intemperate attack on Natalie Davis's *The Return of Martin Guerre*, first published in English a good five years earlier.[4] The same issue of *AHR* carried a reply by Natalie Davis, entitled '"On the lame"'.[5]

As often in historical narrative, the sequence of events to which this exchange attaches deserves our attention. In the previous year, 1987, Natalie Davis had been President of the American Historical Association – only the second woman to achieve this position.[6] Her presidential address also appeared in the 1988 *American Historical Review* (I will come back to that address). Five years after the appearance of Natalie Davis's much-lauded book, in the official publication of the American Historical Association, a male historian takes it upon himself formally to challenge the credentials as a historian of the woman who has achieved the remarkable feat (for a woman) of presiding over the learned society of his (predominately male) profession.

Since 1983, a number of historians and (especially) text critics have turned their attention to Davis's *The Return of Martin Guerre* and its method of historical inquiry.[7] Like Montaigne (one of the earliest commentators on the Arnaud du Tilh imposture) these scholars are drawn to the story because it illustrates compellingly the problem of *uncertainty of identity* – an uncertainty of *male* identity, since it was on the problem of correctly identifying Martin Guerre, husband, head of family, householder in the Artegat community (and whose responsibility that identity was) that the court case, and the written accounts to which it gave rise, hinged.[8] Set against the absolute finality of the punishment, uncertainty hovers as anxiety over the narrated case and its verdict: 'Montaigne writes that the condemnation of the alleged impostor seemed to him reckless. . . . For, writes Montaigne, if you are going to execute people, you must have luminously clear evidence – "A tuer les gens, il faut une clarté lumineuse et nette" – and there was no such clarity in the trial of Martin Guerre."[9]

By contrast, Robert Finlay's belated attack on Davis's book is launched on behalf of certainty – the certainty which is supposed to be achieved by the traditional historian's practice. In particular, his offensive against Davis's historical narrative concerns itself with the methodology of her reconstruction of the part played in the Martin Guerre story by Bertrande de Rols, Martin Guerre's wife. When the man to whom she had been married for nine years before his disappearance reappeared, Bertrande de Rols accepted him *as* Martin Guerre, and lived with the imposter, Arnaud du Tilh, apparently without suspicion, bearing him two daughters. Not until her uncle, Pierre Guerre, began proceedings against him in the courts did Bertrande de Rols show any signs of wavering in her commitment to her now husband; and although she was named in the proceedings against him, she continued to serve him as a wife throughout his imprisonment, up to his execution. Her testimony was necessarily crucial to the case; her silence a vital part of the story. For Davis, therefore, Bertrande de Rols is crucially implicated in the construction of Martin Guerre's identity and selfhood, and is bound to figure significantly – as participant, not as cipher – in any historical narrative which does justice to the events.[10] That is to say, for Davis, social relations between the sexes are part of the formation of early modern selfhood, and as such are a key constituent in the historical narrative which crafts *The Return of Martin Guerre*.[11] It is precisely the explicit attention which such an approach inevitably gives to gender, and the key role gender plays within Davis's historical narrative, that Finlay objects to – just this attention to gender which he regards as fictionalising the historical account. Here is a key passage from the concluding sections of Finlay's piece:

> Nothing is cited from Coras's text [the near-contemporary account of the presiding judge at the trial of Arnaud and Bertrande] to support these contentions [concerning Bertrande]. Given the nature of the argument throughout, that is entirely understandable. If the guilty but honorable Bertrande is 'present in Coras's text,' she cannot be there in the usual sense that makes quotation of, or reference to, the text possible. If Coras repressed his recognition of Bertrande's guilt because of alarm at her freedom from sexual constraints, proof of that must be sought in curious omissions and subtle exaggerations in the text regarding Arnaud du Tilh. If Coras believed that the unmasking of 'the new Martin' was a tragedy, his troubling recognition of that cannot be encompassed by traditional forms of scholarly evidence. If 'Bertrande does not seem a woman so easily fooled' in bed by a rogue like Arnaud, it is to be expected that her subsequent deceits would elude documentation. . . . Such arguments, it may be said, make footnotes to sources

quite beside the point. If historical records can be bypassed so thoroughly in the service of an inventive blend of intuition and assertion, *it is difficult to see what distinguishes the writing of history from that of fiction* [my emphasis].[12]

'None of the central points of the book ... *depend* on the documentary record'; 'this Bertrande de Rols seems to be far more a product of *invention* than of historical reconstruction' [my emphases].[13] In other words, Finlay cannot recognise Davis's narrative *as* historical narrative. Or, to come back to the Bruner passage with which I began, Finlay looks in vain for 'continuity, or incremental change, in which the old story is continually modified'. Failing to locate it in Davis's text, he rejects the narrative outright: 'it is difficult to see what distinguishes [this kind of] writing of history from that of fiction'. In *The Return of Martin Guerre*, I propose, we do indeed have (to quote Bruner again) 'structural change, in which a new story emerges'. It is this 'new story', with its association of the 'revolutionary' and 'rupture of the social fabric', which Finlay cannot take on board. And as so often seems to happen, it is around gender that the methodological issues crystallise – it is Davis's version of the woman in her new historical narrative which Finlay resists, which he is prepared confidently to trash on the grounds that her reconstruction is not based on 'adequate' evidence – is merely a 'fiction'.

I argued a moment ago that in focusing his attention on Davis's representation of Bertrande de Rols, Finlay was attacking above all Davis's engagement, within the enterprise of history, with gender. Which brings me back to Natalie Davis's AHA Presidential Address (published, as I said, in the *AHR* earlier in the same year in which the 'Forum on *The Return of Martin Guerre*' appeared, and entitled 'History's two bodies'). The theme of Davis's address is the nature of the relationship between the abstracted concept of the historical pursuit, and the particular practice of history as it is *embodied* in the individual historian of stature, with her particular interests, beliefs and prejudices. The subject of the address, then, is the balance to be held between idealised 'History', and 'the lived experience of the individual historian' (hence the deliberate echo in Davis's title of Kantorowicz's *The King's Two Bodies*). But twice over in its delivered form the Presidential Address turns on the question of gender: once in Davis's careful choice of paralleled but contrasting examples – David Hume and Catharine Macaulay; Marc Bloch and Eileen Power – whose particular political and cultural formation informed their version of history; and once in the physical presence on the podium of Professor Davis herself – the physical femaleness of the historian presiding over the supposed abstract gender neutrality of the discipline. And in her conclusion, Davis takes care to insist that however we choose to represent 'History' (the discipline) for the future, that representation must include both genders:

What I like about [Paul Klee's watercolour, to which Walter Benjamin gave the title] the Angel of History is that, unlike the Muse, an angel has no sex in theology ... and Benjamin's aphorism puts at the core of history an eternal tension – between wholeness and fragmentation – and a multiple vision: ours, the Angel's, and that of the wind from Paradise.[14]

Before I draw my conclusion from this exchange, let me pick up for a moment that image of Natalie Davis on the podium, delivering the American Historical Association presidential address: 'the physical femaleness of the historian presiding over the supposed abstract gender neutrality of the discipline.' The year following Natalie Davis's term as president of the AHA, 1988, also saw the publication of Joan Scott's crucial article on the fortunes of women historians within the American Historical Association: 'American women historians, 1884–1984'.[15] The American Historical Association had, from its foundation in 1884, actively encouraged female membership.

By including women in the AHA, the founders underscored their democratic and levelling impulse, their desire to 'bring all the historical resources of the nation within the purview of [the] Association', and their belief that their science could be mastered by any intelligent person.[16]

But Scott stresses the fact that in spite of its explicitly egalitarian statements and policies, the position of women within the AHA was always *unequal*:

The AHA formally endorsed inclusiveness and spoke a language of universality that nonetheless rested on differences. Representing the typical historian and the typical historical actor as a (white) male made women a particular and troubling exception. Their likeness to the universal type could not be taken for granted; rather it had to be demonstrated, proven, in the behaviour of any individual woman. Thus, whatever their skills and training, women had the further challenge of repudiating the disabilities assumed to attach to their sex. This was no easy task, whatever strategy was adopted. One could choose to ignore systems of differentiation, accepting their limits and operating within them; but this, of course, left the systems in place and often placed a great burden on the individual woman, who attributed the treatment she received to her own failings. One could attribute specific instances of discrimination to individual misogyny, and thus avoid systematic analysis. One could acknowledge the way gender differences led to unequal treatment and condemn them as violations of democratic principles either individually or collectively. One could affirm the difference of women and elevate it to a position of complementarity or even superiority to men. Either in the name of equality or in the name of difference, collective action by women could be politically extremely effective; but it carried with it the potential for underscoring the fact of women's separate and different identity, of pointing up rather than playing down the contrast between historians and women historians. [17]

'The history of professional women historians since 1884' (Scott continues) 'illustrates all of these strategies.'

The only exception to the AHA's continuous record of including women in its membership, whilst marginalising them in its activities, and above all in its choice of officers and senior figures, was the election to the AHA presidency, in 1943, of Nellie Neilson. 'Yet the election of Nellie Neilson to the AHA presidency did not signal the beginning of a new era. . . . [I]t would still be many years before women were regularly included in positions of power in the AHA and not until 1987 that a second woman assumed the office of President.'[18] And if this was the fortune of the women historians, it was also the fortune, apparently, of women *in* history – in those historical narratives supposedly so reassuringly grounded in factual detail, precise documentation, archive and footnote. John Higham's *History*,[19] 'a story of the discipline from its institutionalization in 1884', produces a historical narrative of the succession of leading historians in America from which the AHA's women members are almost entirely erased:

> No works by women are included in any of the summaries of historio-graphic debates; Mary Beard appears in two footnotes as the author of a book about her husband and as co-author with him of a book entirely credited to him in the text; and Nellie Neilson's presidency is not so much as acknowledged even in passing.[20]

This, then, is the background against which we need to set the exchange between Finlay and Davis.

In her reply to Finlay, '"On the lame"' (a title with magnificently multiple resonances),[21] Davis never deviates from the narrative strategy she had originally adopted in *The Return of Martin Guerre* – she continues to stress the multivalency of the text, 'the doubling of a text that, for Finlay, must always be single-minded, objective and transparent'.[22] She persists in representing the historian's task as one fundamentally of textual study – of close, nuanced reading of sources, interpretation, reading between the lines of the surviving evidence, interpolating the cultural and social history out of which the text was produced:

> When a sixteenth-century writer uses words like 'prodigious,' 'tragedy,' and 'tragicomedy,' the historian must pay attention, for they are hot and expanding terms of that day. . . . When a judge comments that the burning of the body of a criminal like Arnaud is justified 'so that the memory of so miserable and abominable a person be annihilated and lost' and then publishes an account of such a criminal under the title *Memorable Decree*, the historian asks what that means. . . . And when a jurist-author invents a new kind of book – for the *Arrest Memorable* is

a new kind of writing on crime and the law – the historian wonders why. . . . I am thus engaging in the historian's common practice of conjecturing from evidence on the basis of assumptions about psychological process. . . . Finlay discusses neither evidence nor assumptions but just snorts that they are 'unfounded.' . . . Robert Finlay has no doubts about what is true in the case of Martin Guerre.[23]

By unweaving and then reweaving her historical narrative before her reluctant suitor, Davis reveals the way in which Robert Finlay has failed to recognise the discontinuity in the historical narrative itself which sets her account apart from his own – reveals how he has chosen simply to deny the new narrative which 'ruptures the social fabric' (and inscribes women fully within the historical narrative) in the name of a 'truth' which merely names the 'old story'. 'The rights and wrongs in the Guerre case are . . . crystal clear to Finlay . . . [but] these are Finlay's moral understandings, not mine', writes Davis; 'They come . . . from his inattentiveness to the whole argument of my book and his deafness to my authorial voice.'[24]

So now let me draw out of this episode a provocative suggestion. The scholar of women's history is perceived by the historians (who we now know are *not* innocently ungendered) as writing truth (in a historical subdiscipline) when her narrative can be accommodated to the incrementalist version of 'changing history', as writing fiction when that narrative contributes to 'a breakdown in previously accepted understanding' – when it 'ruptures the social fabric'. In the terms of my title: Penelope's suitors accept her woman's labour as long as they believe she is completing one continuously produced tapestry. When it becomes clear that she has repeatedly unwoven that tapestry and rewoven a different one – it is not the tapestry they thought it was, her project was not theirs, but a tactical reweaving – their support turns to anger. Or, put slightly differently, when the scholar of women's history adds incrementally to the fund of knowledge of the past which is still shaped by a largely traditional historical narrative, her work is (on the whole) accepted as providing important extra pieces for a jigsaw which continues to relate an emerging male identity in past time. But when her work produces an account in which once familiar events *no longer make sense*, we may judge that something more gravely disruptive of traditional history is taking place.

So now let us look at the difference it might make if we carried over the distinction between incremental history and rupturing history to specific examples (which, in keeping with my continuing interdisciplinary commitment, I draw from both history and text studies). Within what I am calling 'incremental historical narrative', the social historians' declared interest in marginalised groups has led recently to a spate of discussions about disruptive women, and especially the category of 'scold' or 'shrew' in early modern

England. David Underdown identifies the *scold* as disruptive of early modern order, on the confident assumption that 'she' is a (marginal) phenomenon recognisable separately from, and in advance of, any incident which leads to prosecution or neighbourly intervention:

> Let us begin with the scold: the person (usually a woman)[25] who disturbs the peace by publicly abusing family members or neighbours. *Such people had always existed, of course,* but before the middle of the sixteenth century the authorities do not seem to have been particularly concerned about them, and they were dealt with by the routine processes of presentment to the ecclesiastical or manor court, with penance or small fines as the customary punishments. From the 1560s, however, many places began to show increasing concern about *the problem* [my emphases].[26]

Here, the scold is a perennial problem in the community, who attracts the attention of the authorities (manorial leets or local ecclesiastical courts) at some historical moments but not at others. And her persistence as a feature of the social life of early modern England is regarded as understandable, on grounds of the oppressive position in which women found themselves in the social hierarchy. Within the subdiscipline of women's history we can all learn to understand why assertive women tend to become tiresomely disruptive of social harmony.[27]

But we might prefer to describe the situation in another way. The label 'scold', applied to a neighbour in a deposition, designated her as the culpable figure (pointed the finger of blame) in the narration of a fraught incident involving several parties, sharpening the contours of a predictably blurred and confused collision of circumstances, involving opposed individuals and households. According to this version, scolds were women who 'brought their rejection of women's "quiet" and obedience out of the household and into public view' only in the sense that the court, whose records provide the social historian's 'data', administered specific penalties against a woman who had been publicly recognised as such – to whom the label 'scold' had been attached, and deemed fitting to this particular example of 'disorderly' behaviour.[28] Silent on the circumstances which gave rise to the outburst, the depositions which label individual women as 'scolds' merely construct a convenient classification within the terms of the court records, for the purpose of handing down penalties aimed generally at controlling behaviour in the community. In the spirit of our new 'rupturing historical narrative', I suggest, we need to approach the 'scold' in such a way as to keep in play both the figurative, cultural, controlling version of the unruly woman (as opposed to the 'chaste' silent woman) and the historical event in which 'interpersonal tensions' led to a public complaint, a demand for redress, or a formal charge being laid.

If we renarrate the 'scolding' depositions in the ecclesiastical court records in response to an incident in which a woman figures, rather than as a description of it, I think we begin to see that the occasions on which a woman may be said to 'scold' or to be 'curst and shrewd' in her talk are various, but that they have in common her intervention outside the home, as a woman, in public social relations, in a way which causes tensions in which her femaleness is at once recognised, and is the source of difficulty (which is what usually leads to a charge).[29] But even here, I think, 'intervention' gives too strong a sense of the woman's original agency in the events – as opposed to the agency she *acquires* when the events are redescribed for the court (hence the similarity with the Martin Guerre story, also a record of a court case). Here I think I am beginning to move from record to representation: we see the shape of an incident, outside the home, or on its doorstep, in which a woman plays a part; we see the developing interpersonal tensions, the flash-point, and the outcome (generally 'disorderly'); then the entire incident is redescribed to give the woman a particular type of agency (moral and figurative) in the incident – an agency which designates her as culpable.

Inevitably, such a suggestion needs fuller illustration from the records than I can possibly offer here. But I have come across a suggestive case in the Wiltshire records which will make my point (a case with some of the textual possibilities of 'doubling' which Davis finds in Coras's *Arrest Memorable*). In the Marlborough quarter sessions for 1648 the following petition was received:

> The humble peticon of certayne of the Inhabitants of Stert and others whose names are hereunder written. Humbly sheweth & complayneth.
>
> That William Willis and Edith his wife (as well by way of comon imbarretry as otherwise) have byn for divers yeares past & yet are, comon and notorious disturbers of the peace. That they have incited ag[ain]st theire neghbors divers frivolous & vexatious suites, thereby enforceing them to excessive expences. That the said Edith is & stand-eth convicted for a comon scould as appears by the records of this Court.
>
> That they still continue theire litigious & wrangling course.
>
> That this peticon to this Court p[ro]ceeds meerly out of a desire of neighbourly & peaceable lyving & not for any other respect.
>
> They doe therefore pray yor wo[rshi]pps to inflict on them such punishment as they deserve or otherwise to deale w[i]th them as in yor wor[shi]pps grave wisdom shalbe thought most convenient.
>
> And they shall pray &c.[30]

The editor of the printed records adds:

> This bears four signatures but has a note added as follows:-
> Whereas I have foremerly ben desired to undertake ye decideing of certaine differences between Wm. Willis of Stert and Willm Gittings of Erchfount I find that upon examination of Witnesses on both sides ye

said Wm. Willis through the instigation (as I conceive) of his wife who (as I have often heard) is guilty of ye aforesaide complaints to be very much averse from a peaceable life. (Signed) RICHARD NAB.[31]

On the face of it, there is nothing to distinguish this entry from the following one, from the Marlborough quarter sessions for 1649:

Wee whose names are under written doe certifie that Al[i]ce Harper the weife of Richard Harper of Steple Ashton is a most troblesome and p[er]verse wooman she being a common scould having from time to time abused with her tongue the best men and women in the towne of Steple Ashton and now upon our knowledge shee hath abused John Markes and his weife he being a Tithing man of the aforesaid towne for executing his office most viperous with her tongue and giveing them such bad and groce language as no tongue can well expresse, they liveing in such good repute and estate as they doe, he haveing divers times served all offices in the aforesaid towne of Steple Ashton honestly and justly all the dayes of their lives hitherto amongst us. Wee leaving it to yor Wor: consideracon. July 28th, 1649.

(Signed by Geo: Markes & nine others).[32]

And, indeed, there is nothing to indicate that the two cases are not largely similar: in both cases a couple has trouble with the neighbours, that trouble focusing on the wife's behaviour, and in both cases the wife is indicted as a common scold on the testimony of neighbours. But in the case of the Willises we have two previous petitions surviving in the records, this time from the couple themselves to the Court. In the presentments at Marlborough quarter sessions on 6 October 1646, the Willises petitioned as follows:

The humble petition of Willm Willis & Edith his wife. These are to show & declare unto you all his Ma[jes]ties Justices of the peace what wronges & injuries Robert Ruddle of Sterte with many more that he hath sett on have done yor poore petitioners Willm Willis & Edith his wife. The first wronge he hath laid violent handes upon yor petitioner Edith Willis & he hath made confession of it & with my crying out against him my dog coming out he threw his hatchett att my dog & had almost kill my dog which thing Mr. Topp knowes well. Ye next abuse w[hi]ch was done me by some of Robert Ruddles company w[hi]ch he had sett on was, I was coming with fruitt from ye Vize for Mr Topp a woman with 3 or 4 sett upon me in ye Kings hie way and beat me most lamentable so yt I was almost Chokt with my owne blood & I had dyed with it had not Mrs. Topp made me divers medicines to doe me good. I lay by it w[i]th this abuse twelve months to or great hindrance & Charge I being not able to help myself. Some of these woemen that did me this great wrong I had two biles [bills] of inditement & did put them into ye Quarter Sessions & have waited for justice ever since. Upon the bills of inditem[en]t w[hi]ch were putt in with very sufficient witnesses yet could I never obtain any justice for my wrongs. Sir John Glanfeild did promise us that if we would have a Tryall in Malborow Sessions last past that we should never receave any wrong more but we can make it appear that ye same parties w[hi]ch were indited tooke a false oath att ye same Sessions & have done us since abundance of wronge my Childe likewise receivd abundance of wronge by one of their Company ye Smith threw a hott iron at him and wounded him soe yt we could see into his bowells & ye child lay by it 1/2 a yeare w[hi]ch was great expence & charge unto us. Now we desire yor Worships that you would cause them to show unto you how any kind of waies we have misbehaved or selves unlesse it hath bine for ye asking of some satisfaction for ye great wrongs they have done us. Yor poore petitioners are quite undone unless now you will be please that there be granted by you a right examinacon.[33]

In the Devizes quarter sessions in April of the following year there is a second petition from the Willises:

Mr Drew said att ye bench we being poore & of a low estate that it was not best for us to goe onward in lawe & soe we being poore could not have justice for or greevance since this by ye setting on of some ye compacted company by one Robert Ruddle of Stert, husbandman (being our adversary) I was very much abused & beaten 3 times w[hi]ch we can make plainlie appeare to yor worships & since ye said Robert Ruddle hath threatned me that I shall be worse use then ever I was & that he would rid ye Parish of us though it did cost him 40£ & that he would make us flee the country w[hi]ch we have sufficient witness for it; some of this compacted company have spoild us & eaten up our gease these 16teen yeares & since that they have robd us within doores & without w[hi]ch they have confessed & we have had two warrants for them, one warrant from Mr. Edward Earnley of Ashlinton & thother from Sir John Earnley of Whettom w[hi]ch warrant is yet in the Constables hand & it is not yet served. Robert Ruddle our adversary served me into Wilton Court & when it came to ye tryall of a judgment I borrowed money & laid it down to him & tould him yt if I owed him any money he should take his due but he could make no debt appeare nor tooke never a pennie; for speaking for justice for this our greevance this compacted company have indited me into the sessions for a common scould & it hath cost us much even to our utter undoing. The said Robert Ruddle did confesse in the presence of Mr. Richard Gilbert of a lamentable abuse that ye said Robert Ruddle did to me Edith Willis ye wife of Willm Willis we have witnesse to prove his confession & for want of the knowledge of inditing a bill we could not try the suite.

We do humbly entreat yor worships for gods cause to consider how

lamentably we have binne abused by this compacted company & that
we may have a right examinacon of this compacted company.
     Yor poore petitioners
                         William Willis & Edith Willis his wife.[34]

I am not suggesting here that the petitions constitute 'mitigating circumstances' for the scolding charge; indeed, I am not suggesting that we 'judge'
the case in any way. What I wish to draw attention to is that the simplicity of
the statement – 'That William Willis and Edith his wife ... have byn for
divers yeares past & yet are, comon and notorious disturbers of the peace. ...
That the said Edith is & standeth convicted for a comon scould as appears by
the records of this Court' – is misleading, as is the inclusion of Edith Willis
under the category 'scold' in a social historian's statistical analysis of the
records. Neither, however, in my view, would a textual account which simply
drew attention to the way in which Edith Willis's litigation with her neighbours could be reduced to the label 'scold' deal adequately with what is going
on here. What we seem to have is *both* Edith Willis acting as free female agent
(and evidently making most of the going in the petitions, which clearly speak
in her first person with occasional support from her husband), *and* Edith
Willis disabled by being relegated to the figurative position of 'scold' in the
text of the final villagers' petition to have the pair publicly condemned as
'comon and notorious disturbers of the peace', together with confirmation
that Edith is a 'comon scold' (we might note that in the second Willis petition
they allege that the charge of scold was made to stand on false supporting
testimony).

I have been arguing that the task of the scholar of women's history at the
present time is to go beyond 'incremental historical narrative', to which she
has been vigorously contributing for nearly a century. My model for a new,
'rupturing historical narrative' has been that offered by Natalie Davis –
crucially in *The Return of Martin Guerre*, more recently, but no less compellingly in
Fiction in the Archives.[35] And it is Natalie Davis once again who brings me to
the matter of women's *voice*. For one of Davis's responses to Finlay is to
maintain that he is deaf to her 'authorial voice'.[36] The question I ask, to close
this penultimate chapter, is whether an 'authentic female voice' might mean
something significantly different, according to whether we locate it in relation
to incremental or to rupturing historical narrative. Finlay is deaf to Davis's
voice – the voice he would hear clearly would have (Davis implies) a more
traditionally moral ring to it.
     The 1599 presentation copy of *The Psalms of Sir Philip Sidney and the Countess
of Pembroke* contains two otherwise unpublished dedicatory poems by Mary
Sidney, apparently for a presentation copy for Queen Elizabeth.[37] Of these
poems Margaret Hannay writes that 'we hear her own voice most clearly
in two poems which may have been unknown to her contemporaries; they

apparently never circulated and exist in one manuscript only'.[38] The poem which interests me is 'To the Angell Spirit of the most excellent Sir Phillip Sidney', addressed to the Countess's dead brother and bearing the final attribution, 'by the Sister of that Incomparable Sidney'.[39]

This is a poem with a compelling authorial voice – an arresting production of selfhood – or so it seems.[40] That selfhood, moreover, is explicitly female – the poem is signed 'By the Sister of that Incomparable Sidney'. The poem directs itself confidently into the public domain, and offers itself openly to the reader's gaze. Consistent with the decorum demanded of the virtuous woman, it does so using a strategy which is well illustrated by a famous letter written by Thomas More in praise of his daughter Margaret Roper's intellectual accomplishment: this poem displays its virtuosity ostensibly only for the author's brother's eyes as her closest male kin.[41] The opening stanzas of the poem run as follows:

> To thee pure sprite, to thee alones addres't
>   this coupled worke, by double int'rest thine:
>   First rais'de by thy blest hand, and what is mine
> inspird by thee, thy secrett power imprest.
>   So dar'd my Muse with thine it selfe combine,
>   as mortall stuffe with that which is divine,
> Thy lightning beames give lustre to the rest,
>
> That heavens King may daigne his owne transform'd
>   in substance no, but superficiall tire
>   by thee put on; to praise, not to aspire
> To, those high Tons, so in themselues adorn'd,
>   which Angells sing in their cœlestiall Quire,
>   and all of tongues with soule and uoice admire
> Theise sacred Hymnes thy Kinglie Prophet form'd.[42]

As the poem goes on, this insistence on the exclusivity of attention of the dead Sidney produces an interesting intensification of the convention that the poem is the most lasting monument to a person (beauty will fade, life ends, but the poem is an eternal monument to the fame of the beloved):

> And sithe it hath no further scope to goe,
>   nor other purpose but to honor thee,
>   Thee in thy workes where all the Graces bee,
> As little streames with all their all doe flowe
>   to their great sea, due tribute's gratefull fee:
>   so press my thoughts my burthened thoughts in mee,
> To pay the debet of Infinits I owe
>
> To thy great worth . . .[43]

This poem is a monument which must lose the author (female) if it is to be the object of attention of any audience other than Sidney himself. So it is written insistently towards his 'sweet sprite', and its achievement will be to bear that mark and obliterate any other 'title' (such as Mary Sidney's):

> Receiue theise Hymnes, theise obsequies receiue;
>   if any marke of thy sweet sprite appeare,
>   well are they borne, no title else shall beare.
> I can no more: Deare Soule I take my leaue;
>   Sorrowe still striues, would mount thy highest sphere
>   presuming so iust cause might meet thee there,
> Oh happie chaunge! could I so take my leaue.[44]

If Mary Sidney can elevate her verse into the spirit of Sidney himself, she thereby changes places with him – leaves the poem, loses her selfhood into his – he lives and she 'takes [her] leave'.[45]

If we take one more look at this poem, we see that Aphthonius's *Progymnasmata* (the standard school(boy's) textbook on rhetorical, public self-presentation) is also relevant to the discursive self-construction:[46] the eleventh exercise in Aphthonius is the imagined first person, emotionally charged speech of intense self-presentation; and the specific examples which Aphthonius chooses are both examples of highly emotionally charged female speech – Hecuba and Niobe. Both women, in fact, are grief stricken at the violent and unnatural deaths of their closest family. Mary Sidney's poem, with perfect rhetorical decorum, presents her self in an appropriately highly wrought state of intense grief:

> Oh, had that soule which honor brought to rest
>   too soone not left and reft the world of all
>   what man could showe, which wee perfection call
> This halfe maim'd peece had sorted with the best.
>   Deepe wounds enlarg'd, long festred in their gall
>   fresh bleeding smart; not eie but hart teares fall.
> Ah memorie what needs this new arrest?[47]

And, indeed, this poem is an outpouring of intense grief, explicitly over the violently mutilated body of the woman's closest family (death from an infected battle wound). It repays quite careful comparison with the Niobe example in Aphthonius.

In incremental history this is indeed the voice of Mary Sidney. To the extent that it conforms closely and with considerable technical proficiency to the requirements of a number of formal conventions for female emotion and female selfhood, it is compelling within a recognisable literary tradition. This, for instance, is how Edmund Spenser dedicates *The Faerie Queene* to the Countess of Pembroke in 1590:

Remembraunce of that most Heroicke spirit,
  The heuens pride, the glory of our daies,
  Which now triumpheth through immortall merit
  Of his braue vertues, crownd with lasting baies,
Of heuenlie blis and euerlasting praies;
  Who first my Muse did lift out of the flore,
  To sing his sweet delights in lowlie laies;
  Bids me most noble Lady to adore
His goodly image liuing euermore,
  In the diuine resemblaunce of your face;
  Which with your vertues ye embellish more,
  And natiue beauty deck with heuenlie grace:
For his, and for your owne especial sake,
  Vouchsafe from him this token in good worth to take.[48]

Mary Sidney's self-presentation is entirely coherent with this version of her, presented in exemplary fashion by a male poet aspiring to her service (but who is unlikely to have had any personal knowledge of her). It is that very coherence which makes Mary Sidney, here, a coherent self, herself.[49]

But I suggest that within our rupturing historical narrative 'To the Angell Spirit of the most excellent Sir Phillip Sidney' gives the scholar of women's history no clue whatsoever to Mary Sidney's authentic voice. To exactly the extent that it seamlessly weaves Mary Sidney into the very fabric of late Elizabethan lyric poetry, it is silent on Mary Sidney *as* self – the self we might detect, infer, interpret and renarrate in the margins, lacunae, omissions and doublings of a less accomplished piece of writing (that is, a piece of writing which less competently inscribes itself entirely within the conventions of the dominant male writing of the period).[50]

In 'American women historians', Joan Scott writes:

> We cannot write women into history ... unless we are willing to enter-
> tain the notion that history as a unified story was a fiction about a
> universal subject whose universality was achieved through implicit pro-
> cesses of differentiation, marginalization, and exclusion. Man was
> never, in other words, a truly universal figure. It is the processes of
> exclusion achieved through differentiation that established man's uni-
> versal plausibility that must, to begin with, constitute the focus for a
> different, more critical history.[51]

Most feminist historians have, I suggest, in our diverse ways recognised that 'history as a unified story was a fiction' – that all history *is* constructed narrative, textually interpreting and recreating – weaving, unweaving and re-weaving – the slender residue of 'evidence' which time has carried down to us. Indeed, we might coin an adage for our scholar of women's history: 'One woman's fact is another man's fiction'. What we have yet to take fully on board, however, is how we should use that recognised fictionality or narrativity of history effectively.

Out of the processes of exclusion, I suggest, we must unweave the comforting accretions of an incremental historical narrative which have given us marginal categories of women, and assimilated women's voices. Fortified with the great wealth of 'incremental women's history', which has recovered and enriched our understanding of women in past time, we must now begin again to reweave the unwoven tapestry, reweave our ruptured historical narrative again and again in pursuit of that new history in which women's and men's interventions in past time will weigh equally – permanently and for all time (or at least until the next structural change in the narrative). It is not yet clear to me where that new historical narrative will lead, but it will surely take us away from the continuing ghettoisation, the marginalisation of women's history within the traditional discipline of which all of us are all too aware. And in the meantime, I salute Natalie Zemon Davis's pioneering work in such gender-equal history as groundbreaking in its rupturing originality.

9

CONCLUSION
What happens in *Hamlet*?

Ophelia. My lord, as I was sewing in my closet,
Lord Hamlet, . . .
. . . comes before me.[1]

The critical reading of Shakespeare is historical twice over. To read Shakespeare historically is to undertake a dialogue with these culturally freighted residues of our own past in order more clearly to illuminate the culture we currently inhabit. To read Shakespeare historically is also always to know that such illumination is provisional, that it will always have to be done again, in order to capture with precision the particular situation of the interlocutor relative to the historicised Shakespearean text – a situation focused by the bright light of contemporary events and our pressing need to understand them in a larger than parochial context. The conceptual struggle between gender and nationality in *Henry V* did not become part of my own dialogue with the play until the disintegration of former Yugoslavia and the personal tragedies of the young Bosnians who entered my classroom forced it upon me. I end this book, therefore, with a small example of the way in which I, like Penelope, have woven and rewoven the tapestry of my own involvedness with Shakespeare and with European contemporary culture – a process which I imagine will go on as long as I continue to care deeply about what happens to the world around me.

At least twice in my published work over the past ten years my attention as a historicising, feminist reader of Shakespeare has been drawn to the figure of Hamlet's mother, Gertrude.[2] She was, indeed, one of the original textual stimuli for my setting out to write *Still Harping on Daughters*: the fact that so much had been made, on behalf of or against the cause of women, of the very little she is given to say in the play was one of the early examples I noted of a pressing need to reconsider our approaches to the female figures in Shakespeare. When I returned to her in 1991 it was to suggest even more strongly that the critical reader's confidence of Gertrude's guilt in the play depended upon culturally customary transferences of blame which remain all too recognisable to us today: we have no difficulty in understanding the way in which blame for the incestuous marriage entered into by Old Hamlet's brother, Claudius, is passed across to Gertrude as if she were its instigator.

Now, as I tackle Gertrude one more time, I do so under the pressure of a question which seems to me an increasingly pressing one in relation to the play, *Hamlet*: Why does it seem to have become necessary, at the very end of the twentieth century, in order to keep our sympathy for the hero (to sustain the tragedy), that we shift the burden of blame from Hamlet and make him blameless? And why does it seem so unavoidable that however we shift our critical terms and methodologies, the burden of blame should settle so inevitably on the fragile shoulders of Gertrude?

Whenever we give attention to the figure of Hamlet's mother it is, I think, as part of an attempt to understand the cultural dynamics of blame and its relation to questions of gender. Virtually silent on her own behalf (Gertrude speaks fewer lines than any other major character in the play), her depth as a protagonist is accumulated out of the responses to her of others. Thus she captures for feminist critics the constructedness of femaleness which has absorbed us for more than a decade.

The crux in the play for all explorations of the condition of Gertrude's so-called 'guilt' is the closet scene of Act 3, scene 4. Here, critics feel, we are bound to find the key to understanding that complexity of feeling which T. S. Eliot captured so vividly in his influential essay on the play:

> The essential emotion of the play is the feeling of a son towards a guilty mother . . . Hamlet (the man) is dominated by an emotion which is inexpressible, because it is in excess of the facts as they appear. . . . Hamlet is up against the difficulty that his disgust is occasioned by his mother, but that his mother is not an adequate equivalent for it; his disgust envelops and exceeds her.[3]

Yet the closet scene is more ostentatiously stage-managed, more contrived within the suffocating court atmosphere of watching, controlling and generalised espionage, than any other scene in the play. The 'intimate' conversation between Hamlet and his mother there is entirely the brain-child of Claudius's master of surveillance, Polonius:

> *Polonius.* . . . if you hold it fit, after the play
> Let his queen-mother all alone entreat him
> To show his grief, let her be round with him,
> And I'll be plac'd, so please you, in the ear
> Of all their conference.[4]

> *Polonius.* My lord, he's going to his mother's closet.
> Behind the arras I'll convey myself
> To hear the process. I warrant she'll tax him home,
> And as you said – and wisely was it said –
> 'Tis meet that some more audience than a mother,

Since nature makes them partial, should o'erhear
The speech of vantage. Fare you well, my liege.
I'll call upon you ere you go to bed,
And tell you what I know.
King.   Thanks, dear my lord.[5]

Gertrude is a decoy, to lure Hamlet into the self-revelation he has adeptly avoided, and which will decide Polonius and Claudius as to whether he is a danger to the state. Like Ophelia in the 'nunnery' scene, Gertude embarks on her audience with her son in the full knowledge that they are deliberately overheard.[6] Unlike Ophelia (who simply 'walks' where Hamlet will 'as 'twere by accident' encounter her), by summoning her son to her most private quarters she formally signals to him that their meeting will be in the strictest confidence. Here, then, are grounds for accusations of betrayal: from the outset Gertrude connives in misleading Hamlet more formally and more fully than does the dutifully obedient Ophelia.

Let us look briefly at some of the implications of our registering Polonius's confident insistence that Hamlet is bound to reveal his emotional all to his mother, and that any analysis of the closet scene ought therefore to take account of the fact that circumstances have been arranged so that this private transaction can be covertly observed.

In *The English Secretorie* (1592) Angel Day defines the closet as follows:

Wee do call the most secret place in the house appropriate vnto our owne priuate studies, and wherein wee repose and deliberate by déepe consideration of all our waightiest affaires, a *Closet*, in true intendment and meaning, a place where our dealings of importance are shut vp, a roome proper and peculier onely to our selues. And whereas into each other place of the house, it is ordinary for euery néere attendant about vs to haue accesse: in this place we do solitarie and alone shutte vp our selues, of this we kéepe the key our selues, and the vse thereof alone do onely appropriate vnto our selues.[7]

Within the organisation of rooms in the English country house of the period, the total privacy of the closet is signified by its location as the final room in a run of chambers serving increasingly 'private' functions – the reception room opening into the retiring room, opening into the bedroom, off which is found the closet (sometimes the closet is even concealed within a chimney piece or the depth of a wall).[8] But as Alan Stewart has recently pointed out, the aura of utter seclusion which the closet acquires depends to some extent on the social formality of the gentlewoman or man's withdrawing to it:

In Lady Margaret Hoby's diary ... the (private) closet is placed in contrast to her (public) bedchamber, where she is often accompanied by her gentlewomen, acting as a sign to distinguish public praying – that is, praying in company – from private, solitary praying which takes place in her closet. For example, on Thursday 13 September 1599 she concludes her day: 'Then I wrought tel almost :6:, and praied with Mr. Rhodes [her chaplain], and priuatly in my Closett'. . . . When Lady Margaret goes into her closet, she does not merely withdraw to privacy, but rather she enacts that withdrawal publicly, and records it textually, indicating a space of secrecy outside the knowledge of the household. . . . The closet is thus constructed as a place of utter privacy, of total withdrawal from the public sphere of the household – but it simultaneously functions as a very *public* gesture of withdrawal, a very public sign of privacy.[9]

Of the domestic spaces occupied or traversed on a daily basis by the early modern gentlewoman, her closet was the sole place over which she ostensibly exercised total control, her one truly privy or private place.

Because what goes on in the closet, is, uniquely amongst the activities in the early modern gentrified household, customarily solitary, a suggestion of the illicit, the indiscreet, certainly the secretive, hovers over those infrequent occasions when men and women encounter one another there, a *frisson* of likely indiscretion audible in Ophelia's anxious account of Hamlet's intrusion 'all unbrac'd' into *her* private quarters in Act 2, scene 1.[10] For beyond Hamlet's dishevelled appearance, his very entry into the entirely unsupervised, solitary intimacy of Ophelia's closet suggests an erotic entanglement. When Hamlet responds to his mother's summons and comes to her closet, he intrudes where customarily a woman would only entertain her husband or lover. For an adult son, intimations of erotic possibility are almost inevitable; the son crosses into the enclosure of his mother's privacy to encounter her as a sexualised subject.

The King of Denmark's close adviser and Councillor of State, Polonius, has no legitimate place within the intimate space of Gertrude's closet; his presence fatally confuses privacy with affairs of state. The erosion of privacy which has already been effected by the constant surveillance which has characterised Claudius and Polonius's management of the state of Denmark here reaches its logical conclusion: the state invades the Queen's inner sanctum, and in the ensuing confusion it is defiled by a botched and mistaken act of violence.

The instructions issued by Polonius to Gertrude are that she should reprimand her son for his behaviour towards Claudius:

> *Polonius.* A will come straight. Look you lay home to him,
>   Tell him his pranks have been too broad to bear with
>   And that your Grace hath screen'd and stood between
>   Much heat and him. I'll silence me even here.
>   Pray you be round.[11]

Performing before Polonius, Gertrude frames her reproach formally; believing himself alone, Hamlet responds familially. The upshot is that the language of public disapproval collides with that of personal hurt, coloured by the present reminders of maternal sexuality:

> *Hamlet*. Now mother, what's the matter?
> *Gertrude*. Hamlet, thou hast thy father much offended.
> *Hamlet*. Mother, you have my father much offended . . .
> *Gertrude*. Have you forgot me?
> *Hamlet*.   No, by the rood, not so.
>   You are the Queen, your husband's brother's wife,
>   And, would it were not so, you are my mother.[12]

Reproved for his offensive behaviour (with the familiar 'thou' of maternal scolding), Hamlet retaliates with the more grievous 'offence' against his deceased natural father of his mother's remarriage to his brother. The marriage is technically illicit, a serious matter under canon law; within the closet it takes on an aura of secrecy and deception, as if it has been 'discovered' by Hamlet (yet the marriage appears to bother no one else in the Court of Denmark). Whereas Hamlet, as he proceeds fully to reveal, continues to suffer the deeper smart of the usurped place of the two men whose part he takes – his father supplanted by Claudius in his mother's bed and himself supplanted on the throne by Claudius, who also now stands in affection between himself and his mother.

In a landmark essay on *Hamlet*, Jacqueline Rose suggested that Eliot's judgement of the play as an aesthetic failure ('Hamlet is up against the difficulty that his disgust is occasioned by his mother, but that his mother is not an adequate equivalent for it; his disgust envelops and exceeds her') can be turned around – that the intensity of feeling produced in Hamlet by his mother's sexual inscrutability captures the essence of femininity. For Hamlet, Gertrude is unmanageable in the enigmatic and indecipherable quality of her sexuality, 'the Mona Lisa of literature':

> By choosing an image of a woman [the Mona Lisa] to embody the inexpressible and inscrutable content which he identified in Shake-speare's play, Eliot ties the enigma of femininity to the problem of interpretation itself. . . . Freud himself picks up the tone in one of his more problematic observations about femininity when he allows that critics have recognised in the picture:
>
> > the most perfect representation of the contrasts which dominate the erotic life of women; the contrast between reserve and seduction, and between the most devoted tenderness and a sensuality that is ruthlessly demanding – consuming men as if they were alien beings.

What other representation, we might ask, has so clearly produced a set of emotions without 'objective correlative', that is, in excess of the facts as they appear? T. S. Eliot's reading of *Hamlet* would therefore seem to suggest that what is in fact felt as inscrutable, unmanageable or even horrible (ecstatic in both senses of the term) for an aesthetic theory which will only allow into its definition what can be controlled or managed by art is nothing other than femininity itself.[13]

Rose names the problem for Hamlet in the closet scene as femininity, and identifies the 'buffoonery, ecstasy, the excessive and unknowable' of his subsequent behaviour as the recognisable response of a man who cannot deal with that problem.

If we set this version of Hamlet's difficulty in relation to Gertrude within the context I have been describing, what do we get? In the terms of intimacy, privacy and enclosure away from the public domain which I have been exploring, the problem which confronts Hamlet in the closet scene is one of contradictory, inconsistent and incompatible messages. Hamlet is summoned to the intimate space into which his mother has (publicly) withdrawn: he crosses into what he believes to be the domestic sphere, expecting the entire secrecy of an intense conversation between mother and son. But the presence of an intruder means that privacy is already absent, his exchanges already coloured by public interpretation as they are uttered. The competing and conflicting signs which Hamlet receives from his mother are the product of an insecure separation of private and public domains, intimate and state spaces. The enigma of femininity (in Freud's and Rose's terms) lies in this insufficiently clear demarcation of discourses and domains – in the elision of the demands of social and secret (sexual) intercourse.

When the intimacies of the early modern closet are interpreted from a public perspective, the intimate transaction is perceived as erotically charged. Just as Hamlet's uncomprehending buffoonery in Ophelia's closet was readily interpreted as thwarted eroticism, so Hamlet's retreat from his mother's closet – backwards, in disorder, dragging a dead body – implies an erotic situation he has been unable to deal with. In other words, I am suggesting that the physical spaces of intimacy in the early modern play readily lend themselves to a psychoanalytic interpretation – or rather a reinterpretation from the perspective of a world which no longer honours spatial thresholds between differing registers of publicness and privacy.

'Is it the King?' asks Hamlet, after he has run through with his rapier the figure concealed behind the tapestry hanging. And indeed, the only person Gertrude might reputably have entertained in her closet is her husband. As if to underscore this limitation, the ghost of Hamlet's father appears 'in his nightgown' – in the kind of state of undress which only a woman's most intimate companion would be entitled to wear in such a place. In response, Hamlet fills the space of intimacy with an excess of sexually explicit accusation levelled against his mother in respect of her conduct with Claudius, accusations in which his constant invoking of the mismatch between brother and brother renders both men vividly present:

Look here upon this picture, and on this,
The counterfeit presentment of two brothers.
See what a grace was seated on this brow,
Hyperion's curls, the front of Jove himself,
An eye like Mars to threaten and command,
A station like the herald Mercury
New-lighted on a heaven-kissing hill,
A combination and a form indeed
Where every god did seem to set his seal
To give the world assurance of a man.
This was your husband. Look you now what follows.
Here is your husband, like a mildew'd ear
Blasting his wholesome brother.[14]

The effect is yet again to produce a redundancy of male presences in Gertrude's closet, competing for her personal attentions. Alongside the body of Polonius and the distressed person of her son, the physical attributes of two husbands are vividly conjured up, two consorts in the innermost space of the erotic and potentially carnal, eliciting from Hamlet the accusation: 'O shame, where is thy blush?'

What is excessive in this closet is the presence of all these men, together with the withholding of a promise of emotional (or possibly erotic) satisfaction. What the audience experiences is Gertrude's promiscuous entertaining of too many men in her inner chamber, and her reluctance to commit her loyalties except under emotional duress.

'[Hamlet's] disgust envelops and exceeds [his mother]', wrote Eliot. 'The fact that it is a woman who is seen as cause of the excess and deficiency in the play and again a woman who symbolises its aesthetic failure starts to look like a repetition', writes Rose. A troubling excess – emotions too large for the scale of the offences caused – has been a feature of all *Hamlet* criticism since Eliot's classic essay. Hamlet's 'excessive' feelings in terms of desire (inexpressible emotion) immediately make concrete and specific his mother as focus of attention for her guilt – she is pronounced guilty not as a judgement on her actions, but as a condition of her presence in the play in relation to Hamlet – faced with the impossibility of resolving the uncertainties surrounding his father's death Hamlet turns his attention instead upon his mother. If Hamlet's feeling is excessive it is because his sense of his mother's guilt exceeds what could possibly fit the facts of the plot. Or, as another critic puts it, the play's enigma is the gap between 'Hamlet's vehement disgust and the Gertrude who is neither vehement nor disgusting'.[15]

Hamlet's emotion, painfully revealed in the secrecy of the closet, concerning his mother's remarriage is 'excessive' – there is too much of it. Eliot himself related this 'too much' to an editorial argument – there is too much of what Shakespeare is thinking about to pin on to the bare bones of an inferior play by Kyd, with which he is supposedly working.

There is, however, another source of 'excess' in *Hamlet*, which conforms intriguingly closely to Rose's suggestions that 'buffoonery, ecstasy, the excessive and unknowable [are] terms in which we have learnt to recognise (since Freud at least) something necessarily present in any act of writing . . . which only suppresses them . . . at a cost'. The play-text of *Hamlet* with which we all, as critics, work is a conflation of three texts, and at its most conflated in the closet scene.

All modern editions of *Hamlet* use the second quarto of 1604 (Q2) as their core text, and incorporate material from the 1623 first folio (F), together with some material from the first 'bad' quarto of 1603 (Q1). The result is a 'conflated' text, whose component texts are succinctly described in the New Cambridge edition of the play as follows:

> Q1 is generally recognised as a 'bad' quarto: a corrupt, unauthorised version . . . of Shakespeare's play. It runs to 2,154 lines. . . . Q2 is not well printed, but is generally held to be based on Shakespeare's own manuscript, his 'foul-papers'; that is, the completed draft, as opposed to a fair copy, which he submitted to his company. This is the fullest of the three versions, 3,674 lines. . . . The third basic text is . . . the First Folio (F). A number of passages found in the second quarto, amounting to 222 lines, are omitted, but five new passages, totalling 83 lines, are added, giving a total for the play of 3,535 lines.[16]

Editorial practice is, roughly, to take the Q2 text and 'restore' to it the eighty-three lines found only in the first folio (but without deleting the 222 lines which are in Q2 but not in F), thus producing a text 3,757 lines long. A certain number of further lines and emendations are introduced on the basis of Q1. The result is a play-text which if performed in its entirety (as the Royal Shakespeare Company did in 1992) runs for nearly five hours.

Twenty-seven lines in the Q2 version of the closet scene do not occur in F, but are customarily returned to the text by the editor, thus increasing its length significantly. Almost all of these occur in Hamlet's outbursts against his mother. Largely reshaped in the folio version of the play, the restoration of the 'lost' lines from the second quarto has the effect of literally *repeating* many of the sentiments expressed. The excess and repetition to which both Eliot and Rose draw attention, in other words, are a feature of the editorial process of textual conflation and accretion as much as of the dramatist's original design. Every modern edition of *Hamlet* (including the one Eliot was using) has – literally – too much text in the scene between Hamlet and Gertrude; there is textual excess even before the critic sets to work on it. And lo and behold, what an outstandingly alert and sensitive reader like Eliot detects in the scene is excessive emotion – too much emotionally going on in the text to be sustained by the plot structure.

Excess is 'present in the act of writing' in *Hamlet* because the received text contains more than one version of the 'act of writing' the closet scene.[17] This should not, however, deter us in locating the emotional crux of the encounter between Gertrude and Hamlet here, in this scene. For we might well want to argue that it is precisely because the exchanges between them carry such a heavy emotional freight that the dramatist worked over and reworked them in successive stagings, or textual renderings of the play. In any case, it is a tribute to the critical ear of both Eliot and Rose that their insistence on the curiously repetitive and ecstatic nature of Hamlet's pronouncements is matched by the discovery that the text of *Hamlet* is at this point in the play literally excessive.

I failed to note the crucial significance of surveillance for the closet scene in *Hamlet* when I wrote critically about Gertrude previously. My rethinking of 'What happens in *Hamlet*?' begins with this acknowledgement of that in-attention. At a banal level, closets were not the focus of social historians' attention until recently; thus the possibility had been lost of identifying the specificity of location of the scene as crucial for the plot. But there is more to my current rethinking than this. I first noted the critics' unreasonable demand that Gertrude should bear the burden of guilt for Hamlet's crisis of indecision in 1983. Ten years later *Hamlet* criticism (and productions of *Hamlet*) seem mesmerisingly powerless to rid her of blame. As Rose writes elsewhere:

> What requires explanation ... is not that Gertrude is an inadequate object for the emotions generated in the play, but the fact that she is expected to support them. Hamlet's horror at Gertrude (like the horror Eliot sees behind the play) makes her a focus for a set of ills which the drama shows as exceeding the woman *at the same time* as it makes her their cause. It has often been pointed out that Hamlet's despondency seems to centre more on his mother's remarriage than it does on his father's death even after the revelation of his uncle's crime. Eliot does suggest that it is in the nature of the sentiments dealt with in *Hamlet* – a son's feelings towards a guilty mother – that they are unmanageable by art. But he does not ask why it is, in the play as in his own commentary, that the woman bears the chief burden of the guilt.[18]

When *Still Harping on Daughters* came out in 1983 it was contentious enough simply to point out that Gertrude does not deserve the critics' blame for Hamlet's tortured and confused state of mind. The question, 'What happens in *Hamlet*?' asked and answered with such patriarchal confidence by John Dover Wilson in 1935, nowadays requires a more reflective and complicated response. Once it has been pointed out that Gertrude is neither complicit in the murder of old Hamlet nor in any way in control of what has happened to the throne of Denmark, what is it that happens which makes her so enduringly dramatically culpable? The question Rose asks goes further: why does

Gertrude continue to carry the play's burden of guilt so recognisably – so convincingly – today?

I return, then, to my earlier question: what is it in our contemporary version of the tragic which (unlike Aristotle's) requires a blameless hero – a hero whose tragic predicament derives from fatal flaws in others?

I suggest that this critical shift mirrors, and perhaps takes its justification from, a prevailing political tendency to deny responsibility for the oppressed and disadvantaged of all races, genders and sexual preferences, and to transfer to them culpability for their own predicament. At the very moment at which special interest groups have finally compelled us to recognise their presence – have made themselves decisively visible – the dominant critical register (like the political one) has deftly shifted from comfortable paternalistic intolerance to a culture of downright blame.

NOTES

INTRODUCTION

1 *Still Harping on Daughters: Women and Drama in the Age of Shakespeare*, Brighton, Harvester, 1983; 2nd edn, Harvester and Columbia University Press, 1989.

2 Amongst the many pieces of academic good fortune which have allowed me to develop my thinking in rich ways (charismatic teachers, centres of excellence which encouraged freedom of thought, access to excellent, open-shelf access libraries) the one which now strikes me as the most curious (because at times it seemed more like a handicap) is the fact that I could never make up my mind which discipline I wanted to make the centre of my specialist studies. At one time it was regarded as incautious (and not properly career-minded) to have interests in history, in history of science, in neo-Latin studies and in text studies (not to mention the fact that my early training destined me for a career in science). Now I can only count myself as incredibly fortunate to have had access to studies which qualified me to be 'interdisciplinary' in a strong sense.

3 Thus Quentin Skinner showed me that some historians could see a relationship between Renaissance thought as studied by historians and as probed by literary specialists, Keith Wrightson introduced me to the new social history, and in particular drew my attention to the work of Susan Amussen, and Patrick Collinson made me aware of social historians willing to countenance dialogue with specialists in early modern text studies. Their influence during the later years of my time at Cambridge was immeasurable, and I shall always be in their debt.

4 The 'Gender and Power' session at the 1986 combined Shakespeare Association of America and International Shakespeare Association meeting in Berlin, which I co-chaired with Carol Neely, produced some spectacular confrontations (there is a bootleg tape still circulating). The most memorable alliance of feminists and new historicists in which I personally participated was a session at the 1987 Modern Languages Association meeting in San Francisco.

5 For a clear and helpful discussion which makes explicit the basis for his own new historicist work, see Stephen Greenblatt's introduction to his *Learning to Curse: Essays in Early Modern Culture*, London, Routledge, 1990.

6 See my introduction to the revised edition of *Still Harping on Daughters*, 1989. With hindsight it seems blindingly obvious that the discussions of gender and power had several overlapping agendas: our own power (or lack of it) as female Shakespeareans; the fudging of the gender issue in the works of Shakespeare, in the critical tradition, and in the SAA conference proceedings; the uncanny ease with which putting 'power' in the title of a session brought male critics eagerly into the 'gender' forum which they had previously ignored, suggesting that

marginalisation of the disempowered is understood to be universal until it is specified as marginalisation on grounds of gender. At the time, however, I don't believe that any of us (female or male) could see this.

7 Willy Maley, whose helpful comments on a draft of this introduction I grate-fully acknowledge, points out that Shakespeare stands in a confusingly different relationship to England (historically Shakespeare's nation) from the one cur-rently constructed for Britain (the United Kingdom). This point will become clearer later in this introduction.

8 Whether they really had this familiarity is, of course, another matter. Fear of being revealed as an interloper in the élite classroom contributed to Cambridge students' reluctance to confess to any ignorance of any part of Shakespeare's work.

9 It was Carol Neely who first pointed out to me how privileged my position as a teacher was in this respect. I had thanked the students in my Shakespeare seminar for remarks they had made on a draft of the paper I gave at the SAA; she observed that no group of students to whom she taught Shakespeare would have had the confidence to comment on a professor's specialist (and theoreti-cally sophisticated) paper on a Shakespeare play.

10 *Henry V*, Oxford Shakespeare edn, Gary Taylor (ed.), Oxford, Oxford Univer-sity Press, 1982, 4.3.35–6. Conservative Party Conference, 10 October 1989.

11 Anthony Lewis, 'A disaster slogging towards a climax', *International Herald Tribune*, 14–15 August 1993.

12 This box-office success was confined to North America. The film flopped in Britain, finishing sixty-fourth in 1989's top-grossing films in the UK and taking a mere £664,727 (J. Rumbold, 'Profile of Kenneth Branagh', *The Guardian*, 9 November 1992).

13 Kenneth Branagh, *Henry V: A Screen Adaptation*, London, Chatto & Windus, 1989, p. 105.

14 Branagh also wanted his *Henry V* to be a 'truly popular film. The audience that wants to see *Rambo* could also be stimulated by *Henry V*' (Rumbold, 'Profile').

15 The folio text contains the choruses, the opening scene with the plotting clergy and a number of other portions of text which, it has been argued, were 'censored' from the quarto text. See Taylor, pp. 12–26 for the full discussion. A story is needed here from one of my 'other lives': I confess that I did not at first see the significance of the missing 'shame' passage. As I drafted my intro-duction to this book, I simply moved on in my argument to my suspicion that the *International Herald Tribune* writer had the Branagh film in mind, rather than the play-text. Shortly thereafter, however, I took part in a BBC radio discussion on the canonical significance of Shakespeare's *Henry V*, and gave a copy of my draft introduction to the programme's presenter, Paul Allen. It was he who drew my attention to Taylor's piece of buccaneering editing: he was using another edition, and commented on the mismatch between our texts.

16 For an elegant account of this Williamsite version of cultural centrality, which also takes *Henry V* as its text, see G. Holderness, '"What ish my nation?": Shakespeare and national identities', *Textual Practice*, 1991, vol. 5, pp. 74–93.

17 Willy Maley points out that in the film, Kenneth Branagh, an Irishman from Belfast, plays a Welshman (Henry Tudor) playing a proto-British/English King.

18 Stephen Greenblatt, *Shakespearean Negotiations: The Circulation of Social Energy in Renaissance England*, Oxford, Clarendon Press, 1988, p. 1.

19 I am told by members of the Royal Shakespeare Company that Prince Charles was moved to tears by Kenneth Branagh's original stage performance as Henry V, which he attended at Stratford-upon-Avon incognito (something he appar-ently does comparatively often).

20 In 1994 a prominent tea company put out a television commercial which won

public acclaim (a letter from a visiting American in the *Evening Standard* news-paper pronouncing it the most moving evocation of the beauty of Britain she had encountered during her trip, for example) and at least one award. Over serene and sumptuous images of the English countryside an actor reads John of Gaunt's 'this royal throne of kings, this sceptred isle' speech from Act 2 of *Richard II* . . . only the closing line, 'this earth, this realm, this England' has become 'this earth, this realm, this Britain'. On the steady confusion in British ideology of the 'England' which Shakespeare steadily celebrates, and the 'Britain' he is called upon anachronistically to champion in the modern era, see Willy Maley, '"This sceptred isle": Shakespeare and the British problem', in J. Joughin (ed.), *Shakespeare and National Culture*, Manchester, Manchester University Press, forthcoming.

21 Two classic versions of this 'fissured' version of the play from the recent literature are Greenblatt's 'Invisible bullets: Renaissance authority and its subversion, *Henry IV* and *Henry V*', in J. Dollimore and A. Sinfield (eds), *Political Shakespeare: New Essays in Cultural Materialism*, Manchester, Manchester University Press, 1985, pp. 18–47, and Alan Sinfield and Jonathan Dollimore's 'History and ideology, masculinity and miscegenation: the instance of *Henry V*', in A. Sinfield (ed.), *Faultlines: Cultural Materialism and the Politics of Dissident Reading*, Oxford, Clarendon Press, 1992, pp. 109–42.

22 5.2.95–7.

23 5.2.12–20.

24 5.2.316–32.

25 In the related play, *The Famous Victories of Henry the Fifth: Containing the Honourable Battell of Agin-court*, the Dauphin is forced to kneel to Henry and swear fealty in the final scene. See Gary Taylor, Oxford edn, p. 27.

26 At the end of *Twelfth Night*, for instance, the marriage of brother and sister (Sebastian and Viola) to the two independent landowners Olivia and Orsino effects the alliance which Olivia's refusal of Orsino's suit made impossible. Olivia and Orsino are now kin; their estates are bound together by the bonds each has formed with a young, desirable, well-born person (Olivia breaks the news of her marriage to Orsino in these terms: 'think me as well a sister, as a wife, / One day shall crown th'alliance on't, so please you' (5.1.316–17)). In terms of 'blood' and 'kinship', Viola's blood is absorbed into Orsino's line (their children will be heirs to his lands), Olivia's lineage is subordinated to Sebastian's (but his youth and the fact that he is a stranger leaves her line in control). *Twelfth Night*, Arden edn, J. M. Lothian and T. W. Craik (eds), London, Methuen, 1975.

27 5.2.1–10.

28 5.2.196–208.

29 A promise to wed in the presence of a witness (here Alice) was considered binding. See Lorna Hutson, *The Usurer's Daughter*, London, Routledge, 1994, pp. 82–3. But of course here Kate is part of the matter being discussed formally elsewhere, under the terms of the treaty being negotiated: 'Yet leave our cousin Catherine here with us. / She is our capital demand, comprised / Within the fore-rank of our articles' (5.2.95–7).

30 Actually, since Henry insists on his Welshness at several points in the play, the baby will be half-Welsh half-French. Henry also claims Saint George rather than Saint David as his patron saint, although Fluellen regards Henry as a suitable leek-wearer – i.e. as a son of Saint David.

31 Lorna Hutson points out to me that one of Anne Clifford's arguments in support of her right as sole (female) heir to inherit her family's estates (rather than her uncles) was that in marriage her own family blood was a pure stream

which did not mingle with that of either of the husbands she married. This argument was not accepted: once a woman married the blood of the female line was legally understood to merge completely, creating the fiction of a continuing 'pure' male line. Anne Clifford thoroughly embarrasses the legal establishment by drawing attention to the fact that whichever way you choose to look at it, female blood does in fact persist. On Anne Clifford see E. Graham, H. Hinds, E. Hoby and H. Wilcox (eds), *Her Own Life: Autobiographical Writings by Seventeenth-Century Englishwomen*, London, Routledge, 1989, pp. 35–53.

32 Sinfield and Dollimore pick up on the significance of this 'taint' when they suggest that the wooing scenes in *Henry V* emphasise the compulsion Catherine is under, and the fact that her 'conquest' is the 'reward and final validation of Henry's manliness, the symbol of enforced French submission' ('History and ideology', p. 137).

33 A Princeton undergraduate and star member of the college basketball team commented in class that he enjoyed the play as a whole, and admired Henry greatly, but he wished he had not behaved in such a 'girly' way in the wooing scene.

34 Its dramatic function is to show her eagerness to be conquered. In addition, the language lesson naturalises the English language as *the* language of the nation which Henry heads, even though a scene earlier the humour has turned on the competing languages of Welsh, Irish and Scots 'Englishmen'. In fact, the vernacular language of Henry V's court was French, so Shakespeare's 'lesson' is a deliberate anachronism.

35 3.5.27–31.

36 3.4.44–54.

37 As Alan Stewart points out to me, the child of Henry and Kate didn't turn out too well, either – he 'lost France and made his England bleed'. Taylor comments that Catherine is called *madame* nine times in this scene (Oxford edn, p. 182).

38 That is, the English are descendants of the Norman invaders of 1066. Note that there is no suggestion that Norman *men* might have hybridised their line by cross-breeding with English *women*.

39 3.5.5–9.

40 See p. 5.

41 4.5.10–15.

42 3.3.63. For a full exploration of the significance of 'nation' in this scene and its thematic prominence in the play as a whole, see Maley, '"This sceptred isle"'. Maley points out that the *real* enemy in *Henry V* is Ireland, not France, as is also the case in *Lear* (in the source, Cordelia marries the king of Hibernia – Ireland – not France). Around 1600, though, Ireland was a very touchy subject. See also Holderness, '"What ish my nation?"'; Philip Edwards, *Threshold of a Nation: A Study of English and Irish Drama*, Cambridge, Cambridge University Press, 1979.

43 On types of lineage and the various strategies for assuring lineal integrity see David Herlihy, *Medieval Households*, Cambridge, Mass., Harvard University Press, 1985, pp. 82–98.

44 Down to the present day the eldest son of the reigning British monarch is the Prince of Wales.

45 None of them risks claiming Ireland – and there are several explicit references to Ireland's having been Richard II's downfall.

46 A. R. Humphreys (ed.), *The First Part of King Henry IV*, Arden edn, London, Methuen, 1960, 3.1.189 ff.

47 1.2.65–89. I think it is this punctuation of familiar male lines with obscure

women's names to which the audience would have been expected to respond. That in itself confirms the sophistry of the Archbishop's argument rather than following the reasoning itself, which, as Gary Taylor suggests, is too convoluted for stage success.

48 5.2.166–72.

49 E. W. Tillyard's influential *Shakespeare's History Plays*, London, Chatto & Windus, 1944, is a striking example of such 'war effort' criticism.

50 See Sinfield, *Faultlines*; G. Holderness (ed.), *The Shakespeare Myth*, Manchester, Manchester University Press, 1988; Holderness, *Shakespeare Recycled: the Making of Historical Drama*, Brighton, Harvester, 1992; L. Aers and N. Wheale (eds), *Shakespeare in the Changing Curriculum*, London, Routledge, 1991.

51 Terence Hawkes, *That Shakespeherian Rag: Essays in Critical Process*, London, Methuen, 1986; G. Holderness, 'Agincourt 1944: readings in the Shakespeare myth', *Literature and History*, 1984, vol. 10, pp. 24–45.

52 Thus the essay on Shakespeare's learned heroines began as two pieces of research on real fifteenth-century women humanists: 'Isotta Nogarola: woman humanists – education for what?', *History of Education*, 1983, vol. 12, pp. 231–44; and '"O decus Italiae virgo" or, the myth of the learned lady in the Renaissance', *The Historical Journal*, 1985, vol. 28, pp. 799–819.

53 S. Zimmerman, *Erotic Politics: Desire on the Renaissance Stage*, London, Routledge, 1992.

54 'Fiction and friction', in T. C. Heller, M. Sosna and D. E. Wellbery (eds), *Reconstructing Individualism: Autonomy, Individuality, and the Self in Western Thought*, Stanford, Stanford University Press, 1986, pp. 30–52.

55 For my own practice as a historian see most recently *Erasmus, Man of Letters: The Construction of Charisma in Print*, Princeton, Princeton University Press, 1993.

1 'WHY SHOULD HE CALL HER WHORE?'

1 M. R. Ridley (ed.), *Othello*, Arden edn, London, Methuen, 1958, 4.2.139–40.

2 For a similar insistence on studies like the present one as part of an emerging interdiscipline rather than a series of borrowings by literary studies from adjacent disciplines, see S. Mullaney, *The Place of the Stage: License, Play and Power in Renaissance England*, Chicago, University of Chicago Press, 1988, pp. x–xii.

3 Most infamously in L. Tennenhouse, *Power on Display: The Politics of Shakespeare's Genres*, London, Methuen, 1986, p. 127.

4 In this respect, the present work is of a piece with other work in social history and textual studies which focuses attention on the way in which categories of persons outside the dominant élite have been excluded from traditional historical types of explanation. See e.g. the introduction to K. Wrightson, *English Society 1580–1680*, London, Hutchinson, 1982, p. 11.

5 I am conscious that such a type of investigation is crucially related to recent work in social anthropology. See, in particular, V. W. Turner and E. M. Bruner (eds), *The Anthropology of Experience*, Champaign, Illinois, University of Illinois Press, 1986, especially Bruner's introductory essay, 'Experience and its expressions' (pp. 3–30).

6 *Othello*, 2.1.167–79.

7 The play on words is never, as far as I am aware, commented on by editors of the play, though it is precisely the same joke as the one made at Cressida's expense in *Troilus and Cressida* (4.5.54–63): '*Ulysses*. Fie, fie upon her! / There's language in her eye, her cheek, her lip – / Nay, her foot speaks; her wanton spirits look out / At every joint and motive of her body. / O, these

encounterers, so glib of tongue, / That give accosting welcome ere it comes, / And wide unclasp the tables of their thoughts / To every ticklish reader: set them down / For sluttish spoils of opportunity / And daughters of the game. [*Flourish.*] / *All.* The Trojan's trumpet'. Kenneth Palmer's footnote in the Arden edition (London, Methuen, 1982) runs: 'Delius is obviously right: it is for Hector's trumpet that the Greeks have been waiting. A. P. Rossiter suggested the "knavish device" of aural ambiguity – the cry could certainly be heard as The Trojan strumpet – but the trumpet call is what modulates the scene, from facetious comment and moral distaste, on the one hand, to serious chivalric action, on the other' (*Angel with Horns and other Essays* (ed. G. Storey), London, Longman, 1961, pp. 247–8). In other words, Palmer both acknowledges the innuendo and brushes it aside as irrelevant. See also *The Merchant of Venice* 5.1.122 (and the insinuating response, 'We are no tell-tales madam').

8 See S. Kappeler, *The Pornography of Representation*, Cambridge, Polity Press, 1986. This is also, I think, what Coppélia Kahn highlights in her work on the pressure of male fantasy as a deterministic discourse in Shakespeare's plays (*Man's Estate: Masculine Identity in Shakespeare*, Berkeley, California, University of California Press, 1981).

9 Retrieve, because the pursuit of such an 'agent' as the residual trace of 'lived experience' in text and document has been the constant goal of Left criticism committed to the theoretical positions of Raymond Williams and E. P. Thompson; but most of this work has not been done on early modern material. See J. Swindells and L. Jardine, *What's Left? Women in Culture and the Labour Movement*, London, Routledge, 1989.

10 There is a nice example of just this distinction in *Hamlet*, Arden edn, Harold Jenkins (ed.), London, Methuen, 1982. During the 'Mousetrap' performance, after the Player Queen has declaimed long and passionately on the wickedness of second marriage ('In second husband let me be accurst; / None wed the second but who kill'd the first' (3.2.174–5)), a topic naturally bound to offend Gertrude, Claudius asks Hamlet, 'Have you heard the argument [do you know the plot of the play]? Is there no offence in't?' 'No, no', replies Hamlet, 'they do but jest – poison in jest. No offence i' th' world' (3.2.227–30). Offensive, possibly; but no real crime is committed.

11 There is a literature going back some way on 'slander' in this play and others, but I am arguing for a more precise distinction than has hitherto been made between utterance (text) and occasion (what I am calling 'event').

12 A. L. Rowse, *Sex and Society in Shakespeare's Age: Simon Forman the Astrologer*, New York, Scribner, 1974, p. 20. Rowse comments that this dream 'has a wider, an anthropological significance: it throws a shaft of light, as nothing else that I know, into the erotic stimulus that the menfolk derived from having a Virgin Queen upon the throne' (my emphasis). This seems to me right – it is men who 'derive the erotic stimulus' from any event in which the Queen figures. Forman's dream cit. L. Montrose, ' "Shaping fantasies": figurations of gender and power in Elizabethan culture', *Representations*, 1983, vol. 2, pp. 61–94, at pp. 62–3.

13 H. de Maisse, *A Journal of all that was accomplished by Monsieur de Maisse Ambassador in England from King Henri IV to Queen Elizabeth Anno Domini 1597*, trans. G. B. Harrison and R. A. Jones, London, Nonesuch Press, 1931, pp. 25–6. The French text is unavailable in print, but fortunately large extracts are reprinted in L. A. Prevost-Paradol, *Elisabeth et Henri IV (1595–1598): Ambassade de Hurault de Maisse en Angleterre au sujet de la paix de Vervins*, Paris, Durand, 1855. The relevant passage here runs: 'Elle avait le devant de sa robe en manteau ouvert et luy voyoit-on toute la gorge et assez bas et souvent, comme si elle eust eu trop chaud, elle eslargissoit avec les mains le devant dudict manteau . . . sa gorge se

montre assez ridée, autant que (la laissoit veoir) le carcan qu'elle portoit au col, mais plus bas elle a encore la charnure fort blanche et fort déliée autant que l'on eust peu veoir' (*Journal*, pp. 240, 241; cit. Prevost-Paradol, p. 151). 'Gorge' here surely means 'throat' rather than 'bosom' (see Robert and Huguet dictionaries), since the elaborate choker necklace she wears largely conceals it. English text cit. in part Montrose, '"Shaping fantasies"', p. 63.

14 de Maisse, pp. 36–7; the relevant passage in French runs: 'Une robe dessous de damas blanc, ceinte et ouverte devant, aussy bien que sa chemise, tellement qu'elle ouvrait souvent cette robe et luy voyait-on tout l'estomac jusques au nombril . . . elle a cette façon qu'en rehaussant la teste elle met les deux mains à sa robe et l'entrouvre, tellement qu'on luy veoit tout l'estomac' (*Journal*, p. 256; cit. Prevost-Paradol, p. 155). It is not clear here whether what is revealed is *décolleté* or stomacher (on the dress of black taffeta, over which the over-dress of white damask is worn) but it is clear that de Maisse is disturbed by the gestures of revealing. In a third audience Elizabeth once again wears an embroidered over-dress, this time over a white dress embroidered with silver, 'Echancrée fort bas et le sein descouvert' (*Journal*, p. 279; cit. Prevost-Paradol, p. 168). At the fourth and final audience, 'Elle estoit ce jour-là habillee de toile d'argent comme de coustume, ou gaze, que nous appelons en françois; sa robe estant blanche et la sapronelle de soye d'or de couleur viollette. Elle avoit une très-grande quantité de bagues sur elle tant sur la tête qu'au dedans de son collet, à l'entour des bras et aux mains, avec une très-grande quantité de perles, tant autour du col qu'en bracelets, et avait deux carcans, un à chaque bras, qui estoient de fort grand prix' (*Journal*, p. 316; cit. Prevost-Paradol, pp.180–1). In this last case Elizabeth's dress is clearly high-fronted (since the 'very great quantities' of jewels around her neck hang over her collar) – it is anything lower than this which draws the ambassador's attention. English of first passage cit. in part Montrose, '"Shaping fantasies"', p. 64.

15 Montrose, '"Shaping fantasies"', p. 64.

16 In fact, it turns out to belong to the twentieth-century English translation of de Maisse's diary far more than to the original French, although one would still want to take note of Hurault de Maisse's difficulty with the breach of decorum (in his terms) of a woman of Elizabeth's age receiving him with anything other than a gown which entirely concealed her body.

17 See for instance the illustrations in Lyndal Roper, 'Discipline and respectability: prostitution and the Reformation in Augsburg', *History Workshop*, 1985, vol. 19, pp. 3–28. 'Respectability' is probably a good term, historically, to describe what is going on (undermining it) in the late sixteenth-century passages describing Elizabeth.

18 See Roper, 'Discipline and respectability', p. 20. And see in particular Diane O. Hughes's compelling account of Italian sumptuary laws assigning extravagant dress exclusively to prostitutes as a badge of their trade, and as a disincentive to 'honest' women's wearing lavish clothing (D. O. Hughes, 'Distinguishing signs: ear-rings, Jews and Franciscan rhetoric in the Italian renaissance city', *Past and Present*, 1986, vol. 112, pp. 3–59). See also polemicists like Stubbs, who also suggest that all women who wear extravagant dress are potentially whores. Warren Boutcher gives me another example from Florio's translation of Montaigne's *Essais*. Florio renders Montaigne's description (in the essay 'De l'institution des enfans') of Angelique, 'vestue en garce, coiffee d'vn attifet emperle' as 'disguised and drest about the head like vnto an impudent harlot, with embroyderies, frizelings, and carcanets of pearles' (French from E. Courbet and C. Royer (eds), *Les essais de Montaigne* (5 vols), Paris, Lemerre, 1872–1900, I, p. 198; English from J. Florio, *The Essayes of Morall, Politike and*

Militarie Discourses of Lo: Michaell de Montaigne, London, J. Simms, 1603, sig. H3r).
The English makes finery inappropriate to rank figure for 'impudent harlot[ry]'.

19 The soiled smock of the Forman passage is a standard euphemism for sexual (or at least moral) laxity and sluttishness; see e.g. *Piers Plowman*.

20 Throughout this chapter I use 'equivalent' in inverted commas, to remind the reader that when words 'weigh equally' it may not mean that there is an identity between the events the text recalls.

21 And that is the point the critic wishes to make in the article in question. So although I am drawing attention to problems for my way of approaching Shakespeare historically, in this kind of juxtaposition I am not commenting on the argument in the context of an investigation of 'figurations of gender and power' which argues the case that the Queen's 'pervasive [female] cultural presence was a condition of the play's imaginative possibility'.

22 Rowse (op. cit., pp. 66–7) gives us a clear indication of what kinds of 'event' did occasion it: 'That morning Forman arrested Sefton [a cleric, with whom Forman was engaged in protracted lawsuits] for the money he had lent him, "and I had a silver bowl for my money". When Forman went to the Queen's Attorney, "he entreated me to stay the matter. And after I went to Avis Allen [with whom he is sexually involved]." He was with her the next day, and on the 20th, "but did not halek [have sex] but spake with her". He himself put the question whether it were best to leave her or no, "and not to continue her love in hope", i.e. of marriage. It was at this time, 23 January 1597, that he had his suggestive dream of the Queen.'

23 See the Lutheran whore of Babylon woodcut in Roper, 'Discipline and respectability'.

24 Here it is instructive, as is so often the case, to listen to the anthropologists. In 'Does the concept of the person vary cross-culturally?', Shweder and Boume summarise the problems encountered by western analyses of non-western selves (citing Geertz on Bali, Read on the Gahuku-Gama and Dumont on India) as follows: 'How are we to interpret this widespread mode of social thought in which the individual is not differentiated from the role [with intentional theatrical connotations], and where the person achieves no abstract, context-independent recognition?' (R. A. Shweder and R. A. LeVine (eds), *Culture Theory: Essays on Mind, Self, and Emotion*, Cambridge, Cambridge University Press, 1984, pp. 158–99, at p. 168). See also Michelle Rosaldo, 'Towards an anthropology of self and feeling': 'Cultural idioms provide the images in terms of which our subjectivities are formed, and, furthermore, these idioms themselves are socially ordered and constrained. . . . Society . . . shapes the self through the medium of cultural terms, which shape the understanding of reflective actors. It follows that in so far as our psychology is wedded to our culture's terms in its accounts of people elsewhere in the world, it is unlikely to appreciate their deeds' (Shweder and LeVine, *Culture Theory*, pp. 137–57, at p. 150). Scrutinising the textual remains of early modern England, we search for subjectivity in our own cultural terms, and fail to appreciate women's deeds.

25 Although the text is not explicit as to Bianca's place of origin, I would argue that it is crucial to the play that Bianca might be described as a 'whore of Venice' (the phrase used by Othello to insult Desdemona, and a popular Renaissance 'type'). Bianca has a household in Cyprus and is Cassio's established courtesan. For a near contemporary account incorporating all the popular stereotype features, see T. Coryate, *Coryate's Crudities* . . . (2 vols), London, William Stansby, 1611; repr. James MacLeHose, Glasgow, 1905, vol. 1, pp. 401–9. On Venetian courtesans see particularly C. Santore, 'Julia Lombardo, "somtuosa

meretrize": a portrait by property', *Renaissance Quarterly*, 1988, vol. 41, pp. 44–83; A. Barzhagi, *Donne o cortigiane? la prostituzione a Venezia documenti di costume dal XVI al XVIII secolo*, Verona, Bertani, 1980; S. Chojnacki, 'La posizione della donna a Venezia nel cinquecento', in *Tiziano e Venezia: convegno internazionale di studi*, Neri Pozza (ed.), Venice, Neri Pozza, 1980, pp. 65–70.

26 This is an alteration of the source story, in which Emilia's rank is higher. The social distance between them is carefully charted in the play in their relationships to the talismanic handkerchief. The intricately embroidered piece is a gift to Desdemona from Othello (who had it from either his mother or his father – in either case it draws attention to Desdemona's acquisition of wealth/goods with marriage (see M. Spufford, *The Great Reclothing of Rural England: Petty Chapmen and their Wares in the Seventeenth Century*, London, Hambledon, 1984)); finding it by chance, Emilia decides to have the work copied to please her husband, who (she thinks) admires it – an act of service which confirms her subordinate, serving status; passed to Bianca by Cassio with the request that she copy the needlework, the gentlewomanly but morally dubious courtesan is outraged (not just that Cassio might have another mistress, but that she be taken for a servant, or a casual prostitute (see Roper, 'Discipline and respectability', for the association with needlework)).

27 Apart from the claim that Desdemona has committed adultery with Cassio, Emilia has been accused of adultery with Othello, and Bianca (although professionally a courtesan) is accused of running a bawdy house and whoring by Iago and Emilia (see p. 30).

28 By 'ordinary' I mean to indicate the fact that the middling sort (women and men) had regular recourse to the ecclesiastical courts in this period. See C. B. Herrup, *The Common Peace: Participation and the Criminal Law in Seventeenth-Century England*, Cambridge, Cambridge University Press, 1987; J. A. Sharpe, *Crime in Early Modern England 1550–1750*, London, Longman, 1984, Chapter 2, 'Courts, officers and documents'; M. Ingram, 'Ecclesiastical Justice in Wiltshire 1600–1640 with special reference to cases involving sex and marriage', unpublished D.Phil. thesis, University of Oxford, 1976.

29 On defamation depositions see J. Sharpe, *Defamation and Sexual Slander in Early Modern England: The Church Courts at York*, Borthwick Papers, 58, York, Universities of York and St Andrew's, 1980. I am grateful to Jim Sharpe for verbal comments on a draft of this paper delivered at the 1987 HETE conference at Canterbury. See also P. Hair, *Before the Bawdy Court: Selections from Church Court and Other Records relating to the Correction of Moral Offences in England, Scotland and New England 1300–1800*, London, Elek, 1972, pp. 256–8; Ingram, 'Ecclesiastical Justice'; R. A. Marchant, *The Church under the Law: Justice, Administration, and Discipline in the Diocese of York, 1560–1640*, Cambridge, Cambridge University Press, 1969; C. A. Haigh, 'Slander and the church courts in the sixteenth century', *Transactions of the Lancashire and Cheshire Antiquarian Society*, 1975, vol. 78, pp. 1–13; R. C. Dunhill, 'Seventeenth century invective: defamation cases as a source for word study', *Devon and Cornwall Notes and Queries*, 1976, vol. 33, pp. 49–51.

30 S. Amussen, 'Gender, family and social order, 1560–1725', in A. Fletcher and J. Stevenson (eds), *Order and Disorder in Early Modern England*, Cambridge, Cambridge University Press, 1985, pp. 196–217, at p. 208. Amussen's article usefully shows the gendering of offences against the social in the Norfolk records. Sharpe, *Defamation*, suggests that in the York records the discrepancy between female and male sexual slurs arises only in the seventeenth century: 'A total of 1,638 cases for defamation are known to have entered the Consistory court in the 1590s, of which 49 per cent involved male plaintiffs and 51 per cent female.

565 such cases entered the Consistory in the 1690s, of which only 24 per cent involved male plaintiffs.'

31 Sharpe, *Defamation*, p. 15.

32 See M. Ingram, 'Ridings, rough music and mocking rhymes in early modern England', in B. Reay (ed.), *Popular Culture in Seventeenth Century England*, London, Croom Helm, 1985, pp. 166–97; Roper, 'Discipline and respectability'; Roper, '"Going to church and street": weddings in Reformation Augsburg', *Past and Present*, 1985, vol. 106, pp. 62–101.

33 *Depositions and other Ecclesiastical Proceedings from the Courts of Durham, extending from 1311 to the reign of Elizabeth*, London, The Publications of the Surtees Society, 1845, p. 89. By contrast, on 4 May 1568 Jasper Arkle of Gosforth made a deposition for defamation against Martin Atchuson, claiming that Atchuson had said publicly 'that he wittinglye solde one stolne shepe skyn in the towne of Newcastell' (p. 89). I am extremely grateful to Keith Wrightson who launched me on the ecclesiastical court records, and continues to give me advice and support in the project of bringing together literature and history in the early modern period.

34 *Depositions*, p. 89.

35 *Depositions*, p. 104.

36 The *OED* gives as an instance of the use of the obsolete 'naughtie packe' the 1540 translation of Vives' *Instruction of the Christian Woman*: 'Call hir a naughtie packe: with that one woorde thou haste taken all from hir, and haste lefte hir bare and foule.' For the 'whore' insinuation in the original 'noughtie pak' see e.g. *A Collection of Seventy-Nine Black-Letter Ballads and Broadsides, Printed in the Reign of Queen Elizabeth, Between the Years 1559 and 1597*, London, Joseph Lilly, 1867, p. 194: 'At Maydstone in Kent there was one Marget Mere, daughter to Richard Mere, of the sayd towne of Maydstone, who being vnmaryed, played the naughty packe, and was gotten with childe, being deliuered of the said childe the xxiiij. daye of October last past, in the yeare of our Lord 1568, at vij. of the clocke in the afternoone of the same day, being Sonday' (the child is a monstrous birth, revealing the mother's sinful behaviour). I am grateful to Carolyn Whitney-Brown for drawing my attention to this example. Ian Archer confirms for me that in the Bridewell records the phrase 'naughty pack' is consistently used as a synonym for 'whore', e.g. *Bridewell Court Book I*, fol. 62: Lewse Hochyn, 'a naughty packe' committing whoredom is punished, and Ellyn Holt, 'a lewd, naughty pack' who 'as a "bribyng drab" went in the name of Nicholas Williams of the Chamber with whom she dwelt, to a butcher for a shoulder of mutton and a breast of veal', likewise (Ian Archer, personal communication, November 1987).

37 *Depositions*, pp. 90–1.

38 See N. Davis, *Fiction in the Archives: Pardon Tales and their Tellers in Sixteenth-Century France*, Cambridge, Polity Press, 1988, for a similar argument about pardon tales. Where depositions survive for the supposed slanderer, they invariably try to undermine the character of the person supposedly defamed.

39 There is a striking example in the Durham records of the inside/outside of the house boundary being breached, and drawing 'outsiders' into a case of wife abuse (then, as now, customarily treated as 'private') (*Depositions*, pp. 97–8): 'Ex parte Agnetis Carr adversus Thomam Carr, maritum suum. WILLIAM BAYKER, of the city of Durham, yoman, aged about 40 years. This examinate was in Durham that present day, when the parties and all their compeny cam home with them frome their mariadge here to Durham, wher they dwelt as man and wif togither, by the common report of the people. Mary, this examinate was not present at their mariadge. He saith that he belyvith that Thomas Carr,

articulate, haith not used nor entretyd the said Agnes, his wyf, as an honestman ought to have doon; for this examinate was personally present at one tyme, enspeciall when the parties had bein at the lawe, and the said Thomas then commanndyd to take hir, the said Agnes his wyfe, home with hym, and to use hir as he aught to doo; and immediatlie after ther home commynge quietly togither, according as thei were comandyd, this examinate, and one John Woodmose, was doon to the market-place, and commyng by the said Carr's doore, the said Agnes was wepinge and sore lammentyng, sainge that hir said husband Thomas wold not suffer hir to tarye that night with hym in his house here in Durham, but comandyd hir then, being towerd night, to goo to Feildehouse, which she said she wolde nott. And at this examinate's coming home he founde the said Agnes in his owne house in the Balye. And, after moch talke that this examinate and his wyf had with hir, this deponent came doon in the streit again to hir said husband Thomas Carr, and reasoned with hym, mervalinge moch that he wold not use and intreit his said wyf accordinge as he was commandyd. And was then well content, saing yt was not well doon to put hir out of his house towerd night frome hym self, which Thomas Car gave this examinate so light and short annswers in such angre and greiff, that this examinate therupon thougth veryly, and yett doith, that he, the said Thomas, had moch misused his wyf; and further to this article he canott depose upon his own knowledg. Mary, the said Agnes, with weping eies, haith affirmed all the resydew of this article to be trewe to this examinate and his wyfe, saing, hir said husband had not used hir as his wyfe, nor wolde sufer hir aither to gyve hym meat and drinck, or take hir self any, but used [her] worse and a servannt, and had hir meat gyvon by a youngwoman one of the said Thomas maid servaunts. Signum + w. BAIKER.'

40 *Othello*, 4.2.81–96.

41 'Would-be copulators', according to Ridley's Arden note.

42 4.2.117–23.

43 4.2.139–40. It is also telling that it should be Emilia who circulates the defamation, like the 'wyfes of the Close'. As the 'low' female servant character in the play, she both loyally supports her mistress and contributes to her undoing (as also in the 'willow' scene).

44 Desdemona's oath on her knees (but only to Iago) that she has never been unchaste 'either in discourse of thought or actual deed' (4.2.155) further emphasises the seriousness of what has happened.

45 4.2.139–49. Ridley, the Arden editor, comments: 'This disposes of any idea that Iago's suspicions of Othello ... were figments, invented during momentary "motive-hunting" and dismissed. They have been real, and lasting, enough for him to challenge Emilia' (*Othello*, Arden edn, p. 159). For the early twentieth-century critic also, apparently, occasions for sexual jealousy are 'actual' as long as they are produced as 'actual' defamation. On Ridley's general tendency to betray deep-seated patriarchal attitudes see L. Jardine, *Still Harping on Daughters: Women and Drama in the Age of Shakespeare*, Brighton, Harvester, 1983, pp. 119–20.

46 5.1.115–24.

47 An interesting piece of supporting material comes here from Santore, 'Julia Lombardo': Julia Lombardo goes to court against a public charge of 'whoring', which is at odds with her comparatively elevated status as courtesan (and would imply loss of important privileges).

48 Thus the defamation links back to the first part of this chapter. In *Still Harping on Daughters* I noted the intrusion in the 'willow scene' of the observation, 'This Lodovico is a proper man', which reintroduces the sensual and 'flaws the "innocence" which a modern audience looks for in Desdemona' (p. 75). The

secondary sense of 'proper' (a manly man) harks back to 1.3.390–6, where it is Cassio whom Iago describes as 'a proper man', and therefore susceptible to an accusation of adultery: 'After some time, to abuse Othello's ear, / That he is too familiar with his wife: / He has a person and a smooth dispose, / To be suspected, fram'd to make women false'.

49 I consider the careful counter-currents of innocence, essential for the final tragic denouement ('Let nobody blame him, his scorn I approve'), in *Still Harping on Daughters*, pp. 184–5.

50 It is particularly poignant that at the opening of 4.2 – immediately prior to the defamation – Othello entirely disregards Emilia's careful laying of evidence by testimony, that she has never seen Desdemona behave suspiciously with Cassio, ending, 'if she be not honest, chaste, and true, . . . the purest of her sex / Is foul as slander' (4.2.17–19). At this point in the play (before the 'case' against Desdemona has been framed as a defamation) such testimony is not sufficient to Othello's jealous demand for 'ocular proof'.

51 See, for instance, 5.2.230, where Iago's response to Emilia's testimony against him is the insult, 'Villainous whore!'

52 4.2.120–1, 163–4. This further highlights the dramatic intensity of the accidental overhearing by Emilia: since Desdemona cannot bring herself to utter the word 'whore', she would never have circulated the charge – as Emilia so energetically does – outside the hearth. This genteel decorum also ensures that from this point on Desdemona is no longer vulnerable to the suspicion of implicit 'knowingness' which was part of the pervasive innuendo of the earlier part of the play (contrast 2.1.109–66 with 5.3.35–105, where Emilia is 'knowing' and Desdemona refrains (apart from that first, triggering reminiscence in 'That Lodovico is a proper [sexy] man')). See Jardine, *Still Harping on Daughters*, pp. 119–20, 75. It has been suggested to me that the decorum of her rank requires that one of her male kin act to clear her name; that it would indeed be unseemly for her to lodge the kind of deposition (as it were) that the rural artisanal woman pronounced. This suggestion is supported by the fact that after Desdemona's death it is specified (irrelevantly, in terms of other plot concerns) how isolated and remote Desdemona was from the protection of any male kin (Gratiano and Lodovico are specified in the dramatis personae as brother and kinsman to Brabantio, respectively), apart from her husband: *Othello* 'I scarce did know you, uncle, there lies your niece . . .' *Gratiano* 'Poor Desdemona, I am glad thy father's dead; / Thy match was mortal to him, and pure grief / Shore his old thread atwain' (5.2.205–7). In 4.1 Lodovico is involved in the incident in which Othello strikes his wife – another type of 'inside' domestic incident between man and wife which once 'outside', the court records show, may require formal action (see above, note 39). But he does not intervene, in spite of his elaborate sustaining of courtesy towards Desdemona, when Othello has dropped all 'good forms'.

53 *Depositions*, pp. 252–3.

54 For a carefully argued account of exploration of the past through 'document' and literary text which agrees with my own see Natalie Davis, '"On the Lame"', *American Historical Review*, 1988, vol. 93, pp. 572–603.

55 Natalie Davis points out that in early modern France 'jealousy' is a demeaning emotion, which is therefore never admissible as justification when male suppliants make pleas for pardon in letters of remission in the public records (*Fiction in the Archives*: 'A peasant wife threw stones at her husband's lover "de chaulde colle", but also "by force of jealousy" ("par force de la jallosie"), thereby mentioning an emotion which men did not admit in slaying their adulterous wives or their wives' lovers. A husband merely said, with a merchant apothecary

of Tours, that he "had previously forbidden his wife the company of the said Estienne". Honor and obedience were at stake for him, not demeaning jealousy."). I am extremely grateful to Professor Natalie Davis, who commented on an early draft of this chapter, and allowed me to see the relevant sections of *Fiction in the Archives* in manuscript. On the punishment of adultery in early modern England see K. Thomas, 'The puritans and adultery; the act of 1650 reconsidered', in D. H. Pennington and K. Thomas (eds), *Puritans and Revolutionaries: Essays in Seventeenth-Century History Presented to Christopher Hill*, Oxford, Clarendon Press, 1978, pp. 252–82. It does not matter, for my argument, that Othello himself perpetrated the defamation (though see the Helen Johnson case, p. 32); it is not archival verisimilitude I am after, but clues to what the community (the audience) would have expected to happen once a defamation was 'audiently' made.

56 3.3.159–96.

57 3.3.365–72. On the contemporary debate about the comparative status of 'ocular proof' and testimony in the English lawcourts of the period see J. Langbein, *Prosecuting Crime in the Renaissance: England, Germany, France*, Cambridge, Mass., Harvard University Press, 1974; J. Langbein, *Torture and the Law of Proof*, Chicago, University of Chicago Press, 1977; J. Bellamy, *Criminal Law and Society in Late Medieval and Tudor England*, New York, St. Martin's Press, 1984. I am extremely grateful to Professor Katharine Maus for drawing my attention to the discussion of 'ocular proof' in law, and clarifying its relevance to *Othello*.

58 And again, 'Iago knows / That she with Cassio hath the act of shame / A thousand times committed; Cassio confess'd it' (5.2.211–13).

59 On the two senses of 'conviction' (being convicted, and clinching the case) in the context of doubt and certainty in the lawcourts, see K. E. Maus, 'Proof and consequences: inwardness and its exposure in the English renaissance', 1991, vol. 34, pp. 29–52.

60 5.2. *passim*. See particularly the point at which Othello recognises that without the certainty, Desdemona's death would be murder, not, what Ridley in the note to this passage calls 'impersonal justice': 'O perjur'd woman, thou dost stone thy heart, / And makest me call what I intend to do / A murder, which I thought a sacrifice' (5.2.64–6). On adultery as 'unlawful' see Chapter 2.

61 For an English audience, Othello is none the less guilty of murder in killing his wife as retribution for her adultery, since English law specified that murder by a husband of his adulterous wife could only be excused if it took place in the first flush of anger. See Davis, *Fiction in the Archives*, Chapter 2.

2 'NO OFFENCE I' TH' WORLD'

1 *Hamlet*, 3.2.224–30. All references are to the Arden edn, ed. Harold Jenkins, London, Methuen, 1982.

2 D. Simpson, 'Literary criticism and the return to "history"', *Critical Inquiry*, 1988, vol. 14, pp. 721–47, at 724–5. For another powerful argument which meshes with Simpson's doubts about the authenticity of discourse theorists' commitment to 'history' see L. Montrose, 'Renaissance literary studies and the subject of history', *English Literary Renaissance*, 1986, vol. 16, pp. 3–12.

3 'In particular, given the current popularity of discourse analysis, it seems likely that for many practitioners the historical method will remain founded in covertly idealist reconstructions' (ibid.).

4 Catherine Belsey, in her paper delivered on the same occasion as an early draft

of this chapter, 'Making histories then and now: Shakespeare from *Richard II* to *Henry V*', gives an elegant account of the ideological motivation for the privileging of a master-narrative version of history in criticism of Shakespeare's 'history' plays (for a similarly astute account of the ideology of Hamlet criticism, see Terence Hawkes, 'Telmah', in *That Shakespeherian Rag: Essays on a Critical Process*, London, Methuen, 1986). Unlike Simpson, however, she sees the possibility of a post-modernist deconstruction which 'uncovers the differences within rationality, and thus writes of it otherwise', and which will thereby 'activate the differences and promote political intervention'. She proposes this as an alternative to both 'the master-narrative of inexorable and teleological development' and 'a (dis)continuous and fragmentary present, a world of infinite differences which are ultimately undifferentiated because they are all confined to the signifying surface of things'.

5 For a challenging account of these developments in cultural history see R. Chartier, *Cultural History: Between Practices and Representations*, trans. L. G. Cochrane, Cambridge, Polity Press, 1988.

6 See, for instance, Clifford Geertz, '"From the native's point of view": on the nature of anthropological understanding', in R. A. Shweder and R. A. LeVine (eds), *Culture Theory: Essays on Mind, Self, and Emotion*, Cambridge, Cambridge University Press, 1984, pp. 123–36; M. Z. Rosaldo, 'Towards an anthropology of self and feeling', ibid., pp. 137–57; R. A. Shweder and E. J. Bourne, 'Does the concept of the person vary cross-culturally?', ibid., pp. 158–99; E. M. Bruner, 'Experience and its expressions', in V. W. Turner and E. M. Bruner (eds), *The Anthropology of Experience*, Urbana, Illinois, University of Illinois Press, pp. 3–30.

7 For a clear account of the way in which political commitment sharpens the focus of feminist historical work, see Jean Howard, 'The new historicism in renaissance studies', *English Literary Renaissance*, 1986, vol. 16, pp. 13–43.

8 See most eloquently N. Davis, *Fiction in the Archives: Pardon Tales and their Tellers in Sixteenth-Century France*, Cambridge, Polity Press, 1987.

9 All of this may seem obvious to historians, but at the boundary between history and text studies it is probably the greatest impediment to collaborative work, so needs to be aired.

10 See Chapter 1.

11 See first of all Clifford Geertz, *The Interpretation of Cultures*, New York, Columbia University Press, 1973, p. 51; then Stephen Greenblatt, *Renaissance Self-Fashioning: From More to Shakespeare*, Chicago, Chicago University Press, 1980, p. 3.

12 Here, for these purposes, I specifically discard the idea that the theatre is a special space, with its own acknowledged rules which are not those of 'everyday life' – see e.g. K. McLuskie, *Renaissance Dramatists*, Brighton, Harvester, 1989, *passim*.

13 See Geertz, *Interpretation of Cultures*, pp. 15–16.

14 See Geertz, *Interpretation of Cultures*, p. 35: 'Whatever else modern anthropology asserts – and it seems to have asserted almost everything at one time or another – it is firm in the conviction that men unmodified by the customs of particular places do not in fact exist, have never existed, and most important, could not in the very nature of the case exist. There is, there can be, no backstage where we can catch a glimpse of Mascou's actors as "real persons" lounging about in street clothes, disengaged from their profession, displaying with artless candor their spontaneous desires and unprompted passions.'

15 This coexistence is made easier by the fact that social anthropologists like Geertz have thoroughly absorbed psychoanalytical theory, and tend to assume

the Freudian subject as the starting point for their discussions of the cultural construction of selfhood. See Geertz, *Interpretation of Cultures*; Rosaldo, 'Towards an anthropology of self and feeling'.

16 'I began with the desire to speak with the dead. This desire is a familiar, if unvoiced, motive in literary studies, a motive organized, professionalized, buried beneath thick layers of bureaucratic decorum: literature professors are salaried, middle-class shamans. If I never believed that the dead could hear me, and if I knew that the dead could not speak, I was nonetheless certain that I could re-create a conversation with them' (Stephen Greenblatt, *Shakespearean Negotiations*, Oxford, Clarendon Press, 1988, p. 1). Greenblatt here deliberately invokes Geertz. Compare: 'We are seeking, in the widened sense of the term in which it encompasses much more than talk, to converse with [our 'native' informants], a matter a great deal more difficult, and not only with strangers, than is commonly recognized. "If speaking for someone else seems to be a mysterious process," Stanley Cavell has remarked, "that may be because speaking to someone does not seem mysterious enough"' (Geertz, *Interpretation of Cultures*, p. 13).

17 See Carol Neely, 'Constructing the subject: feminist practice and the new renaissance discourses', *English Literary Renaissance*, 1988, vol. 18, pp. 5–18.

18 In discussion, at the Essex conference at which I gave the first version of this piece of work, it became clear, I think, that in this respect (and this respect only) feminist critics are currently at an advantage in the critical debate being conducted around historicist and deconstructive critical approaches to text. Since they have a declared political objective, they are entitled to discard methodologies which fail to contribute constructively to it.

19 I find it striking that by 1932, when this essay is included in his collected essays, Eliot is fully aware of Freud, and thus that psychoanalytical reading of the play is established before psychoanalytical theory is explicitly introduced into literary studies.

20 T. S. Eliot, *Selected Essays*, London, Faber, 1932, pp. 144–5.

21 For a clear account of the consistent allocation of blame to the woman in psychoanalytical readings of *Hamlet* and *Measure for Measure* see Jacqueline Rose, 'Sexuality in the reading of Shakespeare', in J. Drakakis (ed.), *Alternative Shakespeares*, London, Methuen, 1985, pp. 95–118.

22 Cedric Watts, *Harvester New Critical Introductions to Shakespeare: Hamlet*, Brighton, Harvester, 1988, pp. xxiv–v.

23 As tends to happen with Shakespeare criticism, I had myself already started work on this theme when I began to notice references to prohibited degrees in the work of others.

24 Watts, *Hamlet*, p. 31.

25 Edmund Gibson, *Codex Juris Ecclesiastici Anglicani*, 2nd edn, 2 vols, Oxford, Clarendon Press, 1761, vol. 1, p. 387.

26 Richard Burn, *Ecclesiastical Law*, 6th edn, ed. Simon Fraser, 4 vols, London, T. Cadell, W. Davies and J. Butterworth, 1797, vol. 2, p. 446.

27 For a clear account of the transition from the prohibited degrees of the Catholic Church to those of Reformation England see J. Goody, *The Development of the Family and Marriage in Europe*, Cambridge, Cambridge University Press, 1983, pp. 134–46 and 168–82.

28 There are exactly comparable tables of consanguinity and affinity for the woman.

29 Indeed, this is how theological dictionaries traditionally describe the rules of affinity – as concerning property.

30 So was Henry's marriage to Anne Boleyn, since he had already had a relation-

ship with her sister (Catholic propaganda, interestingly, claimed more obvious incest: that Anne was in fact Henry's daughter). One of the defamatory claims made against Anne's own reputation was that she had had unlawful sex with her brother.

31 See Goody, *Development*, p. 172: 'Catherine [Howard] was the first cousin of his second wife, Anne Boleyn, who had been executed on the grounds of adultery. Such a marriage was clearly forbidden under the rule of affinity, attributed to the same general prohibition in Leviticus as the levirate, that is, the prohibition on uncovering the nakedness of one's kin. In order to marry Catherine Howard, Henry legalised marriage to all first cousins, not simply cousins of affines, under a statute of 1540 [32 Henry VIII. cap. 38; *Statutes at Large* (London, 1763), pp. 55–6]. The Act declared that when a marriage was consummated, it could not be annulled by reason of pre-contract, or of "degree of kindred or alliance, but those mentioned in the Law of God". Since pre-contract (that is, the virtual equation of the betrothal with marriage) was no longer to be considered grounds for annulment, the Act therefore set aside one of the reasons for dissolving the marriage of Anne Boleyn (who was said to have been "pre-contracted") and therefore legitimised her daughter Elizabeth. But more immediately it legitimised the king's latest union.'

32 *Depositions and other Ecclesiastical Proceedings from the Courts of Durham, extending from 1311 to the reign of Elizabeth*, London, The Surtees Society, 1845, p. 59. The 'marks' made by both deponents indicates that they were illiterate (a fact which is confirmed within Edward Ward's deposition).

33 Goody uses part of this case in his discussion of prohibited degrees (Goody, p. 178). However, he takes this as evidence that 'the public at first paid no great attention to "unlawful" marriages, indeed even encouraged them'. But I think this is not to read the 'direction' of the depositions sufficiently carefully.

34 See N. Davis, *The Return of Martin Guerre* (Cambridge, Mass., Harvard University Press, 1983) for a clear case in which an unlawful relationship goes unreported in the community until a charge is brought by an individual who regards the 'marriage' as depriving him of something (land) due to him: 'The new Martin was not only a husband, but also an heir, a nephew, and an important peasant proprietor in Artigat. It was in these roles that the trouble finally began' (p. 51).

35 A number of tales are told concerning the legislative status of the Tudor tables of prohibited degrees. The most common one is that the canons of 1603 were drawn up hastily upon Elizabeth's death, since at her death it was suddenly realised that there was now no body of valid ecclesiastical law (her own legislation having been specified as for the duration of her reign). Owing to an oversight, the 1603 canons did not go through Parliament until some three years later, when it was realised that the clergy was probably operating outside statute law, and the situation was rectified. Patrick Collinson, however, has recently suggested to me that these canons in fact never went on to the statute book – that in fact the Tudor and Stuart governments left church law in a kind of deliberate limbo. Goody gives a good clear account of the pragmatic nature of the Henrician reforms in prohibited degrees which suggests that it was well understood that the legal status of the reforms was dubious (op. cit., pp. 168–82). Houlbrooke suggests that 'the prohibited degrees of kinship (reduced in 1540) at no stage offered an easy way out of marriage' (R. Houlbrooke, *The English Family 1450–1700*, London, Longman, 1984, p. 115). See also A. Macfarlane, *Marriage and Love in England: Modes of Reproduction 1300–1840*, Oxford, Oxford University Press, 1986, Chapter 11, 'Status rules concerning marriage' (pp. 245–62). All of this is really to suggest that (1) there was at the very least some vagueness about how to operate the various competing demands of

common law, statute and canon law, and (2) 'moral' and 'legal' demands might readily be perceived to be in opposition, the legal contrary to custom, or the moral dubious within the technical law.

36 *Hamlet*, 1.2.146–57. And see the *Book of Common Prayer*, cit. Jenkins, *Hamlet*, p. 319, n. 14. For another example of explicit affinity incest in the drama see Spurio's relationship with his stepmother in Tourneur's *The Revenger's Tragedy*. There, as here, the unlawfulness of the relationship is emphasised by the repeated formula from the tables of affinity: '*Spurio*. I would 'twere love, but 't 'as a fouler name / Than lust; you are my father's wife, your Grace may guess now / What I call it' (1.2.129–31). In *Cymbeline* Cymbeline tries both to force Imogen to divorce her true husband, Posthumous, and to enter into an incestuous marriage with her stepbrother, Cloten.

37 1.5.42–6; 80–3.

38 Watts, *Hamlet*, p. 32.

39 See my discussion of 'It is the cause' in *Othello*, p. 34.

40 I have in mind Macfarlane on status rules concerning marriage, and Houlbrooke on prohibited degrees. See also D. Cressy, 'Kinship and kin interaction in early modern England', *Past and Present*, 1986, vol. 113, pp. 38–69, for a very careful study of the different modes of operation of close kin networks and distant kin networks in relation to wills.

41 In Hamlet's case this comes in Act 5: 'He that hath kill'd my king and whor'd my mother, / Popp'd in between th'election and my hopes' (5.2.64–5).

42 For an extended discussion of the 'elective' monarchy in Denmark, see Harold Jenkins in the Arden edition. I point out for brevity that Scotland was an elective monarchy: the eldest son of the reigning monarch was removed at birth to the care of the Earl of Marr. In due course the clans were assembled, and he was 'elected' heir to his father.

43 1.1.82–107.

44 1.2.1–9, 14.

45 1.2.64–7, and then see 109–12: 'You are the most immediate to our throne, / And with no less nobility of love / Than that which dearest father bears his son / Do I impart toward you.'

46 The specific offence is committed against Hamlet senior and Hamlet junior. See Stephen Greenblatt, 'Psychoanalysis and renaissance culture', in P. Parker and D. Quint (eds), *Literary Theory/Renaissance Texts*, Baltimore, Md., Johns Hopkins University Press, 1986, pp. 210–24, at p. 219: 'The ghost of Old Hamlet – "of life, of crown, of queen at once dispatched" – returns to his land to demand that his son take the life of the imposter who has seized his identity.' There seems to be a useful notion here of 'Hamlet' as an identity, a nexus of relations that Hamlet junior ought to occupy. See René Girard, 'Hamlet's dull revenge', also in Parker and Quint, pp. 280–302, at pp. 285–6: 'This significance of twins and brothers ... must be present ... if we are to interpret correctly the scene in which Hamlet, holding in his hands the two portraits of his father and his uncle ... tries to convince his mother that an enormous difference exists between the two. There would be no Hamlet "problem" if the hero really believed what he says. It is also himself, therefore, that he is trying to convince.'

47 Watts, *Hamlet*, p. 31.

48 That is, 'been offensive to'.

49 That is, 'committed an offence against'.

50 See Myles Coverdale's translation of Heinrich Bullinger: 'A woman may not marry her Husbandes brother' (*The Christen State of Matrymonye, wherein housebandes and wyues maye lerne to kepe house together wyth loue*, London, Abraham Vele, 1552, sig. C.ii.ʳ).

51 3.4.7–41.

52 In this account the possible murder of the king is a secondary issue.

53 On murder by wife or child as petty treason see J. I. Sharpe, *Crime in Early Modern England, 1550–1750*, London, Longman, 1984.

54 Had Hamlet an heir himself his position would be strengthened (the play stresses Gertrude's maturity). I have come to think that this is the emphasis which so insistently produces Ophelia as a fallen woman – were she pregnant she would threaten the (new) line in Denmark. Once she is dead she is recuperated as undoubted virgin: 'Yet here she is allow'd her virgin crants [funeral garlands], / Her maiden strewments, and the bringing home / Of bell and burial' (5.1.225–7). On funeral rites specific to the death of an unwed woman see C. Gittings, *Death, Burial and the Individual in Early Modern England*, London, Routledge, 1988, pp. 117–18.

55 As Hamlet senior consistently maintains.

56 3.2.239–60.

57 3.2.168–225.

58 See e.g. for convenience L. Jardine, *Still Harping on Daughters: Women and Drama in the Age of Shakespeare*, Brighton, Harvester, 1983, pp. 83–4; L. Stone, *An Elizabethan: Sir Horatio Palavicino*, Oxford, Clarendon Press, 1956, pp. 289–99; G. Duby, *Medieval Marriage: Two Models from Twelfth-Century France*, trans. E. Forster, Baltimore, Md., Johns Hopkins University Press, 1978; Macfarlane, *Marriage and Love*, pp. 231–8; Goody, *The Development of the Family*, pp. 60–8; and especially Houlbrooke, *The English Family*, pp. 207–15.

59 One might argue that as *feme coverte* Gertrude is strictly disabled under the law in any civic action involving Claudius.

60 The intensity of the blame this occasions stands comparison with the blame which drives Ophelia insane – the murder of a father by the daughter's 'husband' (an act of petty treason, carried out by a king's son). Early modern inheritance law consistently reflects anxiety as to whether mothers can be expected to act reliably on their male offspring's behalf in the absence of a male head of household. See Chapter 3.

61 3.4.158. Note the intimate setting of the confrontation between Gertrude and Hamlet in which he is entirely explicit about his mother's sexual activity.

3 CULTURAL CONFUSION AND SHAKESPEARE'S LEARNED HEROINES

1 *Othello*, 2.1.124–39. Quoted from Arden Shakespeare, ed. M. R. Ridley, London, Methuen, 1958. I am extremely grateful to the following people for taking the time to read and comment on earlier versions of this chapter: Natalie Zemon Davis, Julia Swindells, Stephen Greenblatt, Gareth Stedman-Jones, Frank Whigham.

2 Stephen Greenblatt discusses this passage as part of Iago's 'ceaseless narrative invention', and comments on the birdlime image as 'a covert celebration of [Iago's] power to ensnare others' (*Renaissance Self-Fashioning: From More to Shakespeare*, Chicago, Ill., University of Chicago Press, 1980, p. 233). I am suggesting that Desdemona is also 'fashioned' by this exchange, but that female self-fashioning certainly does not act to her own advantage.

3 Lisa Jardine, 'Isotta Nogarola: women humanists – education for what?', *History of Education*, 1983, vol. 12, pp. 231–44; '"O decus Italiae virgo" or, The myth of the learned lady in the Renaissance', *The Historical Journal*, 1985, vol. 28, pp. 799–819; A. Grafton and Lisa Jardine, *From Humanism to the Humanities: The*

Liberal Arts in Fifteenth- and Sixteenth-Century Europe, London, Duckworth, 1986, Chapter 2.

4 Recent scholarly and historical work suggests that the similarities between sixteenth-century English and fifteenth-century Italian attitudes towards the education of women in the Renaissance are greater than the differences. See Patricia H. Labalme (ed.), *Beyond Their Sex: Learned Women of the European Past*, New York, New York University Press, 1980; Retha M. Warnicke, *Women of the English Renaissance and Reformation*, Westport, Conn., Greenwood Press, 1983; *Women in the Renaissance*, special issue of *English Literary Renaissance*, 1984, vol. 14, no. 3; Margaret P. Hannay (ed.), *Silent But for the Word: Tudor Women as Patrons, Translators, and Writers of Religious Works*, Kent, Ohio, Kent State University Press, 1985.

5 Natalie Davis, *Society and Culture in Early Modern France*, Stanford, Calif., Stanford University Press, 1975. See in particular, 'Woman on top', pp. 124–51; and 'City women and religious change', pp. 65–95. See also '"Women's history" in transition: the European case', *Feminist Studies*, 1976, vol. 3, pp. 83–103; 'Women in the crafts in sixteenth-century Lyon', *Feminist Studies*, 1982, vol. 8, pp. 46–80.

6 See, for instance, the essays collected in Berenice A. Carroll (ed.), *Liberating Women's History: Theoretical and Critical Essays*, Urbana, Ill., University of Illinois Press, 1976; and those in Renate Bridenthal and Claudia Koonz (eds), *Becoming Visible: Women in European History*, London, Houghton Mifflin, 1977; also J. Kelly, *Women, History, and Theory: The Essays of Joan Kelly*, Women in Culture and Society Series, Chicago, Ill., University of Chicago Press, 1984. For examples of more recent work which, in my view, more fully assimilates Davis's approach, see, for instance, S. Amussen, 'Gender, family and the social order, 1560–1725', in Anthony Fletcher and John Stevenson (eds), *Order and Disorder in Early Modern England*, Cambridge, Cambridge University Press, 1985, pp. 196–217; Lyndal Roper, 'Discipline and respectability: prostitution and the Reformation in Augsburg', *History Workshop*, 1985, vol. 19, pp. 3–28.

7 Such work includes the following: Juliet Dusinberre, *Shakespeare and the Nature of Women*, London, Macmillan, 1975; Catherine M. Dunn, 'The changing image of women in Renaissance society and literature', in Marlene Springer (ed.), *What Manner of Woman: Essays on English and American Life and Literature*, New York, Gotham Library, 1977, pp. 15–38; Lisa Jardine, *Still Harping on Daughters: Women and Drama in the Age of Shakespeare*, Brighton, Harvester Press, 1983; Simon Shepherd, *Amazons and Warrior Women: Varieties of Feminism in Seventeenth-Century Drama*, Brighton, Harvester Press, 1981; Linda Woodbridge, *Women and the English Renaissance: Literature and the Nature of Womankind, 1504–1620*, Brighton, Harvester Press, 1984; Carol Neely, *Broken Nuptials in Shakespeare's Plays*, New Haven, Conn., Yale University Press, 1985.

8 Actually I think work by social historians like Jim Sharpe and Susan Amussen shows that similar problems concerning prior assumptions have to be overcome when assessing such 'documentary' evidence as Assizes records, or Depositions in the ecclesiastical courts. See J. A. Sharpe, *Defamation and Sexual Slander in Early Modern England: The Church Courts at York*, Borthwick Papers, 58, York, Borthwick Institute of Historical Research, 1980; *Crime in Seventeenth-Century England: A County Study*, Cambridge, Cambridge University Press, 1983; Amussen, 'Gender, family and the social order, 1560–1725'.

9 Woodbridge, *Women and the English Renaissance*, p. 129.

10 See Dusinberre, *Shakespeare and the Nature of Women*, and Jardine, *Still Harping on Daughters*.

11 I tend to use the term 'textual critic' in order to remind myself that all written

evidence from the period – 'documentary' or 'literary' – requires an equal amount of alert critical scrutiny.

12 The only other candidate I am aware of, besides the two I discuss here, is Marina in *Pericles*.

13 Elizabeth Frances Rogers (ed.), *St. Thomas More: Selected Letters*, New Haven, Conn., Yale University Press, 1961, pp. 154–5. The final paragraph of the letter refers to Margaret's imminent confinement, and hopes that the child will be 'like to his mother in everything except sex. Yet let it by all means be a girl, if only she will make up for the inferiority of her sex by her zeal to imitate her mother's virtue and learning'!

14 See, for instance, the passage from Erasmus's *Christiani matrimonii institutio*, Julia O'Faolain and Lauro Martines (eds), *Not in God's Image: Women in History*, London, Virago, 1979, p. 194.

15 See Jardine, ' "O decus Italiae virgo" '.

16 *All's Well That Ends Well*, 1.1.33–45. All quotations from this play are from the Arden edn, ed. G. K. Hunter, London, Methuen, 1959. I follow Hunter's construing of the second sentence.

17 In *Pericles* Shakespeare almost entirely erases Marina's explicit learnedness in the liberal arts, which in his source is the means of her preserving her chastity in the brothel – 'Deep clerks she dumbs' (Arden edn, ed. F. D. Hoeniger, London, Methuen, 1963, 5.1.5) is the one remaining trace of 'learning' – replacing it by skill at music, embroidery and dance (traditionally decorous signs of womanly virtue). I think it is a significant alteration which supports the case I argue here. The ability to win arguments and debate extempore is less securely 'moral' in a woman than sewing and singing. I am grateful to Elizabeth Archibald for drawing my attention to the association of learning with the heroine of the Apollonius of Tyre source story.

18 See G. K. Hunter's gloss on 'virtuous qualities': 'The antithesis between *mind* and *virtuous qualities* is between inherited nature and the qualities imparted by training. *Virtuous qualities* does not mean "fine moral qualities", but "the qualities of a virtuoso skill, capacity, technical prowess". Hoby translates Castiglione's *virtuose qualità* by "vertuous qualities" . . . where the modern translator has "admirable accomplishments" ', Arden edn, p. 5, n. 39.

19 Baldassare Castiglione, *The Book of the Courtier*, trans. Sir Thomas Hoby, ed. J. H. Whitfield, London, J. M. Dent & Sons, 1974, p. 195.

20 The idea of the 'woman on top' is discussed further by Karen Newman in 'Portia's ring: unruly women and structures of exchange in *The Merchant of Venice*', *Shakespeare Quarterly*, 1987, vol. 38, pp. 19–33, at p. 28 ff.

21 1.3.65–90.

22 In the folio text Helena is in fact 'Helen' for most of the play.

23 See Richard P. Wheeler's account of this scene, *Shakespeare's Development and the Problem Comedies: Turn and Counter-Turn*, Berkeley, Calif., University of California Press, 1981, pp. 50–4, e.g.: 'Sexual desire for men in such comedies tends to be deflected away from the hero into the language and sometimes the actions, of secondary figures, especially clowns or fools' (p. 50). Wheeler relates the competing versions of Helena to the complexities of male desire, using a psychoanalytical model and quoting Freud liberally to support his reading. Our readings often agree closely, but I would contend that the confused responses to woman which psychoanalysis internalises to the individual subject (and thus effectively prevents women from challenging) may also be produced as culturally constructed and historically specific.

24 I have argued this case for the scene in which Desdemona exchanges sexual banter with Iago in *Othello*. See *Still Harping on Daughters*, pp. 119–20.

25 Throughout Act 1 Helena is curiously explicit about the carnal nature of her love for Bertram, including, of course, the entire exchange with Parolles, which the audience understands to refer to her own case ('Are you meditating on virginity?' 'Ay', 1.1.108–9).

26 1.3.227–30.

27 It is significant in this context that Bertram has gone to Paris as the King of France's ward on the death of his father. Wardship explicitly meant the taking of the heir into the protective custody of his liege lord – and away from the custody of his mother (who is assumed to be unreliable) – during his minority.

28 2.1.192–9.

29 2.3.111–16.

30 Earlier, Bertram has protested that the King has forbidden his ward to leave the court to become a soldier, but has condemned him to play 'the forehorse to a smock', 2.1.30 – to be commanded by women.

31 What I here call the 'historically precise' disruptiveness of Helena's action appears to map on to (or mirror) the account Wheeler gives in terms of incest and 'the threat of paternal sexuality'. The King is 'restored to vigorous manhood' (Wheeler, *Shakespeare's Development*, p. 81) by Helena; she 'has raised [him] up', etc. She is the King's (sexual) choice, but it is Bertram who is commanded to possess Helena's body (a command Bertram treats as incompatible with his own virility).

32 2.1.168–72.

33 On defamation depositions lodged by women against such sexual slurs see Amussen, 'Gender, family and the social order, 1560–1725'; Sharpe, *Defamation and Sexual Slander in Early Modern England: The Church Courts at York* (cited in note 8). On the depositions in general see P. E. H. Hair, *Before the Bawdy Court: Selections from Church Court and other Records relating to the Correction of Moral Offences in England, Scotland and New England, 1300–1800*, London, Elek, 1972; Martin Ingram, 'Ecclesiastical justice in Wiltshire, 1600–1640, with special reference to cases involving sex and marriage', unpublished Oxford University D.Phil. thesis, 1976; Ronald A. Marchant, *The Church under the Law: Justice, Administration, and Discipline in the Diocese of York, 1560–1640*, Cambridge, Cambridge University Press, 1969; C. A. Haigh, 'Slander and the church courts in the sixteenth century', *Transactions of the Lancashire and Cheshire Antiquarian Society*, 1975, vol. 78, pp. 1–13; R. C. Dunhill, '17th century invective: defamation cases as a source for word study', *Devon and Cornwall Notes and Queries*, 1976, vol. 33, pp. 49–51. For printed texts of some depositions see *Depositions and other Ecclesiastical Proceedings from the Courts of Durham, extending from 1311 to the reign of Elizabeth*, The Surtees Society, London, 1845.

34 For an account of the complexity of the use of witches and cursing women in Shakespeare's history plays see G. Bernhard Jackson, 'Topical witches, amazons, and Shakespeare's Joan of Arc', *English Literary Renaissance*, 1988, vol. 18, pp. 40–65.

35 2.1.77–84.

36 See Wheeler, *Shakespeare's Development*, p. 75.

37 5.3.303–8.

38 4.4.21–5.

39 Arden edn, pp. xxx–xxxii. See W. W. Lawrence, *Shakespeare's Problem Comedies*, London, Macmillan, 1931. See also Wheeler, *Shakespeare's Development*, p. 23.

40 I think one might argue that it is significant that Helena and Portia 'borrow' their knowledge from two of the professions whose very terms of reference, as public practices that require a university training, define them as exclusively male spheres. The fact that the King of France suffers from a 'fistula' – an

abscess, usually in the region of the rectum (his virility, it is repeatedly hinted, is impaired) – further underlines the fact that Helena cannot with propriety treat his ailment.

41 The ring exchange explicitly precedes the completion of the marriage (which finally takes place at the end of Act 5). It is crucial for the ring circulation of the plot that the ring signifies betrothal – a pledge to complete the marriage to its bearer at a future date. At the end of 3.2 Portia instructs Bassanio, before he returns to Venice, to 'First go with me to church, and call me wife', but insists he leave before the marriage is consummated (3.2.302, 308–10, 321); that is to say, before the final ratification of the marriage (and this is underlined by the insistence on haste ten lines later). The loss of the ring calls the completion of the marriage into question. On the vital importance of the wedding night in both pre- and post-Reformation wedding rituals see Christiane Klapisch-Zuber, 'Zacharias, or the ousted father: nuptial rites in Tuscany between Giotto and the Council of Trent', in *Women, Family, and Ritual in Renaissance Italy*, trans. Lydia Cochrane, Chicago, Ill., University of Chicago Press, 1985, pp. 178–212; Lyndal Roper, '"Going to Church and Street": weddings in Reformation Augsburg', *Past and Present*, 1985, vol. 106, pp. 62–101. As both of these authors stress, the terms 'husband' and 'wife' are customarily used from betrothal onwards, but the contractual obligations are not secure until the marriage has been consummated.

42 This is, of course, the same ring trick which Helena used to dupe Bertram into giving away his family ring. In both cases, the yielding up of a ring to a woman is the first stage in a contract to be completed by consummation. For a discussion of the ring exchange in *The Merchant of Venice* which squares well with my own argument, see Karen Newman, 'Portia's ring', pp. 25–32.

43 *The Merchant of Venice*, 3.2.170–4. All quotations from this play are from the Arden edn, ed. John Russell Brown, London, Methuen, 1955.

44 By analogy with 'quitclaim', to discharge from a former claim.

45 5.1.147–50.

46 For the woman in breeches as figure of misrule see Natalie Zemon Davis, *Society and Culture in Early Modern France*; Lisa Jardine, *Still Harping on Daughters*; and, for a telling account of the misrule element in *The Merchant of Venice*, see Karen Newman, 'Portia's ring'.

47 5.1.129–31.

48 5.1.146–54.

49 5.1.257–65.

50 See my account of women and inheritance in the Renaissance period, in *Still Harping on Daughters*, Chapter 3. See also Newman, 'Portia's ring', pp. 25 ff.

51 1.2.20–6.

52 Compare Isabella's complaint at having no choice in marriage in Middleton's *Women Beware Women*, Revels edn, ed. J. R. Mulryne, London, Methuen, 1975, 1.2.166–76.

53 3.2.251–62; 296–301. This is also, tellingly, the moment at which Portia urges Bassanio to leave to help Antonio before the marriage is consummated – that is, before the property and substance she here places at Bassanio's disposal actually pass from her possession to his. In other words, Portia remains explicitly in charge of 'wealth' throughout the play.

54 Throughout the play much is made of Bassanio's upstart status as Portia's suitor, purchased with Antonio's borrowed money. Launcelot Gobbo's characterization of him as one who 'gives rare new liveries' (takes on and apparels a large retinue, 2.2.104–5, 109–12), for instance, might be compared with Jack's presumptuous behaviour in Deloney's *Jack of Newbury*.

55 In the source story for *The Merchant of Venice* (from the first story of the fourth day of ser Giovanni's *Il Pecorone*), Portia is an enchantress, whose power over men has led to the sexual subjugation, followed by death, of a whole sequence of suitors (reprinted in the Arden edn, pp. 140–53).
56 5.1.294–5. A full exploration of woman's 'knowingness' in this play would include a treatment of Jessica's social/sexual duping of Shylock.
57 5.1.297–307.
58 3.2.149–74.
59 Cuckoldry taunts on the way to the marriage ceremony were not an unheard-of occurrence. See Roper, '"Going to Church and Street"'; Martin Ingram, 'Ridings, rough music and mocking rhymes in early modern England', in Barry Reay (ed.), *Popular Culture in Seventeenth Century England*, London, Croom Helm, 1985, pp. 166–97.
60 For the contrived and exclusive rhetoric of 'worth', see Frank Whigham, *Ambition and Privilege: The Social Tropes of Elizabethan Courtesy Theory*, Berkeley, Calif., University of California Press, 1984.

4 TWINS AND TRAVESTIES

1 *Twelfth Night*, Arden edn, J. M. Lothian and T. W. Craik (eds), London, Methuen, 1975, 3.4.389–93.
2 Thomas Middleton, 'Micro-Cynicon', in A. H. Bullen (ed.),*The Works of Thomas Middleton* (8 vols), New York, AMS Press, 1899, vol. 8, pp. 132–3. I am grateful to Alan Bray, in whose work I first saw this poem. See Alan Bray, *Homosexuality in Renaissance England*, London, Gay Men's Press, 1982; 2nd edn, 1988.
3 Jean E. Howard, 'Sex and social conflict: the erotics of The Roaring Girl', in Susan Zimmerman (ed.), *Erotic Politics: Desire on the Renaissance Stage*, London, Routledge, 1993, pp. 170–89; Valerie Traub, *Desire and Anxiety: Circulations of Sexuality in Shakespearean Drama*, London, Routledge, 1992.
4 For the transgressive version see Jonathan Dollimore, 'Subjectivity, sexuality, and transgression: the Jacobean connection', *Renaissance Drama*, 1986, n.s. vol. 17, pp. 53–81. For the 'actual' affirmation version see M. B. Rose, 'Women in men's clothing: apparel and social stability in *The Roaring Girl*', *English Literary Renaissance*, 1984, vol. 14, pp. 367–91, and Jean E. Howard, 'Crossdressing, the theatre, and gender struggle in early modern England', *Shakespeare Quarterly*, 1988, vol. 39, pp. 418–40.
5 Most of the texual accounts of cross-dressing (whether on the stage or in the street), like the 'ingling' verse just cited and the Rainolds poem I use in *Still Harping on Daughters*, are clearly already adjusted to the fictional tropes of cross-dressing/illicit desire. Even sumptuary rules (as cited by Howard and others) aspire to control excesses which threaten good order – which is to say, dress which *signifies*, on which disorder is inscribed. The deposition relating to Mary Frith is a good example of the textual difficulties: in the record (whose narrative shape is controlled by the recording clerk and 'his Lordship', the bishop (?) who interrogates) the 'immodest and lascivious speeches', and 'shame of her sexe' collide with the slender textual traces of her refusal to accept the charge 'being pressed', 'whether she had not byn dishonest of her body & hath not also drawne other women to lewdnes by er perswasions & by carrying her self lyke a bawde'. To cross-dress is to signify as (to 'carry oneself' as) a bawd (deposition transcribed in full in P. Mulholland (ed.), *The Roaring Girl*, Revels Plays, Manchester, Manchester University Press, 1987, pp. 262–3). The spate of 'Moll Frith' plays which accompanied her court appearance seize upon the

event's bawdy potential – for example, by suggesting she might 'take her own part' in the play (which 'part', and how related to stage cross-dressing?) and that she would play the viol on stage (the lewd possibilities of viol playing are considerable, as pointed out by Jean Howard ('Sex and social conflict'). In a paper for the 1989 meeting of the Shakespeare Association of America, Peter Stallybrass quoted Augustine Philips's will in which he left his apprentice various specified desirable items of clothing and his 'bass viol'. Here too it seems possible that the legacy has been adjusted to the tropes of (intimate) devoted service – the bass viol and the shared items of dress suggestively connoting the closeness of the master–servant relationship.

6 Lisa Jardine, *Still Harping on Daughters: Women and Drama in the Age of Shakespeare*, Brighton, Harvester, 1983; 2nd edn, 1989.

7 Since this was the argument, I think that Valerie Traub is not correct in attributing fundamental heterosexism to my discussion of boy players in *Still Harping on Daughters*. See Traub, *Desire*, pp. 93–4. On the other hand, as the present piece shows, I do believe that Shakespeare critics as a whole, including myself, have (as Traub points out) wrongly assumed that the Shakespearean stage was committed to reproductive sex as the norm for erotic interest.

8 It is fascinating that this exactly corresponds to Mary Douglas's 'dirt is matter out of place'. See Mary Douglas, *Purity and Danger*, London, Routledge & Kegan Paul, 1966.

9 See Roger Ascham, *The Scholemaster*, London, John Day, 1570 and its 'morals' source, Xenophon's *Cyropaedia*. I am grateful to Lorna Hutson for making the vulnerability of the 'youth' clear to me, and for all the helpful discussion we had during the writing of this chapter.

10 Throughout this piece I use the contemporary term 'sodomy' rather than the nineteenth-century 'homosexuality', or any of its cognates. In this I follow Bray, *Homosexuality*, and V. L. Bullough, 'The sin against nature and homosexuality', in V. L. Bullough and J. Brundage (eds), *Sexual Practices and the Medieval Church*, Buffalo, New York, Prometheus, 1982, pp. 55–71.

11 To see how far back this goes as a fictionalising of 'loose' women transgressively entering the male preserve see Knighton's *Chronicon* (1348), quoted in E. Rickert, *Chaucer's World*, Oxford, Oxford University Press, 1949, p. 217. I am grateful to Rob Pope for bringing this passage to my attention.

12 This is, I now think, a more correct version of what I wrote earlier: 'The dependent role of the boy player doubles for the dependency which is women's lot, creating a sensuality which is independent of the sex of the desired figure, and which is particularly erotic when the sex is confused' (Jardine, *Still Harping on Daughters*, p. 24). As Valerie Traub has pointed out, this earlier formulation inadvertently gives priority to heterosexual desire (as the dominant mode). See Traub, *Desire*, especially pp. 93–4.

13 Bray, *Homosexuality*, p. 51.

14 For a clear account of the consistent use of the terms 'family' and 'household' to designate those who cohabit under a single roof as dependants of one adult male in the eighteenth century see N. Tadmor, '"Family" and "friend" in *Pamela*: a case study in the history of the family in eighteenth-century England', *Social History*, 1989, vol. 14, pp. 289–306. In Bray, *Homosexuality*, see especially the clear account on pp. 44–6.

15 'The overall pattern in the circulation of members between [households of specified levels of wealth in fifteenth-century Florence] was similar for men and for women, but there are also some significant differences in the movements of the two sexes. The richest households tend to gather in both boys and girls as

they age, from birth up to their middle teens. At exact age 15 the 25 per cent of wealthy households contain 45 per cent of the boys and 43.5 per cent of the girls (as opposed to 39 per cent and 35 per cent respectively of the cohort of babies, age 0–2). This drift of children primarily means that wealthy households were taking in orphaned relatives. The incoming children probably also included many young relatives who had lost their fathers, and whose mothers had remarried and deserted them [sic]. The mother joined the household of her new husband, but usually did not take her children with her. The kindred of her late husband had to look to their care. . . . If we had data on servants and apprentices [registered with their household of birth in the Florentine census] we would undoubtedly observe an even more massive drift of young persons into and out of the homes of the wealthy. We know from other sources that "life-cycle" servants were numerous in Florence, as widely in traditional society. These young people, girls especially, spent their years of late childhood in service; they thereby earned their keep and accumulated from their earnings the dowry they needed for marriage' (David Herlihy, *Medieval Households*, Cambridge, Mass., Harvard University Press, 1985, p. 153).

16 Ralph Houlbrooke, *The English Family 1450–1700*, London, Longman, 1984, p. 173. See Peter Laslett, 'Mean household size in England since the sixteenth century', in P. Laslett and R. Wall (eds), *Household and Family in Past Time*, Cambridge, Cambridge University Press, 1972, pp. 125–58, table, p. 130. See also R. Wall, 'The age of leaving home', *Journal of Family History*, 1978, vol. 3, pp. 181–202.

17 Bray, *Homosexuality*, pp. 50–1.

18 Houlbrooke, *The English Family*, p. 150.

19 M. St Clare Byrne (ed.), *The Lisle Letters: An Abridgement*, Harmondsworth, Middx, Penguin, 1985, pp. 126–7.

20 Bray, *Homosexuality*, p. 51.

21 Susan Amussen, *An Ordered Society: Gender and Class in Early Modern England*, Oxford, Blackwell, 1988, pp. 35–6. See also Bray, *Homosexuality*, p. 45; and Paul Griffiths's work on early modern adolescence ('"At their own hande" and "out of service": residual lumps of young people in early modern England', paper delivered to the Cambridge Early Modernists, April 1990).

22 Houlbrooke, *The English Family*, p. 147. For the classic statement see Laslett, 'Mean household size': 'The seventeenth century patriarchal family had many of the characteristics of the patriarchal household. It included not only wife and children, but often younger brothers, sisters, nephews and nieces: male superiority and primogeniture were unquestioned. Most striking was the presence of very large numbers of servants, whose subjection to the head of household was absolute' (p. 10).

23 Ben Jonson, *Epicoene or The Silent Woman*, New Mermaids edn, ed. R. V. Holdsworth, London, Ernest Benn, 1979, 1.1.10–17.

24 Bray, *Homosexuality*, p. 48.

25 Ibid.

26 For a brilliant account of the ambiguities concerning the relationship between service and sexual favours contained within the early modern patriarchal household, see Cynthia Herrup's paper on the trial of the Earl of Castlehaven (forthcoming).

27 Bray, *Homosexuality*, p. 77.

28 Bray, *Homosexuality*, p. 69. On sexual exploitation of servants in general see, most recently, Amussen, *An Ordered Society*, p. 159. In *Othello*, the shared bed in service, used by Iago to enflame Othello's jealousy, fully exploits the sexual accessibility of the bedfellow: 'I lay with Cassio lately. . . . In sleep I heard him

say "Sweet Desdemona. / Let us be wary, let us hide our loves;" / And then, sir, would he ... kiss me hard, / As if he pluck'd up kisses by the roots, / That grew upon my lips, then laid his leg / Over my thigh, and sigh'd, and kiss'd' (3.3.419–31).

29 Peter Stallybrass, 'Transvestism and the "body beneath": speculating on the boy actor', in Zimmerman (ed.), *Erotic Politics*, 1992, pp. 64–83.

30 There is a steady, interesting insistence in the text on the good birth of the twins, and of their having full purses at their disposal. This seems to place them pivotally between the household economy and that of the market-place. Although employment in the former was, historically, as precarious as that in the latter (wage-labour), there is no question that in the play-text only the household is seen as a suitable 'place' for Viola and Sebastian. On wage-labour versus service see A. L. Beier, *Masterless Men: The Vagrancy Problem in England 1560–1640*, London, Methuen, 1985.

31 'My father was that Sebastian of Messaline whom I know you have heard of. He left behind him myself and a sister, both born in an hour' (2.1.16–19); 'My father ... died that day when Viola from her birth / Had number'd thirteen years'; 'O, that record is lively in my soul! / He finished indeed his mortal act / That day that made my sister thirteen years' (5.1.240–6).

32 1.5.157–64. See also the Duke's emphasis on the extreme youth of Cesario when he cautions him against marrying an older woman (2.4.24–39). In the same passage the Duke calls Viola 'boy'. Sebastian (mirror-image of the cross-dressed Viola) is consistently referred to as 'youth' (for example, 3.4.368).

33 See Beier, *Masterless Men*, for a gloss on the security of service versus the insecurity of waged labour (the temporarily full purse).

34 It perfectly fulfils the trope of serving devotion, as represented in saints' lives and romance. See Jardine, *Still Harping on Daughters*.

35 In terms of tropes, here is the moralisers' trope of the vulnerable boy captured in service by dominating female householders. See Ascham and, of course, Plautus's *Menaechmi* and Secchi's *Gl'Ingannati* (both of which link this play with *A Comedy of Errors*). In *Two Gentlemen of Verona* the two tropes are run into one, when Julia takes the name Sebastian (a straightforward signifier of male dependency and vulnerability) in order to pursue her fickle lover in faithful service. See Beier, *Masterless Men*: 'Regarding [living-in service] we are told that the master/servant relationship was the lynch-pin of a patriarchal society in which "every relationship could be seen as a love-relationship".'

36 1.4.1–7.

37 In the source story the heroine, dressed as a boy, fears she may be asked by her master for 'bedroom favours'. For a related discussion of the ambiguities of 'love' in the context of patronage see John Barrell, 'Editing out: the discourse of patronage and Shakespeare's twenty-ninth sonnet', in *Poetry, Language and Politics*, Manchester, Manchester University Press, 1988, pp. 18–43, on 'love' and patronage in Shakespeare's sonnet 29.

38 1.4.24–42.

39 2.4.110–16.

40 5.1.132–6.

41 5.1.320–5.

42 *Shakespeare's Sonnets*, ed. Stephen Booth, New Haven, Conn., Yale University Press, 1977, p. 20.

43 For the crucial part played by anxieties about resolving debt and credit in structuring the plots of plays of the period see Lorna Hutson, *The Usurer's Daughter: Male Friendship and Fictions of Women in Sixteenth-Century England*, London, Routledge, 1994.

44 5.1.265–71. I think the 'women's weeds' line is quite close in its possibilities to the seductively transgressive Pyander.

45 See Chapter 6.

46 5.1.137.

47 John Manningham's diary (1602) records a performance he saw of the play: 'A good practise in it to make the steward beleeue his Lady widdowe was in Loue wth him by counterfayting a lett^r / as from his Lady in generall tearmes telling him what shee liked best in him / and p[re]scribing his gesture in smiling his apparraile / &c./. And then when he came to practise making him beleeue they tooke him to be mad' (*Twelfth Night*, Arden edn, p. xxvi). Manningham's mistaken memory ('widow' when Olivia in fact mourns the deaths of her father and brother) confirms the fact that as a figure she is recognisably the independent woman of means whose own will and desires figure troublingly strongly in choice of husband (and thus continuation of the paternal line).

48 Olivia's femaleness is also the cause of her steward Malvolio's being prepared so readily to mistake his service relationship with his mistress for the possibility of passionate 'love' between them.

49 Johannes Jhan's school ordinance (1565), cit. Lyndal Roper, 'Blood and codpieces: masculinity in the early modern German town', in *Oedipus and the Devil: Witchcraft, Sexuality and Religion in early modern Europe*, London, Routledge, 1994, pp. 107–24.

50 Roper, *Oedipus and the Devil*, p. 107.

51 Roper, *Oedipus and the Devil*, pp. 119–20.

52 Roper, *Oedipus and the Devil*, p. 116.

53 5.1.315–25.

54 So, my final note addresses the vexed question of Middleton's *The Roaring Girl*. On this reading, Moll is neither male nor female, or both male and female, confusing the several traditions which represent economic dependency via cross-dressing in private and in public. So the joke about the promise that Moll herself would come and play her own part in the play, in place of the boy who 'actually' takes it, is that it simply makes no difference to the 'performance'. Either way, the figure is replete with erotic possibilities.

5 READING AND THE TECHNOLOGY OF TEXTUAL AFFECT

1 Myles Coverdale, *Certain most godly, fruitful, and comfortable letters of such true Saintes and holy Martyrs of God, as in the late bloodye persecution here within this Realme, gaue their lyues for the defence of Christes holy gospel: written in the tyme of theyr affliction and cruell imprysonment*, London, John Day, 1564, sig. A.ii.^{v}.

2 J. H. P. Pafford (ed.), *The Winter's Tale*, Arden edn, London, Methuen, 1963, 1.1.22–9.

3 This piece of work has been shaped by extensive discussion with Lorna Hutson, particularly about the links between Erasmus's textbook treatment of letter writing and the technology of textual affect in *King Lear*. I am deeply grateful to Lorna for the intellectual support she has always given to my work.

4 See Chapter 1.

5 There are, however, some suggestive pointers, prompting enquiry into the influence of Erasmus and an Erasmian concern with the rhetorical production of feeling on Shakespeare in Emrys Jones, *The Origins of Shakespeare*, Oxford, Clarendon Press, 1977, pp. 9–13. It might be argued that all Shakespeare criticism has, until comparatively recently, been fundamentally about 'feeling', in the sense

that it set out to match intensity of emotion in the Shakespearean text to the sensibility of the critic's own period. The difference between such an approach and the one I have in mind here is, of course, that such criticism was committed to the view that feeling was transhistorical – that feeling elicited by the text in the nineteenth or twentieth century was necessarily that feeling which it had elicited when first written and performed. I would like to thank Emrys Jones and Barbara Everett for extremely helpful suggestions made to clarify points in a version of this piece of work delivered to their graduate seminar at New College Oxford in January 1994.

6 I have in mind the fact that the entire Erasmus literature is grounded upon P. S. Allen's monumental compilation of Erasmus's letters: the *Opus epistolarum Des. Erasmi Roterodami* (12 vols), Oxford, Clarendon Press, 1906–1958. For the purposes of such work, Erasmus scholars almost inevitably treat these letters as pure content – the transparent transmission of authentic detail concerning Erasmus's life, thought and work. See my *Erasmus, Man of Letters: The Construction of Charisma in Print*, Princeton, NJ, Princeton University Press, 1993.

7 In their different ways, Deborah Warner, directing the play in 1992 at the National Theatre, and Max Stafford Clark, directing it at the Royal Court in 1993, both still structure their productions around this emotional intensity. In the case of Max Stafford Clark's production, which aspired to contemporise the play (with the divided map used to evoke the current disintegration of the nation state in the Balkans), this investment in a transhistorical emotional core was particularly striking.

8 Jean-Claude Margolin and Pierre Mesnard (eds), *Opera omnia Desiderii Erasmi Roterodami, Ordinis primi, tomus secundus*, Amsterdam, North-Holland Publishing Company, 1971 [hereafter ASD I-2], p. 225. On some of Erasmus's indebtednesses in defining letter writing in the *De conscribendis epistolis* see J. Monfasani, 'Three notes on renaissance rhetoric', *Rhetorica*, 1987, vol. 5, pp. 107–18; 'Two Greek sources for Erasmus's *De conscribendis epistolis*', pp. 115–18.

9 I suspect that nowadays we reserve the form of 'affect at a distance' which Erasmus associates with the letter for telephone communication.

10 It is this nonchalance concerning 'feigning' in order to achieve 'sincerity' which we shall see causing difficulty and anxiety in *King Lear*.

11 Erasmus, *Epistolae Hieronymi*, Basle, Froben, 1524, I, p. 218.

12 For example, Barlandus produced a slim manual on letter writing in the 1520s, consisting of three commented letters of Jerome's, of which the first is the letter to Nitias.

13 James F. Brady and John C. Olin (eds), *Collected Works of Erasmus*, vol. 61, Toronto, University of Toronto Press, 1992, p. 109.

14 *Collected Works of Erasmus*, vol. 61, pp. 109–10.

15 As so often happens with Erasmus (who likes to leave reading clues everywhere), there is surviving evidence that precisely the Jerome *annotatio artis* was in Erasmus's mind at the time he was putting together the Schürer *De copia/Parabolae* volume. In an unpublished letter of September 1514, Erasmus approaches Gregor Reisch, the original editor appointed by Schürer to oversee the complete edition of the works of Jerome. Erasmus's purpose is politely to decline to edit the letters volume collaboratively, and tactfully to gain control of that volume (on which he had already done a good deal of work) himself. One of the points on which Erasmus expresses strong feeling is Reisch's proposed arrangement of the works, and in particular the order in which the genuine Jerome letters should be arranged: 'I see that you feel as I do about this divinely inspired man. I do not reject your order of arrangement, but I would not be able to follow it without considerable labour on my part – I would have to

reorganise everything, and my own system would then be ruined. Finally, there are many letters which for coherence need to be grouped together differently. For instance, Jerome himself wants the letter to Nepotianus to follow the one he wrote to Heliodorus. . . . I have added summaries of the individual letters, and commentaries, so that even people without much education can read them more easily' (*my translation*, Allen, 2, 28 (ep 308)). The internal connection between the letter to Heliodorus and that to Nepotianus is established because Jerome cross-refers from the letter to Nepotianus to 'the previous letter', concerning the importance of its rhetorical structure. Erasmus's reason for placing these two letters side by side is nothing to do with their chronology. In the letter to Nepotianus Jerome refers back to the high rhetorical style of the letter to Heliodorus, which he explicitly says he wrote many years earlier: 'Again and again you ask me, my dear Nepotianus, in your letters from over the sea, to draw for you a few rules of life, showing how one who has renounced the service of the world to become a monk or a clergyman may keep the straight path of Christ, and not be drawn aside into the haunts of vice. As a young man, or rather as a boy, and while I was curbing by the hard life of the desert the first onslaughts of youthful passion, I sent a letter of remonstrance to your reverend uncle, Heliodorus, which, by the tears and complainings with which it was filled, showed him the feelings of the friend whom he had deserted. In it I acted the part suited to my age, and as I was still aglow with the methods and maxims of the rhetoricians, I decked it out a good deal with the flourishes of the schools. Now, however, my head is grey, my brow is furrowed, a dewlap like that of an ox hangs from my chin, and, as Virgil says, 'The chilly blood stands still around my heart' (*Collected Works of Erasmus*, vol. 61, p. 134). Erasmus juxtaposes the letters precisely *because* of the attention Jerome draws, in the letter to Nepotianus, to the rhetorical contrivedness of the letter to Heliodorus. So we know, conveniently, that at the very moment at which Erasmus was composing the letters to Wimpfeling, Schürer and Gilles, and putting together the Schürer *De copia/Parabolae* volume (September to December 1514), he was also thinking about the Jerome letter to Heliodorus and its technology of affect, and putting together its *annotatio artis* – its rhetorical commentary.

16 I should say here that this is the only one of the letters which has such an *annotatio artis* in addition to its primary commentary. Nevertheless, the fact that this is the first letter suggests that Erasmus attached importance to establishing the possibility of such commentaries. Characteristically, in volumes annotated by Erasmus, commentaries tail off and become perfunctory some little way into the edition.

17 Jacques Chomarat, *Grammaire et Rhetorique chez Erasme*, 2 vols, Paris, Societé d'Edition 'Les Belles Lettres', 1981, vol. I, p. 537.

18 *Collected Works of Erasmus*, vol. 61, p. 123.

19 *Collected Works of Erasmus*, vol. 61, pp. 124–5.

20 *Collected Works of Erasmus*, vol. 61, p. 126.

21 ASD I-2, p. 353.

22 *Collected Works of Erasmus*, vol. 61, p. 124.

23 The *annotatio artis* contains a discussion of persuasive and hortatory epistolary writing which is repeated almost verbatim in the *De conscribendis epistolis*. 'And first to say something about the kind of subject, it belongs to the hortatory genre. . . . This is so close to the persuasive kind of discourse that Aristotle did not think that there was any distinction between the two. In my judgment, however, there is some difference. For the aim of persuasion is to influence the will; the aim of exhortation is to encourage and enable. Persuasion is directed at the irresolute, exhortation at the inactive. We persuade when we show what it

is advantageous to do, we exhort when we add emotion to our discourse. . . .
Exhortation has this special feature: it is more fiery and has a large admixture
of the laudatory, which however Jerome does not use in this letter. For men are
incited above all by two factors, praise and the fear of disgrace' (*Collected Works
of Erasmus*, vol. 61, p. 124).

24 Craig R. Thompson (ed.), *Collected Works of Erasmus*, vol. 24, Toronto, University of Toronto Press, 1978, pp. 348, 354.

25 For another relevant link between the *De copia* and letters (this time Seneca's),
see my *Erasmus, Man of Letters*, Chapter 5.

26 For evidence of such careful 'staging' of a text by means of the accompanying
letters and verses, in which Erasmus was closely involved, see the exchanges of
letters soliciting endorsements for Thomas More's *Utopia*.

27 One further piece of cross-referring by Erasmus links Jerome and familiar
letters to the Schürer volume. In Book two of the *De copia* there is a section
entitled *De parabola*, which provides the structural context for the insertion of
parabolae (comparisons) of the kind collected in the companion text in the
volume. The example Erasmus chooses to illustrate this technique is Cicero's
use, in the *Pro Murena,* of an extended comparison as follows: 'Those just
sailing into harbour after a long sea-voyage eagerly give information to those
setting out about the likelihood of storms and the pirate situation and what the
different places are like, because it is natural to feel kindly towards those who
are about to face the dangers which we have just escaped. What then should be
my feelings, who am just coming into sight of land after a terrible tossing,
towards this man who, as I can see, must go out to face dreadful storms?'
(*Collected Works of Erasmus*, vol. 24, p. 621). He goes on immediately to point
out that Jerome closely imitates this passage of Cicero's in the letter to Heliodorus, and cites that passage also in its entirety (*Collected Works of Erasmus*, vol.
24, pp. 621–2).

28 For example: 'It was possible, when I was with you, to see in one city the
virtues of all the most celebrated city-states: Roman severity, Athenian wisdom,
and the self-restraint of Lacedaemon' (amplification of place), *Collected Works of
Erasmus*, vol. 3, trans. R. A. B. Mynors and D. F. S. Thomson, ed. James K.
McConica, Toronto, University of Toronto Press, 1976, p. 26; 'That incomparable young man Jakob Sturm, who adds lustre to his distinguished family by
his own high character, crowns his youth with a seriousness worthy of riper
years, and gives great charm to uncommon learning with his incredible
modesty' (amplification of person), *Collected Works of Erasmus*, vol. 3, p. 27; 'Do
not forget Ottmar, a man who seemed to me well read without ostentation,
who with the rapid trilling on his pipes that outdid the very nightingale so
ravished me that I seemed rapt in ecstasy' (amplification of person), *Collected
Works of Erasmus*, vol. 3, p. 29.

29 The only other letters to or from Wimpfeling in Allen are equally formal,
endorsing, or seeking endorsement of, printed works. P. S. Allen, *Opus Epistolarum Erasmi*, vol. 1, p. 463 (ep 224) (Wimpfeling defends himself against anti-
Erasmian sentiments in a letter appended to Schürer's edition of the *Moriae
encomium* (1511)); Allen, *Opus Epistolarum Erasmi*, vol. 2, p. 180 (ep 382) (unpublished; Wimpfeling tells Erasmus he has mentioned him favourably in his *Catho-
logus* of writers); Allen, *Opus Epistolarum Erasmi*, vol. 2, pp. 187–8 (ep 385)
(Erasmus's nine-line courtesy reply, published in a volume of Mantuan edited
by Wimpfeling).

30 *Collected Works of Erasmus*, vol. 3, p. 33.

31 This is inevitably the point at which a note is needed to indicate how totally the
historical context of both letters and poems is lost as they are presented (or

rather, not presented) in *Collected Works of Erasmus*. Allen already obscures the relationship between the four letters by reassigning them to their (effectively spurious) chronological positions within his *Opus Epistolarum Erasmi*. Thus Erasmus's letter to Wimpfeling is separated from the letter which elicited it as formal response, and the preface to Schürer follows rather than precedes these letters. Allen does, however, indicate that the poems alluded to are included with the text of the letter in the Schürer volume. *Collected Works of Erasmus* omits these notes, and instead refers the reader to Reedjik's collected edition of Erasmus's poems for the texts. It is no longer clear that they were, to all intents and purposes, produced for the volume. As far as the history of the book is concerned, we have altogether lost the book. The book is replaced by pseudo-biography.

32 *Collected Works of Erasmus*, vol. 3, p. 29.
33 *Collected Works of Erasmus*, vol. 3, pp. 43–4.
34 The second edition of the *Parabolae* was printed by Martens at Louvain and edited by Gilles, suggesting that this text was truly his gift.
35 Erasmus expresses closely similar sentiments to Thomas More.
36 *Collected Works of Erasmus*, vol. 3, pp. 43–6.
37 For a somewhat similar argument about textual strategies for manipulating feeling in the period see K. Meerhoff, 'Rhetorica: creativiteit', in M. Spies and K. Meerhoff, *Rhetorica: Strategie en creativiteit*, Amsterdam, Amsterdam University Press, 1993, pp. 25–53.
38 'I will neither wish that the love of your freends . . . nor yet mine authoritie that I have ouer you, should do me any good at all, to compasse this my request, if I shall not proue unto you by most plain reasons . . . to be necessary for you at this time to marry' (*Wilson's Arte of Rhetorique (1560)*, G. H. Mair (ed.), Oxford, Clarendon Press, 1909, p. 40).
39 *Certain most godly, fruitful, and comfortable letters*. I am grateful to Lorna Hutson and Alan Stewart for finding this passage. Here, as always, their breadth of reading and alertness to reference has proved invaluable.
40 Sig. A.ii.$^{r-v}$.
41 See Jardine, *Erasmus, Man of Letters*, pp. 60–2.
42 4.3.9–15. This scene is not in the 1623 folio.
43 4.3.24–32.
44 2.2.159–64: 'Approach, thou beacon to this under globe, / That by thy comfortable beams I may / Peruse this letter. . . . I know 'tis from Cordelia, / Who hath most fortunately been inform'd / Of my obscured course.'
45 3.1.46–7: 'If you shall see Cordelia, – / As fear not but you shall – show her this ring.'
46 Leo Salingar has suggested to me that the letter Macbeth sends to Lady Macbeth in Act 1 scene 5 of the play, informing her that the witches' prophecy has already begun to come true, also conforms to this Erasmian model. The audience experiences the full emotional intensity of the incident for Macbeth by watching the histrionic and rhetorical response of his wife to the *letter* ('Glamis thou art, and Cawdor . . . '). It is also worth noting that the most familiar type of such a letter (to which, in a sense, Macbeth's letter conforms) is the intimate love letter. In the sixteenth century it was already customary for a love letter to be a particularly significant 'gift' from a lover (see A. Macfarlane, *Marriage and Love in England 1300–1840*, Oxford, Basil Blackwell, 1986, pp. 301–3).
47 1.4.330–8.
48 1.4.31–5.
49 It would be attractive to argue that the exemplary letter received by Cordelia,

and written by Kent, in Act 4 scene 3, which exists only in one text of the play, was an addition for dramatic effect, which, however, is actually not strictly in character with Kent's 'bluntness' elsewhere.

50 1.5.1–7.
51 2.4.26–36.
52 2.1.118–24.
53 2.2.15–17, 33–5.
54 2.2.92–7.
55 Lorna Hutson points out that in the earlier chronicle play, *King Leir* (registered in 1605) letters already structure the contest for authority here between Goneril and Lear. But in *King Leir* Goneril *intercepts* letters intended to warn Lear, and *substitutes* letters addressed to her sister 'which contayne matter quite contrary to the other: ther shall she be given to understand, that my father hath detracted her, given out slanderous speeches against her; and that hee hath most intollerably abused me, set my Lord and me at variance, and made mutinyes amongst the commons'. And she instructs the messenger to lay false oath if necessary, to ensure that her letters are accepted as true: 'These things (although it be not so) / Yet thou must affirme them to be true, / With othes and protestations as will serve' (Geoffrey Bullough, *Narrative and Dramatic Sources of Shakespeare*, vol. 7, London, Routledge & Kegan Paul, 1973, pp. 360–1). Here it is plotting by means of letters (instrumentally), rather than rhetorical effect through letters, which secures the desired outcome.
56 Tony Grafton points out to me that Justus Lipsius stressed this misleading quality as potentially exploitable in familiar letters.
57 I owe this insight to Lorna Hutson.
58 3.3.8–11.
59 3.7.42–9.
60 The same letter is sent on from Cornwall to Albany at the beginning of Act 3, scene 7, as evidence that the French have landed.
61 1.1.90–4.
62 For a full version of this argument see Lorna Hutson, *The Usurer's Daughter*, London, Routledge, 1994.
63 At the very beginning of the play, when Kent is not known to Edmund, Gloucester instructs Edmund, 'remember him heareafter as my honourable friend': '*Edm.* My services to your Lordship. *Kent.* I must love you, and sue to know you better. *Edm.* Sir, I shall study deserving. *Glou.* He hath been out nine years, and away he shall again' (1.1.26–32). In other words, Edmund has to build the bonds of kin and service with learnt knowledge of affect.
64 4.2.82–7.
65 4.5.19–22.
66 1.1.84–8.
67 2.3.21.
68 4.3.25–6.

6 ALIEN INTELLIGENCE

1 *The Merchant of Venice*, Arden edn, 1.3.8–25.
2 The Althusserian memories in this formulation are, of course, deliberate.
3 In Spring 1994 a Royal Shakespeare Production of *The Merchant of Venice* in London precipitated an impassioned public controversy between David Thacker (the director) and the playwright Arnold Wesker. Wesker argued that in a climate of revived anti-Semitism in Europe it was more appropriate to rewrite

Shakespeare's play entirely than to tinker (as he maintained Thacker had done) with the original play in ways which threatened to increase rather than to diminish the anti-Semitism of the original.

4 Since I wrote this chapter I have become aware that it was probably prompted by my remembered (or rather, remembered and forgotten) reading of Stephen Greenblatt's 'Marlowe, Marx, and anti-Semitism', in *Learning to Curse: Essays in Early Modern Culture*, London, Routledge, 1990, pp. 40–58, especially pp. 44–5. Thus, I suspect, are intellectual schools born: struck by a compelling argument a critic revises her entire approach to a canonical text, and then promptly erases the memory of the formative work, to rediscover the idea as her own!

5 N. M. Bawcutt (ed.), *The Jew of Malta*, Revels edn, Manchester, Manchester University Press, 1978, 1.1.49–65.

6 1.1.85–8.

7 That precision extends to Barabas's being surprised that the two argosies have not encountered one another on the way (they necessarily take closely similar routes), and his expressing displeasure that they have not sailed in convoy to reduce the risk of interception by Turkish privateers.

8 2.3.220–5, 242–7.

9 K. R. Andrews, *Trade, Plunder and Settlement: Maritime Enterprise and the Genesis of the British Empire*, Cambridge, Cambridge University Press, 1984, pp. 93–7 and Richard Hakluyt, *The Principal Navigations, Voiages, Traffiques and Discoveries of the English Nation* (3 vols), London, 1598–1600, Glasgow, 1903–5. For this section of the chapter I draw extensively on Andrews, *Trade, Plunder and Settlement*, Chapter 4, 'The Levant'.

10 The system of 'factors' appears to originate with the Fugger trading empire.

11 Marlowe is apparently also accurate in suggesting that a Jew would be particularly well placed for trading in the Levant. See Andrews, *Trade, Plunder and Settlement*, p. 100: 'The ambassadors, consuls and factors in the Levant built up over the decades a valuable fund of commercial experience applicable in many respects to other parts of Asia. That they generally failed to bridge the cultural gap between Turkey and England or to develop meaningful contact with the Turkish people was not mainly their fault. . . . Factors' acquaintance was for the most part limited to "dragomen" (interpreters, often of Italian extraction), Jews, Armenians, Greeks and other Europeans.' See also Ramsay, *English Overseas Trade*, pp. 52–3.

12 Lawrence Stone, *The Crisis of the Aristocracy, 1558–1641*, abridged edn, Oxford, Oxford University Press, 1967, p. 242.

13 See L. Schick, *Un grand homme d'affaires au début du XVIème siècle: Jacob Fugger*, Paris, SEVPEN, 1957, pp. 159–60. It seems to me possible that Marlowe alludes directly to this kind of intervention by financiers in establishing ruling houses at 1.1.128–34: 'I must confess we come not to be kings. . . . Give us a peaceful rule, make Christians kings, / That thirst so much for principality.' The merchants had a strong vested interest in stable governments as a trading base.

14 For a clear account of the credit network on which, by the late years of the sixteenth century, England depended economically, see E. Kerridge, *Trade and Banking in Early Modern England*, Manchester, Manchester University Press, 1988.

15 I mention this last (to which I will return) because in spite of the brevity of the mention (2.3.156–63) it occurs precisely in a context where it is the most plausible kind of transaction to be taking place between Christian and Jew.

16 1.2.59–62.

17 See Robert Brenner, *Merchants and Revolution: Commercial Change, Political Conflict, and London's Overseas Traders, 1550–1653*, Princeton, NJ, Princeton University

Press, 1993, pp. 617–18 for later comment on the differential status of alien and denizen merchants.

18 See Brenner, *Merchants and Revolution*, pp. 7–8.

19 In Marlowe's play this is consistently represented by Barabas's asides to the effect that he serves only himself, and his commitment to his family to the exclusion of the state.

20 1.1.102–14.

21 L. Pearsall Smith, *The Life and Letters of Sir Henry Wotton*, 2 vols, Oxford, Clarendon Press, 1907, vol. I, pp. 255–6.

22 Ibid.

23 L. Hutson, *The Usurer's Daughter: Male Friendship and Fictions of Women in Sixteenth-Century England*, London, Routledge, 1994.

24 'Edward II: the pliant king' (Marlowe conference, University of Kent, Canterbury, 6 July 1993), unpublished paper. See also 'The early modern closet discovered', *Representations*, 1995, vol. 50, pp. 76–100.

25 W. H. Sherman, *John Dee: The Politics of Reading and Writing in the English Renaissance*, Amherst, Mass., University of Massachusetts Press, 1995. See also Sherman and Jardine, 'Pragmatic readers: knowledge transactions and scholarly services in late Elizabethan England', in P. Roberts and A. Fletcher (eds), *Religion, Culture and Society in Early Modern England: Essays in Honour of Patrick Collinson*, Cambridge, Cambridge University Press, 1994, pp. 102–24.

26 2.3.156–63.

27 2.3.141–2,153–4.

28 Scholars have tended to be a bit coy about expectation of gain in exchange for the supply of intellectual goods. Several documents survive from the 1590s which indicate an undertaking to supply skilled providers of knowledge as a service arrangement.

29 Kerridge, *Trade and Banking*, pp. 98–9.

30 M. Kiernan (ed.), *Sir Francis Bacon: The Essayes or Counsels, Civill and Morall*, Oxford, Clarendon Press, 1985, pp. 124–9, at p. 125. For early sixteenth-century anxiety about exchange of money without transaction of goods see *A treatise concerning the staple and the commodities of this realm* (c. 1519–35): 'The bredyng of so many marchaunts in London, risen owt of pore mens sonnes, hath bene a mervelous destruction to the holl reme. . . . So wer all yong merchaunts, comyng owt of ther presntishod and cowd have no wages of ther masters, compellid to borrow clothes of clothe makers for respite, and caried the same clothes to the marts beyonde see to sell, and ther must nedes sell theym, and the money to bestow it on wares to bryng home to sell, to make money to pay ther creditors at ther dayes . . . that in short time they distroyed the price of wollen clothes, causyng all the old merchaunts to fall from byeng and sellyng clothes. Than began old merchaunts to forsake occupieng of clothes to occupie their money by exchaunge, which is not only pleyn usury, but also it hath and yit doth helpe to distroye the welth of the kyng, of his lords and comons, for that occupieng hynderith the reame both ways outward and inward' (reprinted in R. H. Tawney and E. Power (eds), *Tudor Economic Documents*, 3 vols, London, Longman, 1924, vol. 3, pp. 90–114 and pp. 106–7. Cit. Barry Taylor, *Vagrant Writing: Social and Semiotic Disorders in the English Renaissance*, London, Harvester, 1991, pp. 50–1.

31 ' "The usurer never adventureth or hazardeth the losse of his principal: for he wil have all sufficient securitie for the repaiment and restoring of it backe againe to himselfe." Interest was another matter. It was the gain that accrued to a man from his interest in a transaction, and could arise in a number of ways. A sleeping partner, who put up money for a venture in which he ran the risk of

losing all or part of his investment, was no usurer, and his gain was not usury, but interest, under the title of *periculum sortis*. He who lent charitably to someone in need what he could otherwise have used profitably in industry or commerce, was permitted reasonable compensation for his opportunity lost, under the title of *lucrum cessans* or cessant gain. He who by lending incurred expenses he would not otherwise have borne, such as the transport of coins, covering loans necessitated by the extension of credit, the keeping of accounts, scrivener's fees, and insurance premiums, had a right to compensation, under the title of *damnum emergens*. . . . He who lent and was not repaid on the agreed day, might claim interest on the delay, *titulus morae*, under title of *mora*. When the contract of loan itself stipulated a penalty for such delay, interest might be charged, under title of *poena conventionalis*. In both cases the lender had to forbear suing for recovery of his loan, and the interest he received was in return for this forbearance. Lawful gains might also be made from ordinary transactions on genuine outland bills of exchange, because of the slight but real risk of loss of part or all of the money advanced and the uncertain amount of any possible gain, due to fluctuations in the exchanges' (Kerridge, *Trade and Banking*, pp. 34–5).

32 This treatment is based on two articles by Raymond de Roover: 'What is dry exchange? a contribution to the study of English mercantilism', and 'Cambium ad Venetias: contribution to the history of foreign exchange', in J. Kirshner (ed.), *Business, Banking and Economic Thought in Late Medieval and Early Modern Europe*, Chicago, Ill., University of Chicago Press, 1974, pp. 183–99 and pp. 239–59.

33 From 1571 charging interest of 10 per cent was legalised in England, largely to prevent the charging of higher percentages on illegal loans. But the moral anxiety persisted, and elsewhere in Europe canon law continued to prohibit the charging of interest. As I understand it, in England, in any case, it was not possible to go to law to require repayment of interest due if the capital sum was repaid.

34 Brenner, *Merchants and Revolution*, pp. 55–6.

35 See Brenner, *Merchants and Revolution*, p. 82: 'Insofar as offices were available, merchants rarely received them. The important exception to this rule was in state finance, and here the Levant-East India traders were overwhelmingly dominant. As Robert Ashton has shown, the farmers of the customs came to play an increasingly crucial role in providing credit for a crisis-ridden government in the 1620s and 1630s.'

36 4.1.63–74.

37 4.2.78–82.

38 Brenner, *Merchants and Revolution*, pp. 80–1.

39 1.2.53–6.

40 Since the Knights Templar operated an early banking system (see Kerridge, *Trade and Banking*, p. 1) I suspect that there is further reference, now lost to us here, to early modern financial transactions.

41 2.2.26–9.

42 2.2.9–18.

43 Although there was a flourishing slave trade dominated by the Spanish, it dealt in natives of West Africa, who were shipped to the Caribbean to work the sugar plantations. See Andrews, *Trade, Plunder and Settlement*, pp. 116–28.

44 One of the pieces of knowledge which Wotton offers Zouche is the ground plan of the Emperor's summer palace. Plans and maps of fortifications were an important kind of 'intelligence' provided by travellers to the authorities back home.

45 1.1.1–24.

46 See the equivocation on who is kind and who is a friend in the transacting of the original bond between Antonio and Shylock in Act 1.

7 COMPANIONATE MARRIAGE VERSUS MALE FRIENDSHIP

1 Thomas Overbury, 'Character of a good wife', cit. A. Macfarlane, *Marriage and Love in England: Modes of Reproduction 1300–1840*, Oxford, Blackwell, 1986, p. 179. Alan Stewart points out to me that this quotation is reminiscent of the standard Ciceronian *amicitia* line on shared adversity. For generalised discussions of the 'good wife' in the period see M. J. M. Ezell, *The Patriarch's Wife: Literary Evidence and the History of the Family*, Chapel Hill, University of North Carolina Press, 1987.

2 See K. Wrightson, *English Society 1580–1680*, London, Unwin Hyman, 1982, pp. 90–104; Macfarlane, *Marriage and Love*; R. A. Houlbrooke, *The English Family 1450–1700*, London, Longman, 1984, pp. 96–126; S. D. Amussen, *An Ordered Society: Gender and Class in Early Modern England*, Oxford, Blackwell, 1988. On the ideology of the companionate marriage see V. Wayne, introduction to *The Flower of Friendship: A Renaissance Dialogue Contesting Marriage by Edmund Tilney*, Ithaca, NY, Cornell University Press, 1992, pp. 13–37.

3 Wrightson, *English Society*, p. 100.

4 Apart from humane social historians in general, feminist historians have been naturally hostile to arranged marriages because agnatic kinship structure suggests that such arrangements are made by men and for men. But of course female kin were also extremely active in 'matchmaking', and the future financial security of a daughter was as important to the strategic choice as was perpetuating the male line. See Ezell, *The Patriarch's Wife*, pp. 20–35.

5 On the importance of intimacy for the organisation of the Tudor and Stuart court see D. Starkey (ed.), *The English Court from the Wars of the Roses to the Civil War*, London, Longman, 1987, especially chapters 3–6.

6 See L. Hutson, *The Usurer's Daughter*, London, Routledge, 1994; A. Stewart, *The Bounds of Sodomy*, Princeton, NJ, Princeton University Press, forthcoming.

7 So although social historians like Wrightson and Macfarlane suggest that it 'seems reasonable to conclude that among the greater part of the common people marriage partners were freely chosen, subject to the advice of friends and a sense of obligation to consult or subsequently inform parents if they were alive and within reach' (Wrightson, *English Society*, p. 78, cit. Macfarlane, *Marriage and Love*, p. 124), Wrightson's full discussion of flexible arrangements for 'consent' from parents (or in the absence of parents, 'friends') to marriages largely formed by two young people does, I think, suggest that the economic need for some form of lineal endorsement means that 'love' between partners still conforms more closely to the lineal model than appears at first sight.

8 *King Lear*, Arden edn, 1.1.95–104.

9 See Macfarlane, *Marriage and Love*, p. 282; J. P. Cooper, in J. Goody, J. Thirsk and E. P. Thompson (eds), *Family and Inheritance: Rural Society in Western Europe 1200–1800*, Cambridge, Cambridge University Press, 1976, pp. 192–327.

10 Thus this kind of 'love' follows the agnatic lineal model: 'The daughter is treated as a marginal member of her father's lineage, and after her marriage, her children will leave it entirely; their allegiance passes to her husband's line' (D. Herlihy, *Medieval Households*, Cambridge, Mass., Harvard University Press, 1985, p. 82).

11 *King Lear*, 1.1.139–42.

12 Starkey, *The English Court.*

13 For a related argument about Jacobean drama and social anxiety see S. J. Wiseman, '"Tis Pity She's A Whore: representing the incestuous body', in L. Gent and N. Llewellyn (eds), *Renaissance Bodies: The Human Figure in English Culture c.1540–1660*, London, Routledge, 1990, pp. 180–97.

14 Shakespeare, sonnet 29.

15 J. Barrell, 'Editing out: the discourse of patronage and Shakespeare's twenty-ninth sonnet', in *Poetry, Language and Politics*, Manchester, Manchester University Press, 1988, pp. 18–43.

16 G. Ungerer, *A Spaniard in Elizabethan England: The Correspondence of Antonio Perez's Exile*, 2 vols, London, 1976.

17 See L. Jardine and A. T. Grafton, '"Studied for action": how Gabriel Harvey read his Livy', *Past and Present*, 1990, vol. 129, pp. 3–51; L. Jardine and W. Sherman, 'Pragmatic readers: knowledge transactions and scholarly services in late Elizabethan England', in P. Roberts and A. Fletcher (eds), *Religion, Culture and Society in Early Modern England: Essays in Honour of Patrick Collinson*, Cambridge, Cambridge University Press, 1994, pp. 102–24.

18 Shakespeare, sonnet 20.

19 A. Bray, *Homosexuality in Renaissance England*, London, Gay Men's Press, 1982; 'Homosexuality and the signs of male friendship in Elizabethan England', *History Workshop Journal*, 1990, vol. 19, pp. 1–19. In *Sodometries: Renaissance Texts, Modern Sexualities*, Stanford, Stanford University Press, 1992, Jonathan Goldberg claims that the instability of the term (and understanding of) 'sodomy' in the period gives the critic licence to interpret all ambivalent sexuality in Renaissance texts along a sodomitical axis. While at times this produces a somewhat 'perverse' reading, it has the virtue of destabilising the comfortable modern heterosexual bias of most criticism, including some of my own (Goldberg, *Sodometries*, pp. 112–15).

20 'Use', here, in other words, has the sense of 'use up' or consumption. Whereas in male friendship there is prolonged reciprocity with the pay-off endlessly deferred.

21 This is what Goldberg wants to argue in *Sodometries*. Valerie Traub argues along similar lines that in Shakespeare's sonnets the purity of homoerotic attraction is in tension with reproductive sex which is tainted by its inevitable association with the female body. The anxiety she detects is there, I am arguing, but I am tracing it to a different source. See V. Traub, *Desire and Anxiety: Circulations of Sexuality in Shakespearean Drama*, London, Routledge, 1992, pp. 140–4.

22 Alan Stewart suggests comparison with a recent article by Lauro Martines, 'The politics of love poetry in renaissance Italy'.

23 Ungerer, *A Spaniard*, pp. 219–20.

24 Alan Haynes, *Invisible Power: The Elizabethan Secret Services 1570–1603*, Stroud, Alan Sutton, 1992, p. 105. See also J. M. Archer, *Sovereignty and Intelligence: Spying and Court Culture in the English Renaissance*, Stanford, Calif., Stanford University Press, 1993.

25 *Othello*, Arden edn, 1.3.180–9.

26 *Much Ado About Nothing*, Arden edn, ed. A. R. Humphreys, London, Methuen, 1981: 'I will assume thy part in some disguise, / And tell fair Hero I am Claudio, / And in her bosom I'll unclasp *my* heart, / And take her hearing prisoner with the force / And strong encounter of *my* amorous tale' (1.1.301–5, my emphasis).

27 1.3.56–60.

28 Within the conventions of parentally negotiated marriage matches there was a place for proxy wooing. A trusted and personable emissary could seek to endear

the proposed partner to the intended spouse whose geographical distance or other impediment made personal wooing inappropriate. Holbein's intensely 'humane' portrait of Christina of Denmark is part of such a proxy wooing process – the ambassador 'falls for' the designated princess and the trusted painter records a 'likeness' which captures the personal qualities which recommend her. But where a more personal kind of service relationship pertains, this kind of wooing in one's own person on behalf of another ceases to be appropriate.

29 2.1.179. Leonato too believes that Don Pedro woos for himself: 'Daughter, remember what I told you: if the Prince do solicit you in that kind [with a marriage proposal], you know your answer' (2.1.61–2).

30 They also suggest real-life models like the supposedly notorious Dr Crooke for the mercenary madhouse proprieter, Alibius.

31 According to a manuscript note by Malone in his copy of the 1653 quarto, *The Changeling* was licensed for performance in 1622: 'Licensed to be acted by the Lady Elizabeth's servants at The Phoenix, May 7, 1622. by Sir Henry Herbert Master of the Revels' (Bodleian Mal. 246(9)). The earliest performance recorded is in January 1623/4 at Court; the play enjoyed a considerable success up to the closure of the theatres in 1642, and again after 1660. Contemporary accounts suggest that it owed its popularity to the performance of Antonio – the feigning madman, identified as the titular 'changeling' (fool, half-wit) in the list of *dramatis personae* in the 1653 printed text of the play. If so, then seventeenth-century taste valued *The Changeling* for precisely that part of the play which modern critics find least interesting. Recent criticism focuses almost exclusively on the main plot, in which the 'changelings' are those who are turncoats and traitors to rank and lineage – De Flores and Beatrice-Joanna: 'Commonly the childe expresseth his sire, and posterity (if not chaungeling) covets to tread the steps of their ancestours' (Lawrence Humphrey, *The Nobles* (1563), cit. Leo Salingar, 'The Changeling and the drama of domestic life', *Dramatic form in Shakespeare and the Jacobeans*, Cambridge, Cambridge University Press, 1986, pp. 222–35).

32 In John Reynolds's main source story, the fourth of five 'tragicall histories' in the first book of *The Triumphs of Gods Revenge against The Crying and Execrable Sinne of Wilfull and Premeditated Murther* (entered in the Stationers' Register on 7 June 1621), the distinction between Don Alonso Piracquo, the suitor of good local standing, and Don Pedro de Alsemero, the son of a professional soldier, who has acquired a considerable fortune through trading in the Indies, with a reputation for bravery but no public presence in Alicante, is equally carefully drawn.

33 R. A. Houlbrooke, *The English Family 1450–1700*, London, Longman, 1984, pp. 73–4.

34 5.3.150–3. Compare Webster's *The Duchess of Malfi*, 2.5.24–5: 'The smarting cupping-glass, for that's the means / To purge infected blood, such blood as hers.'

35 2.1.154.

36 2.1.8–14.

37 2.2.81–2.

38 2.2.86–7.

39 2.2.129–33.

40 4.2.94–102.

41 3.4.130–7.

42 The Duchess's future husband Antonio, in the same play, is also such a servant. The first scene between them plays heavily on this 'balance sheet' version of

obligation. When the Duchess finally declares her love to Antonio it is with the words, 'Being now my steward, here upon your lips I sign your Quietus est'. Whereas male service always leaves deferred obligations unfulfilled, when a woman is involved good service inevitably leads to a 'quietus est' – an acquittal of service, and an explicit (rather than erotically deferred) service/use.

43 5.3.86–7.
44 For the household significance of the closet see Stewart, *The Bounds of Sodomy*. For the importance of such 'privy' chambers in structuring social relations and facilitating decision making in an élite household see Starkey, *The English Court*.
45 2.2.6.
46 4.1.17–23.
47 Marjorie Garber (seen in typescript).
48 5.3.140–2.
49 1.2.52–3.
50 1.2.54–6.
51 A. Friedman, *House and Household in Elizabethan England: Wollaton Hall and the Willoughby Family*, Chicago, Ill., University of Chicago Press, 1989.
52 4.3.115–18.
53 5.1.126–7.
54 2.2.57–64.
55 3.3.248.
56 2.1.96–9.
57 5.3.186–7.
58 5.3.216–17.
59 5.3.220–7.
60 See P. Hammer, '"The Bright Shininge Sparke": The Political Career of Robert Devereux, 2nd Earl of Essex, c.1585–c.1597', unpublished Cambridge Ph.D. thesis, 1991.
61 Which raises the question of whether accusations of sodomy against men in intimate service were political mobilisations of an equivalently powerful anxiety against arrangements which were not, in fact, illegal unless they could be shown to be seditious, but where the endlessly deferred expectation of some unspecified 'fulfilment' could readily be eroticised. This is relevant to recent work by Jonathan Goldberg and others, which sees actual sodomitical activity wherever a charge of such was laid against someone (see Goldberg, *Sodometries*).
62 See Chapter 6.

8 UNPICKING THE TAPESTRY

1 E. M. Bruner, 'Ethnography as narrative', in V. W. Turner and E. M. Bruner (eds), *The Anthropology of Experience*, Urbana, Ill., University of Illinois Press, 1986, pp. 139–55, at pp. 151–3. For a feminist perspective on recent work in social anthropology see Henrietta Moore, *Feminism and Anthropology*, Cambridge, Polity Press, 1988. As ever, I am indebted to Bill Sherman for making me aware of the ethnographic and anthropological debates and for reading and commenting on a first draft of this chapter.
2 The rewriting of this chapter from its original oral form has benefited from the constructive attitude and comments of many participants in the 1991 'Attending to Women in the Early Modern Period' conference at the University of Maryland, College Park. I mention especially Judith Bennett, Barbara E. Bowen, Margaret Hannay and Mary Ellen Lamb.
3 There are, of course, currently many 'emerging narratives' of women's history,

but my contention is that ultimately these will be seen to be aspects of a single 'new historical narrative'.

4 Robert Finlay, 'The refashioning of Martin Guerre', *AHR*, 1988, vol. 93, pp. 553–71; Natalie Zemon Davis, *The Return of Martin Guerre,* Cambridge, Mass., Harvard University Press, 1983.

5 Natalie Zemon Davis, '"On the lame"', *AHR*, 1988, vol. 93, pp. 572–603.

6 The first was Nellie Neilson in 1943. See Joan Scott's article, 'American women historians, 1884–1984', in Joan Scott, *Gender and the Politics of History*, New York, Columbia University Press, 1988, pp. 178–98.

7 See, in particular, Stephen Greenblatt, 'Psychoanalysis and renaissance culture', in P. Parker and D. Quint (eds), *Literary Theory/Renaissance Texts*, Baltimore, The Johns Hopkins University Press, 1986, pp. 210–24; Terence Cave, 'Odysseus's scar', *Recognitions*, Oxford, Oxford University Press, 1988, pp. 12–17. G. Bruckner, *Giovanni and Lusanna: Love and Marriage in Renaissance Florence*, London, Weidenfeld & Nicolson, 1986, pp. vii–ix.

8 Terence Cave suggests that 'recognition' is a key plotting device in such stories of problematic identity and place in the household. This is a similar move to Davis's, when she suggests in *The Return of Martin Guerre* that the wooden leg of the pursuer of guilt is a familiar plot device. Cave's treatment of the Martin Guerre story is juxtaposed with the story of the return of Odysseus (once again calling into play my title), in a chapter entitled (after Eric Auerbach) 'Odysseus' scar'. Amongst treatments of the Guerre story aside from Davis's, Cave's is unusual in at least noting Bertrande's role: 'Any reading of Martin Guerre's story is bound to make Bertrande central to the uncertainty of the recognition.... Central, yet always, in a male-dominated society, peripheral: which is exactly why she is a blind spot' (p. 15).

9 Stephen Greenblatt, 'Psychoanalysis and renaissance culture', p. 215; Michel de Montaigne, 'Des boyteux', in M. Rat (ed.), *Essais*, 2 vols, Paris, Garnier, 1962, vol. 2, pp. 478–9. However much establishing the identity of Martin Guerre was shown to *depend* on the testimony of wives and sisters (and thus to be vacillating, insecure), the construction of selfhood thereby illuminated was within a recognisable tradition of (male) history.

10 For a clear account of this version of selfhood see Natalie Davis, 'Boundaries and the sense of self in sixteenth-century France', in T. C. Heller, M. Sosna and D. E. Wellbery (eds), *Reconstructing Individualism: Autonomy, Individuality and the Self in Western Thought*, Stanford, Calif., Stanford University Press, 1986, pp. 53–63.

11 Joan Kelly specifies 'the social relations between the sexes' as the key topic for the study of women in the Renaissance in *Women, History and Theory: The Essays of Joan Kelly*, Chicago, Ill., Chicago University Press, 1984.

12 Finlay, 'The refashioning of Martin Guerre', p. 569.

13 Finlay, 'The refashioning of Martin Guerre', pp. 569–70.

14 Davis, 'History's two bodies', *AHR*, 1988, vol. 93, pp. 1–30, at pp. 29–30.

15 Scott, 'American women historians, 1884–1984'. Actually, this was first published as 'History and difference' in *Daedalus*, 1987, vol. 116, no. 4, pp. 93–118. See Scott's footnote, 'American women historians', p. 178.

16 'American women historians', p. 181.

17 'American women historians', pp. 186–7.

18 'American women historians', pp. 185–6.

19 J. Higham, *History*, Englewood Cliffs, NJ, Prentice Hall, 1965.

20 'American women historians', p. 189.

21 'On the lame' is the title of Montaigne's *essai*, in which he touches on the Martin Guerre story; 'On the lame' is also the story of the lost husband who returns, on a wooden leg, and 'catches up with' the imposter none the less (see

The Return of Martin Guerre, p. 122, and illustration, p. 121); it also suggests a halting quality to Finlay's argument.

22 '"On the lame"', p. 596.

23 '"On the lame"', pp. 596–7.

24 '"On the lame"', p. 598.

25 In spite of this caveat, scolds are consistently assumed by Underdown and others to be women. The same is true of the court records; disorderly male behaviour is described differently.

26 David Underdown, 'The taming of the scold: the enforcement of patriarchal authority in early modern England', in A. Fletcher and J. Stevenson (eds), *Order and Disorder in Early Modern England*, Cambridge, Cambridge University Press, 1985, pp. 116–36, at p. 119.

27 See also S. Amussen, *An Ordered Society: Gender and Class in Early Modern England*, Oxford, Blackwell, 1988, pp. 122–3; J. A. Sharpe, *Crime in Early Modern England 1550–1750*, London, Longman, 1984, reworked in *Early Modern England: A Social History 1550–1760*, London, Edward Arnold, 1987, pp. 88–93. I make the same unguarded assumption myself in *Still Harping on Daughters: Women and Drama in the Age of Shakespeare*, Brighton, Harvester Press, 1983, and would now want to reconsider what I had to say there about scolds; for example, p. 106: 'The woman with a sharp tongue breaks the social order: she is strictly disorderly. Discordant, disruptive, unruly, she threatens to sabotage the domestic harmony which depends upon her general submissiveness.' Catherine Belsey takes a very similar line in *The Subject of Tragedy* (London, Routledge, 1985) in the chapter entitled 'Silence and speech'.

28 The quotation is from Amussen, *An Ordered Society*, p. 122. Amussen also adopts the classificatory version of 'scolds': 'Only one group of women was consistently punished for repudiating feminine meekness. These were scolds' (ibid.).

29 I find Habermas's description of recognised behaviour in his *Theory of Communicative Action* helpful here.

30 B. H. Cunnington (ed.), *Records of the County of Wilts being extracts from the Quarter Sessions Great Rolls of the Seventeenth Century*, Devizes, George Simpson, 1932, p. 199.

31 Ibid.

32 *Records of the County of Wilts*, p. 217.

33 *Records of the County of Wilts*, p. 166.

34 *Records of the County of Wilts*, pp. 188–9.

35 Natalie Davis, *Fiction in the Archives: Pardon Tales and their Tellers in Sixteenth-century France*, Stanford, Calif., Stanford University Press, 1987. This work has been more vigorously and immediately attacked by 'incremental' historians than *The Return of Martin Guerre*, probably because by now some of the political and gender implications of Davis's historical narrative are plain to reviewers. For a recent example of rupturing historical narrative in the spirit of Davis's see Lyndal Roper, *The Holy Household: Women and Morals in Reformation Augsburg*, Oxford, Oxford University Press, 1989.

36 '"On the lame"', p. 598.

37 On these two poems in particular see Margaret P. Hannay, '"Doo what men may sing": Mary Sidney and the tradition of admonitory dedication', in M. P. Hannay (ed.), *Silent but for the Word: Tudor Women as Patrons, Translators, and Writers of Religious Works*, Kent, Ohio, Kent State University Press, 1985, pp. 149–65. See also M. P. Hannay, *Philip's Phoenix: Mary Sidney, Countess of Pembroke*, Oxford, Oxford University Press, 1990. For the poems see Gary F. Waller (ed.), *The Triumph of Death and Other Unpublished and Uncollected Poems by Mary Sidney, Countess of Pembroke (1561–1621)*, Salzburg Studies in English Literature 65, Salz-

burg, University of Salzburg, 1977, pp. 87–95; 'To the angell spirit' is printed in J. C. Rathmell (ed.), *The Psalms of Sir Philip Sidney and the Countess of Pembroke*, New York, Anchor Books, 1963. See also Gary F. Waller, *Mary Sidney, Countess of Pembroke: A Critical Study of her Writings and Literary Milieu*, Salzburg, University of Salzburg, 1979.

38 Hannay, '"Doo what men may sing"', p. 149.

39 Although I choose to focus on the better-known poem, the poem which precedes it, 'Even now that Care', addressed to the Queen, fits my argument equally well, and fits my title even better. In it, Mary Sidney becomes Penelope, weeping for the absent co-author of the Psalms: 'How can I name whom sighing sighes extend, / and not unstopp my teares eternall spring? / but hee did warpe, I weau'd this webb to end; / . . . And I the Cloth in both our names present' (Waller, *The Triumph of Death*, pp. 88–9).

40 The following argument is a collaborative one, developed with Lorna Hutson during a course on renaissance literature which we taught together to second- and third-year English students at Queen Mary and Westfield College, University of London in spring 1990.

41 For the More letter see Chapter 3.

42 Waller, *The Triumph of Death*, p. 92.

43 Waller, *The Triumph of Death*, p. 93.

44 Waller, *The Triumph of Death*, p. 95.

45 It might be interesting to include as 'background' to such a reading the fact that as Countess of Pembroke, Michael Brennan argues, Mary Sidney used the elevation of her dead brother Philip to enhance the reputation for cultivation of the *Pembrokes*; in other words, she is also entitled to speak out for her line (her father-in-law). Again, her own selfhood is not the issue. See M. G. Brennan, *Literary Patronage in the English Renaissance: The Pembroke Family*, London, Routledge, 1988.

46 See Ray Nadeau, 'The Progymnasmate of Aphthonius in translation', *Speech Monographs*, 1952, vol. 19, pp. 264–85.

47 Waller, *The Triumph of Death*, p. 92.

48 Spenser's *Faerie Queene*, ed. J. C. Smith, 2 vols, Oxford, Clarendon Press, 1909, vol. 2, p. 495.

49 I am extremely grateful to Mary Ellen Lamb for providing me with a transcript of her workshop summary of the argument of my original paper, which greatly helped me to clarify my own thoughts in reworking my discussion of 'Angell spirit'.

50 'Even now that Care', by contrast, does not appear to be 'enabled' by the devices Mary Sidney adopts in an attempt decorously to efface her female authorship. Rather, it struggles syntactically with several attempts to insert a 'he' as subject of the poem (as donor of the Psalms, as suitor for the Queen's patronage, as divine originator of the Psalms themselves). This might be the text to tackle, in my view, to discover the female author struggling for a voice; significantly, this is a much less well-known poem, deemed 'less successful' *as a poem*.

51 Scott, 'American women historians', p. 197.

9 CONCLUSION

1 *Hamlet*, 2.1.77–84. All quotations are from the Arden edn, ed. Harold Jenkins, London, Methuen, 1982.

2 *Still Harping on Daughters*, Brighton, Harvester, 1983; '"No offence i' th' world":

Hamlet and unlawful marriage', in F. Barker, P. Hulme and M. Iversen (eds), *Uses of History: Marxism, Post-Modernism and the Renaissance*, Manchester, Manchester University Press, 1991, pp. 123–39, revised in this volume as Chapter 2.

3 T. S. Eliot, *Selected Essays*, London, Faber, 1932, pp. 144–5.

4 3.2.183–7.

5 3.3.27–35.

6 The 'accretion', '*Hamlet within*: Mother, mother, mother', of Q2 and F, discarded by modern editors, surely registers the limited, local culpability of Gertrude in conspiring to have her familial exchange with her son spied upon.

7 Angel Day, *The English Secretorie*, London, Richard Iones, 1592, p. 109; cit. Alan Stewart, 'The early modern closet discovered', *Representations*, 1995, vol. 50, pp. 76–100, at p. 83.

8 See, for example, the plan by John Smythson for additions to Haughton House, Nottinghamshire, 1618 and his plan for a terrace range at Bolsover c. 1630, reproduced as plates 191 and 177 respectively in Mark Girouard, *Robert Smythson and the Elizabethan Country House*, New Haven, Conn., Yale University Press, 1983.

9 Stewart, 'The early modern closet discovered', p. 81.

10 Stewart argues compellingly that it is the innuendo surrounding encounters in the closet which fuels the suggestion that the gentleman's private secretary (who licitly works with him in the privacy of his closet) might be having some kind of erotic relationship with his employer.

11 3.4.1–5.

12 3.4.8–16.

13 J. Rose, 'Hamlet – the *Mona Lisa* of Literature', *Critical Quarterly*, 1986, vol. 28, pp. 35–49, at p. 38.

14 3.4.53–65.

15 Cedric Watts, *Harvester New Critical Introductions to Shakespeare: Hamlet*, Brighton, Harvester, 1988, pp. xxiv–xxv.

16 Philip Edwards (ed.), *Hamlet*, Cambridge, Cambridge University Press, 1985, p. 9.

17 We might add that Q1 contains a further, almost entirely distinct version of the most emotionally complex component in this scene, the 'Look here upon this picture' speech. See G. Holderness and B. Loughrey (eds), *The Tragicall Historie of Hamlet Prince of Denmarke* , Brighton, Harvester, 1992, p. 80.

18 J. Rose, 'Sexuality in the reading of Shakespeare: *Hamlet* and *Measure for Measure*', in J. Drakakis (ed.), *Alternative Shakespeares*, London, Methuen, 1985, pp. 95–118, at p. 101.

INDEX